A
A P

With expert rea~~ding~~ to romance, adventure, good health, or career opportunities while gaining valuable insight into yourself and others. Offering a daily outlook for 18 full months, this fascinating guide shows you:

- The important dates in your life
- What to expect from an astrological reading
- How the stars can help you stay healthy and fit
  And more!

Let this sound advice guide you through a year of heavenly possibilities—for today and for every day of 2010!

SYDNEY OMARR'S® DAY-BY-DAY ASTROLOGICAL GUIDE FOR

ARIES—March 21–April 19
TAURUS—April 20–May 20
GEMINI—May 21–June 20
CANCER—June 21–July 22
LEO—July 23–August 22
VIRGO—August 23–September 22
LIBRA—September 23–October 22
SCORPIO—October 23–November 21
SAGITTARIUS—November 22–December 21
CAPRICORN—December 22–January 19
AQUARIUS—January 20–February 18
PISCES—February 19–March 20

IN 2010

SYDNEY OMARR'S®

DAY-BY-DAY ASTROLOGICAL GUIDE FOR

GEMINI

MAY 21–JUNE 20

2010

by Trish MacGregor
with Carol Tonsing

A SIGNET BOOK

SIGNET
Published by New American Library, a division of
Penguin Group (USA) Inc., 375 Hudson Street,
New York, New York 10014, USA
Penguin Group (Canada), 90 Eglinton Avenue East, Suite 700, Toronto,
Ontario M4P 2Y3, Canada (a division of Pearson Penguin Canada Inc.)
Penguin Books Ltd., 80 Strand, London WC2R 0RL, England
Penguin Ireland, 25 St. Stephen's Green, Dublin 2,
Ireland (a division of Penguin Books Ltd.)
Penguin Group (Australia), 250 Camberwell Road, Camberwell, Victoria 3124,
Australia (a division of Pearson Australia Group Pty. Ltd.)
Penguin Books India Pvt. Ltd., 11 Community Centre, Panchsheel Park,
New Delhi - 110 017, India
Penguin Group (NZ), 67 Apollo Drive, Rosedale, North Shore 0645
New Zealand (a division of Pearson New Zealand Ltd.)
Penguin Books (South Africa) (Pty.) Ltd., 24 Sturdee Avenue,
Rosebank, Johannesburg 2196, South Africa

Penguin Books Ltd., Registered Offices:
80 Strand, London WC2R 0RL, England

First Printing, June 2009
10 9 8 7 6 5 4 3 2 1

First published by Signet, an imprint of New American Library,
a division of Penguin Group (USA) Inc.

PUBLISHER'S NOTE
While the author has made every effort to provide accurate telephone numbers and
Internet addresses at the time of publication, neither the publisher nor the author
assumes any responsibility for errors, or for changes that occur after publication.
Further, publisher does not have any control over and does not assume any respon-
sibility for author or third-party Web sites or their content.

If you purchased this book without a cover you should be aware that this book is sto-
len property. It was reported as "unsold and destroyed" to the publisher and neither
the author nor the publisher has received any payment for this "stripped book."

The scanning, uploading and distribution of this book via the Internet or via any
other means without the permission of the publisher is illegal and punishable by
law. Please purchase only authorized electronic editions, and do not participate in or
encourage electronic piracy of copyrighted materials. Your support of the author's
rights is appreciated.

CONTENTS

INTRODUCTION

Seize the Moment

"Timing is everything" is a saying worth repeating this year. Astrology is the art of interpreting moments in time, and astrology fans from the rich and famous to the readers of daily horoscope columns realize that some moments are more favorable for certain actions than others. Knowing that they can plan their actions in tune with the rhythm of the cosmic cycles gives them confidence that they are making wise choices. This could be a challenging year for many, so let this guide help you seize the moment and turn those challenges into opportunities by using the tools astrology provides.

In our toolbox for 2010, you'll find secrets of astrological timing—how to find the most auspicious dates this year. For those who are new to astrology or would like to know more about it, we offer easy techniques to start using astrology in your daily life. You'll learn all about your sun sign and how to interpret the mysterious symbols on a horoscope chart. You can use the convenient tables in this book to look up other planets in your horoscope, each of which sheds light on a different facet of your personality.

Many people turn to astrology to help them find love or figure out what went wrong with a relationship. At your service is the world's oldest dating and mating coach, ready to help you decide whether that new passion has potential or might burn out fast. We'll go through the pros and cons of all the possible sun-sign combinations, with celebrities to illustrate the romantic chemistry.

Contemplating a career change? Our sun-sign chapters can help you build your confidence and focus your job search in

1

the most fulfilling direction by highlighting your natural talents and abilities.

Many readers have explored astrology on the Internet, where there are a mind-boggling variety of sites. Our suggestions are well worth your surfing time. We show you where to get free horoscopes, connect with other astrology fans, find the right astrology software for your ability, and even find an accredited college that specializes in astrological studies.

Whether it's money matters, fashion tips, or ideas for vacation getaways, we'll provide ways to use astrology in your life every day. Before giving yourself or your home a makeover, be sure to consult your sun sign, for the colors and styles that will complement your personality.

To make the most of each day, there are eighteen months of on-target daily horoscopes. So here's hoping this year's guide will help you use your star power wisely to make 2010 a happy, successful year!

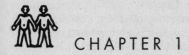

CHAPTER 1

The Top Trends of 2010: Transition Times

Astrologers judge the trends of a year by following the slow-moving planets, from Jupiter through Pluto. A change in sign indicates a new cycle, with new emphasis. The farthest planets (Uranus, Neptune, and Pluto) which stay in a sign for at least seven years, cause a very significant change in the atmosphere when they change signs. Shifts in Jupiter, which changes every year, and Saturn, every two years, are more obvious in current events and daily lives. Jupiter generally brings a fortunate, expansive emphasis to its new sign, while Saturn's two-year cycle is a reality check, bringing tests of maturity, discipline, and responsibility. This year, Jupiter in Pisces and Saturn in Libra are in auspicious signs for most of the year, which should act as a balance to more volatile elements in the comos.

Little Pluto—The Mighty Mite

Though astronomers have demoted tiny Pluto from being a full-fledged planet to a dwarf planet, astrologers have been tracking its influence since Pluto was discovered in 1930 and have witnessed that this minuscule celestial body has a powerful effect on both a personal and global level. So Pluto, which moved into the sign of Capricorn in 2008, will still be called a "planet" by astrologers and will be given just as much importance as before.

Until 2024, Pluto will exert its influence in this practical, building, healing earth sign. Capricorn relates to structures, institutions, order, mountains and mountain countries, mineral rights, issues involving the elderly and growing older—all of which will be emphasized in the coming years. It is the sign of established order, corporations, big business—all of which will be accented. Possibly, it will fall to business structures to create a new sense of order in the world.

You should now feel the rumblings of change in the Capricorn area of your horoscope and in the world at large. The last time Pluto was in Capricorn was the years up to and during the Revolutionary War; therefore this should be an important time in the U.S. political scene, as well as a reflection of the aging and maturing of American society in general. Both the rise and the fall of the Ottoman Empire happened under Pluto in Capricorn.

The Pisces Factor

This year, Jupiter moves from experimental, humanitarian Aquarius to creative, imaginative Pisces. Jupiter is the coruler of Pisces, along with Neptune, so this is a particularly auspicious place for the planet of luck and expansion to be. During the year that Jupiter remains in a sign, the fields associated with that sign are the ones that currently arouse excitement and enthusiasm, usually providing excellent opportunities.

Jupiter in Pisces expands the influence of Neptune in Aquarius; there should be many artistic and scientific breakthroughs. International politics also comes under this influence, as Neptune in Aquarius raises issues of global boundaries and political structures not being as solid as they seem. This could continue to produce rebellion and chaos in the environment. However, with the generally benevolent force of Jupiter backing up the creative side of Neptune, it is possible that highly original and effective solutions to global problems will be found, which could transcend the current social and cultural barriers.

Another place we notice the Jupiter influence is in fashion, which should veer into a Pisces fantasy mood, with more the-atrical, dramatic styles and a special emphasis on footwear. Look for exciting beachwear and seaside resorts that appeal to our desire to escape reality.

Those born under Pisces should have many opportunities during the year. However, the key is to keep your feet on the ground. The flip side of Jupiter is that there are no limits. You can expand off the planet under a Jupiter transit, which is why the planet is often called the "Gateway to Heaven." If some-thing is going to burst (such as an artery) or overextend or go over the top in some way, it could happen under a supposedly lucky Jupiter transit, so be aware.

Those born under Virgo may find their best opportunities working with partners this year, as Jupiter will be transiting their seventh house of relationships.

During the summer months, Jupiter dips into Aries, which should give us a preview of happenings next year. In this headstrong fire sign, Jupiter promotes pioneering ventures, start-ups, all that is new and exciting. It can also promote im-patience with more conservative forces, especially in early summer, which looks like the most volatile time this year. Ju-piter returns to Pisces in September for the rest of the year.

Saturn in Libra

Saturn, the planet of limitation, testing, and restriction, will be moving through Libra, the sign of its exhaltation and one of its most auspicious signs, this year. In Libra, Saturn can steady the scales of justice and promote balanced, responsible judgment. There should be much deliberation over duty, honor, and fair-ness, which will be ongoing for the next two years, balancing the more impulsive energy of other planets. Far-reaching new legislation and diplomatic moves are possible, perhaps resolv-ing difficult international standoffs. As this placement works well with the humanitarian Aquarius influence of Neptune, there should be new hope of resolving conflicts. Previously, Saturn was in Libra during the early 1920s, the early 1950s, and again in the early 1980s.

Continuing Trends

Uranus and Neptune continue to do a kind of astrological dance called a "mutual reception." This is a supportive relationship where Uranus is in Pisces, the sign ruled by Neptune, while Neptune is in Aquarius, the sign ruled by Uranus. When this dance is over in 2011, it is likely that we will be living under very different political and social circumstances.

Uranus in Pisces and Aries

Uranus, known as the Great Awakener, tends to cause both upheaval and innovation in the sign it transits. This year, it is accompanied by Jupiter, as it is preparing to leave Pisces and dip its toe into Aries from June to mid-August. However, the Pisces influence will predominate, since Jupiter will be in Pisces most of the year.

During previous episodes of Uranus in Pisces, great religions and spiritual movements have come into being, most recently Mormonism and Christian Fundamentalism. In its most positive mode, Pisces promotes imagination and creativity, the art of illusion in theater and film, and the inspiration of great artists.

A water sign, Pisces is naturally associated with all things liquid—such as oceans, oil, and alcohol—and with those creatures that live in the water—fish, the fishing industry, fish habitats, and fish farming. Currently there is a great debate going on about overfishing, contamination of fish, and fish farming. The underdogs, the enslaved, and the disenfranchised should also benefit from Uranus in Pisces. Since Uranus is a disruptive influence that aims to challenge the status quo, the forces of nature that manifest now will most likely be in the Pisces area—the oceans, seas, and rivers. We have so far seen unprecedented rainy seasons, floods, mud slides, and disastrous hurricanes. Note that 2005's devastating Hurricane Katrina hit an area known for both the oil and fishing industries.

Pisces is associated with the prenatal phase of life, which is related to regenerative medicine. The controversy over embryonic stem cell research will continue to be debated, but recent developments may make the arguments moot. Petroleum issues, both in the oil-producing countries and offshore oil drilling, will come to a head. Uranus in Pisces suggests that development of new hydroelectric sources may provide the power we need to continue our current power-thirsty lifestyle.

As in previous eras, there should continue to be a flourishing of the arts. We are seeing many new artistic forms developing now, such as computer-created actors and special effects. The sky's the limit on this influence.

Those who have problems with Uranus are those who resist change, so the key is to embrace the future.

As Uranus prepares to enter Aries, an active fire sign, we should have a preview of coming influences over the summer.

Neptune in Aquarius

Neptune is a planet of imagination and creativity, but also of deception and illusion. Neptune is associated with hospitals, which have been the subject of much controversy. On the positive side, hospitals are acquiring cutting-edge technology. The atmosphere of many hospitals is already changing from the intimidating and sterile environment of the past to that of a health-promoting spa. Alternative therapies, such as massage, diet counseling, and aromatherapy, are becoming commonplace, which expresses this Neptune trend. New procedures in plastic surgery, also a Neptune glamour field, and antiaging therapies are giving the illusion of youth.

However, issues involving the expense and quality of health care, medication, and the evolving relationship between doctors, drug companies, and HMOs reflect a darker side of this trend.

Neptune is finishing up its stay in Aquarius and will begin its transit of Pisces, which it rules, in 2011. So this should be a time of transition into a much more Neptunian era, when Pisces-related issues will be of paramount importance.

Lunar Eclipses Are Movers and Shakers

Eclipses could shake up the financial markets and rock your world in 2010. The eclipses in late June and July are the ones to watch as they coincide with a close contact of Jupiter and Uranus in Aries. This is a potentially volatile time, so it would be wise to be prepared. As several recent studies have shown the stock market to be linked to the lunar cycle, track investments more carefully during this time.

New Celestial Bodies

Our solar system is getting crowded, as astronomers continue to discover new objects circling the sun. In addition to the familiar planets, there are dwarf planets, comets, cometoids, asteroids, and strange icy bodies in the Kuiper Belt beyond Neptune. A dwarf planet christened Eris, discovered in 2005, is now being observed and analyzed by astrologers. Eris was named after a goddess of discord and strife. In mythology, she was a troublemaker who made men think their opinions were right and others wrong. What an appropriate name for a planet discovered during a time of discord in the Middle East and elsewhere! Eris has a companion moon named Dysnomia for her daughter, described as a demon spirit of lawlessness. With mythological associations like these, we wonder what the effect of this mother-daughter duo will be. Once Eris's orbit is established, astrologers will track the impact of this planet on our horoscopes. Eris takes about 560 years to orbit the sun, which means its emphasis in a given astrological sign will affect several generations.

CHAPTER 2

How to Find Your Best Times This Year

It's no secret that some of the most powerful and famous people, from Julius Caesar to Queen Elizabeth I, from financier J. P. Morgan to Ronald Reagan, have consulted astrologers before they made their moves. If astrology helps the rich and famous stay on course through life's ups and downs, why not put it to work for you? Anyone can follow the planetary movements, and once you know how to interpret them, you won't need an expert to grasp the overall trends and make use of them.

For instance, when mischievous Mercury creates havoc with communications, it's time to back up your vital computer files, read between the lines of contracts, and be very patient with coworkers. When Venus passes through your sign, you're more alluring, so it's time to try out a new outfit or hairstyle, and then ask someone you'd like to know better to dinner. Venus timing can also help you charm clients with a stunning sales pitch or make an offer they won't refuse.

In this chapter you will find the tricks of astrological time management. You can find your red-letter days as well as which times to avoid. You will also learn how to make the magic of the moon work for you. Use the information in this chapter and the planet tables in this book and also the moon sign listings in your daily forecasts.

Here are the happenings to note on your agenda:

- Dates of your sun sign (high-energy period)
- The month previous to your sun sign (low-energy time)

9

- Dates of planets in your sign this year
- Full and new moons (Pay special attention when these fall in your sun sign!)
- Eclipses
- Moon in your sun sign every month, as well as moon in the opposite sign (listed in daily forecast)
- Mercury retrogrades
- Other retrograde periods

Your Most Proactive Time

Every birthday starts off a new cycle of solar energy for you. You should feel a new surge of vitality as the powerful sun enters your sign. This is the time when predominant energies are most favorable to you. So go for it! Start new projects, and make your big moves (especially when the new moon is in your sign, doubling your charisma). You'll get the recognition you deserve now, when everyone is attuned to your sun sign. Look in the tables in this book to see if other planets will also be passing through your sun sign at this time. Venus (love, beauty), Mars (energy, drive), and Mercury (communication, mental sharpness) reinforce the sun and give an extra boost to your life in the areas they affect. Venus will rev up your social and love life, making you seem especially attractive. Mars amplifies your energy and drive. Mercury fuels your brainpower and helps you communicate. Jupiter signals an especially lucky period of expansion.

There are two downtimes related to the sun. During the month before your birthday period, when you are winding up your annual cycle, you could be feeling especially vulnerable and depleted. So at that time get extra rest, watch your diet, and take it easy. Don't overstress yourself. Use this time to gear up for a big push when the sun enters your sign.

Another downtime is when the sun is in the sign opposite your sun sign (six months from your birthday). This is a reactive time, when the prevailing energies are very different from yours. You may feel at odds with the world. You'll have to work harder for recognition because people are not on your wavelength. However, this could be a good time to work on a team, in cooperation with others, or behind the scenes.

Be a Moon Watcher

The moon is a powerful tool to divine the mood of the moment. You can work with the moon in two ways. Plan by the sign the moon is in; plan by the phase of the moon. The sign will tell you the kind of activities that suit the moon's mood. The phase will tell you the best time to start or finish a certain activity.

Working with the phases of the moon is as easy as looking up at the night sky. During the new moon, when both the sun and moon are in the same sign, begin new ventures—especially activities that are favored by that sign. Then you'll utilize the powerful energies pulling you in the same direction. You'll be focused outward, toward action, and in a doing mode. Postpone breaking off, terminating, deliberating, or reflecting—activities that require introspection and passive work. These are better suited to a later moon phase.

Get your project under way during the first quarter. Then go public at the full moon, a time of high intensity, when feelings come out into the open. This is your time to shine—to express yourself. Be aware, however, that because pressures are being released, other people will also be letting off steam. Since confrontations are possible, take advantage of this time either to air grievances or to avoid arguments.

About three days after the full moon comes the disseminating phase, a time when the energy of the cycle begins to wind down. From the last quarter of the moon to the next new moon, it's a time to cut off unproductive relationships, do serious thinking, and focus on inward-directed activities.

You'll feel some new and full moons more strongly than others, especially when they fall in your sun sign. That full moon happens at your low-energy time of year, and is likely to be an especially stressful time in a relationship, when any hidden problems or unexpressed emotions could surface.

Full and New Moons in 2010

All dates are calculated for eastern standard time and eastern daylight time.

New Moon—January 15 in Capricorn (solar eclipse)
Full Moon—January 30 in Leo

New Moon—February 13 in Aquarius
Full Moon—February 28 in Virgo

New Moon—March 15 in Pisces
Full Moon—March 29 in Libra

New Moon—April 14 in Aries
Full Moon—April 28 in Scorpio

New Moon—May 13 in Taurus
Full Moon—May 27 in Sagittarius

New Moon—June 12 in Gemini
Full Moon—June 26 in Capricorn (lunar eclipse)

New Moon—July 11 in Cancer (solar eclipse)
Full Moon—July 25 in Aquarius

New Moon—August 9 in Leo
Full Moon—August 24 in Pisces

New Moon—September 8 in Virgo
Full Moon—September 23 in Aries

New Moon—October 7 in Libra
Full Moon—October 22 in Aries

New Moon—November 5 in Scorpio
Full Moon—November 21 in Taurus

New Moon—December 5 in Sagittarius
Full Moon—December 21 in Gemini (lunar eclipse)

Timing by the Moon's Sign

To forecast the daily emotional "weather," to determine your monthly high and low days, or to synchronize your activities with the cycles of the moon, take note of the moon's sign under your daily forecast at the end of the book. Here are some of the activities favored and the moods you are likely to encounter under each moon sign.

Moon in Aries: Get Moving

The new moon in Aries is an ideal time to start new projects. Everyone is pushy, raring to go, rather impatient, and short-tempered. Leave details and follow-up for later. Competitive sports or martial arts are great ways to let off steam. Quiet types could use some assertiveness, but it's a great day for dynamos. Be careful not to step on too many toes.

Moon in Taurus: Lay the Foundations for Success

Do solid, methodical tasks like follow-through or backup work. Make investments, buy real estate, do appraisals, or do some hard bargaining. Attend to your property. Get out in the country or spend some time in your garden. Enjoy creature comforts, music, a good dinner, or sensual lovemaking. Forget starting a diet—this is a day when you'll feel self-indulgent.

Moon in Gemini: Communicate

Talk means action today. Telephone, write letters, and fax! Make new contacts; stay in touch with steady customers. You can juggle lots of tasks today. It's a great time for mental activity of any kind. Don't try to pin people down—they too are feeling restless. Keep it light. Flirtations and socializing are good. Watch gossip—and don't give away secrets.

Moon in Cancer: Pay Attention to Loved Ones

This is a moody, sensitive, emotional time. People respond to personal attention and mothering. Stay at home, have a family dinner, or call your mother. Nostalgia, memories, and psychic powers are heightened. You'll want to hang on to people and things (don't clean out your closets now). You could have shrewd insights into what others really need and want. Pay attention to dreams, intuition, and gut reactions.

Moon in Leo: Be Confident

Everybody is in a much more confident, warm, generous mood. It's a good day to ask for a raise, show what you can do, or dress like a star. People will respond to flattery and enjoy a bit of drama and theater. You may be extravagant, treat yourself royally, and show off a bit—but don't break the bank! Be careful not to promise more than you can deliver.

Moon in Virgo: Be Practical

Do practical, down-to-earth chores. Review your budget, make repairs, or be an efficiency expert. Not a day to ask for a raise. Tend to personal care and maintenance. Have a health checkup, go on a diet, or buy vitamins or health food. Make your home spotless. Take care of details and piled-up chores. Reorganize your work and life so they run more smoothly and efficiently. Save money. Be prepared for others to be in critical, fault-finding moods.

Moon in Libra: Be Diplomatic

Attend to legal matters. Negotiate contracts. Arbitrate. Do things with your favorite partner. Socialize. Be romantic. Buy a special gift or a beautiful object. Decorate yourself or your surroundings. Buy new clothes. Throw a party. Have an elegant, romantic evening. Smooth over any ruffled feathers. Avoid confrontations. Stick to civilized discussions.

Moon in Scorpio: Solve Problems

This is a day to do things with passion. You'll have excellent concentration and focus. Try not to get too intense emotionally. Avoid sharp exchanges with loved ones. Others may tend to go to extremes, get jealous, or overreact. Great for troubleshooting, problem solving, research, scientific work—and making love. Pay attention to those psychic vibes.

Moon in Sagittarius: Sell and Motivate

A great time for travel, philosophical discussions, or setting long-range career goals. Work out, do sports, or buy athletic equipment. Others will be feeling upbeat, exuberant, and adventurous. Taking risks is favored. You may feel like gambling, betting on the horses, visiting a local casino, or buying a lottery ticket. Teaching, writing, and spiritual activities also get the green light. Relax outdoors. Take care of animals.

Moon in Capricorn: Get Organized

You can accomplish a lot now, so get on the ball! Attend to business. Issues concerning your basic responsibilities, duties, family, and elderly parents could crop up. You'll be expected to deliver on promises. Weed out the deadwood from your life. Get a dental checkup. Not a good day for gambling or taking risks.

Moon in Aquarius: Join the Group

A great day for doing things with groups—clubs, meetings, outings, politics, or parties. Campaign for your candidate. Work for a worthy cause. Deal with larger issues that affect humanity—the environment and metaphysical questions. Buy a computer or electronic gadget. Watch TV. Wear something outrageous. Try something you've never done before. Present an original idea. Don't stick to a rigid schedule; go with the flow. Take a class in meditation, mind control, or yoga.

Moon in Pisces: Be Creative

This can be a very creative day, so let your imagination work overtime. Film, theater, music, and ballet could inspire you. Spend some time resting and reflecting, reading, or writing poetry. Daydreams can also be profitable. Help those less fortunate. Lend a listening ear to someone who may be feeling blue. Don't overindulge in self-pity or escapism. People are especially vulnerable to substance abuse. Turn your thoughts to romance and someone special.

Eclipses Clear the Air

Eclipses can bring on milestones in your life, if they aspect a key point in your horoscope. In general, they shake up the status quo, bringing hidden areas out into the open. During this time, problems you've been avoiding or have brushed aside can surface to demand your attention. A good coping strategy is to accept whatever comes up as a challenge that could make a positive difference in your life. And don't forget the power of your sense of humor. If you can laugh at something, you'll never be afraid of it.

When the natural rhythms of the sun and moon are disturbed, it's best to postpone important activities. Be sure to mark eclipse days on your calendar, especially if the eclipse falls in your birth sign. This year, those born under Capricorn, Cancer, and Gemini should take special note of the feelings that arise. If your moon is in one of these signs, you may be especially affected. With lunar eclipses, some possibilities could be a break from attachments, or the healing of an illness or substance abuse that was triggered by the subconscious. The temporary event could be a healing time, when you gain perspective. During solar eclipses, when you might be in a highly subjective state, pay attention to the hidden subconscious patterns that surface, the emotional truth that is revealed at this time.

The effect of the eclipse can reverberate for some time, often months after the event. But it is especially important to stay cool and make no major moves during the period known as the shadow of the eclipse, which begins about a week before and lasts until at least three days after the eclipse. After three days, the daily rhythms should return to normal, and you can proceed with business as usual.

This Year's Eclipse Dates

January 15: Solar Eclipse in Capricorn
June 26: Lunar Eclipse in Capricorn
July 11: Solar Eclipse in Cancer
December 21: Lunar Eclipse in Gemini

Retrogrades: When the Planets Seem to Backstep

All the planets, except for the sun and moon, have times when they appear to move backward—or retrograde—as it seems from our point of view on Earth. At these times, planets do not work as they normally do. So it's best to "take a break" from that planet's energies in our life and to do some work on an inner level.

Mercury Retrograde: The Key Is in "Re"

Mercury goes into retrograde most often, and its effects can be especially irritating. When it reaches a short distance ahead of the sun several times a year, it seems to move backward from our point of view. Astrologers often compare retrograde motion to the optical illusion that occurs when we ride on a train that passes another train traveling at a different speed—the second train appears to be moving in reverse.

What this means to you is that the Mercury-ruled areas of your life—analytical thought processes, communications, scheduling—are subject to all kinds of confusion. Be prepared. Communications equipment can break down. Schedules may be changed on short notice. People are late for appointments or don't show up at all. Traffic is terrible. Major purchases malfunction, don't work out, or get delivered in the wrong color. Letters don't arrive or are delivered to the wrong address. Employees will make errors that have to be corrected later. Contracts don't work out or must be renegotiated.

Since most of us can't put our lives on "hold" during Mercury retrogrades, we should learn to tame the trickster and make it work for us. The key is in the prefix re-. This is the time to go back over things in your life, reflect on what you've done during the previous months. Now you can get deeper insights, and spot errors you've missed. So take time to review and re-evaluate what has happened. Rest and reward yourself—it's a good time to take a vacation, especially if you revisit a favorite place. Reorganize your work and finish up projects that are backed up. Clean out your desk and closets. Throw away what you can't recycle. If you must sign contracts or agreements, do so with a contingency clause that lets you reevaluate the terms later.

Postpone major purchases or commitments for the time being. Don't get married (unless you're remarrying the same person). Try not to rely on other people keeping appointments, contracts, or agreements to the letter; have several alternatives. Double-check and read between the lines. Don't buy anything connected with communications or transportation (if you must, be sure to cover yourself).

Mercury retrograding through your sun sign will intensify its effect on your life.

If Mercury was retrograde when you were born, you may be one of the lucky people who don't suffer the frustrations of this period. If so, your mind probably works in a very intuitive, insightful way.

The sign in which Mercury is retrograding can give you an idea of what's in store—as well as the sun signs that will be especially challenged.

Mercury Retrogrades in 2010

Mercury has four retrograde periods this year, since it will be retrograde as the year begins. During the retrograde periods, it will be especially important to watch all activities which involve mental processes and communication.

December 26, 2009, to January 15 in Capricorn
April 17 to May 11 in Taurus
August 20 to September 12 in Virgo
December 10 to December 30 from Capricorn to Sagittarius

Venus Retrograde: Relationships Are Affected

Retrograding Venus can cause your relationships to take a backward step, or you may feel that a key relationship is on hold. Singles may be especially lonely, yet find it difficult to connect with someone special. If you wish to make amends in an already troubled relationship, make peaceful overtures at this time. You may feel more extravagant or overindulge in shopping or sweet treats. Shopping till you drop and buying what you cannot afford are bad at this time. It's *not* a good time to redecorate—you'll hate the color of the walls later. Postpone getting a new hairstyle. It only lasts for a relatively short time this year; however, Scorpio and Libra should take special note.

Venus Retrogrades in 2010

Venus retrogrades from October 8 to November 18, from Scorpio to Libra.

Use the Power of Mars

Mars shows how and when to get where you want to go. Timing your moves with Mars on your side can give you a big push. On the other hand, pushing Mars the wrong way can guarantee that you'll run into frustrations around every corner. Your best times to forge ahead are during the weeks when Mars is traveling through your sun sign or your Mars sign (look these up in the planet tables in this book). Also consider times when Mars is in a compatible sign (fire signs with air signs, or earth signs with water signs). You'll be sure to have planetary power on your side.

Mars began a lengthy retrograde in extravagant Leo on December 20, 2009. Your patience may have been tested more than usual during last year's festivities. The Mars retrograde in Leo will last until March 10, during which time there are sure to be repercussions on the international level.

Mars Retrogrades in 2010

Mars turns retrograde in Leo on December 20, 2009, until March 10, 2010.

When Other Planets Retrograde

The slower-moving planets stay retrograde for many months at a time (Jupiter, Saturn, Neptune, Uranus, and Pluto).

When Saturn is retrograde, it's an uphill battle with self-discipline. You may not be in the mood for work. You may feel more like hanging out at the beach than getting things done.

Neptune retrograde promotes a dreamy escapism from reality, when you may feel you're in a fog (Pisces will feel this, especially).

Uranus retrograde may mean setbacks in areas where there have been sudden changes, when you may be forced to regroup or reevaluate the situation.

Pluto retrograde is a time to work on establishing proportion and balance in areas where there have been recent dramatic transformations.

When the planets move forward again, there's a shift in the atmosphere. Activities connected with each planet start moving ahead; plans that were stalled get rolling. Make a special note of those days on your calendar and proceed accordingly.

Other Retrogrades in 2010

The five slower-moving planets all go retrograde in 2010.

Jupiter retrogrades from July 23 in Aries to November 18 in Pisces.

Saturn retrogrades from January 13 in Libra to May 30 in Virgo.

Uranus retrogrades from July 5 in Aries to December 5 in Pisces.

Neptune retrogrades from May 31 to November 7 in Aquarius.

Pluto retrogrades from April 6 to September 13 in Capricorn.

CHAPTER 3

Introduction to Astrology

Astrology is a powerful tool that can help you discover and access your personal potential, understand others and interpret events in your life and the world at large. You don't have to be an expert in astrology to put it to work for you. It's easy to pick up enough basic knowledge to go beyond the realm of your sun sign into the deeper areas of this fascinating subject, which combines science, art, spirituality, and psychology. Perhaps from here you'll upgrade your knowledge with computer software that calculates charts for everyone you know in a nanosecond or join an astrology group in your city.

In this chapter, we'll introduce you to the basics of astrology. You'll be able to define a sign and figure out why astrologers say what they do about each sign. As you look at your astrological chart, you'll have a good idea of what's going on in each portion of the horoscope. Let's get started.

Know the Difference Between Signs and Constellations

Most readers know their signs, but many often confuse them with constellations. *Signs* are actually a type of celestial real estate, located on the *zodiac*, an imaginary 360-degree belt circling the earth. This belt is divided into twelve equal 30-degree portions, which are the *signs*. There's a lot of confusion about the difference between the *signs* and the *constellations* of the zodiac, patterns of stars which originally marked the twelve divisions, like signposts. Though a *sign* is named after the *constellation* that once marked the same area, the constellations are no longer in the same place relative to the earth that they were many centuries ago. Over hundreds of years, the earth's orbit has shifted, so that from our point of view here on earth, the constellations seem to have moved. However, the signs remain in place. (Most Western astrology uses the twelve-equal-part division of the zodiac, though there are some other methods of astrology that still use the constellations instead of the signs.)

Most people think of themselves in terms of their sun sign. A *sun sign* refers to the sign the sun is orbiting through at a given moment (from our point of view here on earth). For instance, if someone says, "I'm an Aries," the sun was passing through Aries when that person was born. However, there are nine other planets (plus asteroids, fixed stars, and sensitive points) that also form our total astrological personality, and some or many of these will be located in other signs. No one is completely "Aries," with all their astrological components in one sign! (Please note that, in astrology, the sun and moon are usually referred to as "planets," though of course they're not. Though there is some controversy over Pluto, it is still called a "planet" by astrologers.)

As we mentioned before, the sun signs are *places* on the zodiac. They do not *do* anything (the planets are the doers). However, they are associated with many things, depending on their location on the zodiac.

How Do We Define a Sign's Characteristics?

The definitions of the signs evolved systematically from four interrelated components: a sign's element, its quality, its polarity or sex, and its order in the progression of the zodiac. All these factors work together to tell us what the sign is like.

The system is magically mathematical: the number 12—as in the twelve signs of the zodiac—is divisible by 4, by 3, and by

2. There are four elements, three qualities, and two polarities, which follow one another in sequence around the zodiac.

The four elements (earth, air, fire, and water) are the building blocks of astrology. The use of an element to describe a sign probably dates from man's first attempts to categorize what he saw. Ancient sages believed that all things were composed of combinations of these basic elements—earth, air, fire, and water. This included the human character, which was fiery/choleric, earthy/melancholy, airy/sanguine, or watery/phlegmatic. The elements also correspond to our emotional (water), physical (earth), mental (air), and spiritual (fire) natures. The energies of each of the elements were then observed to relate to the time of year when the sun was passing through a certain segment of the zodiac.

Those born with the sun in fire signs—Aries, Leo, Sagittarius—embody the characteristics of that element. Optimism, warmth, hot tempers, enthusiasm, and "spirit" are typical of these signs. Taurus, Virgo, and Capricorn are "earthy"—more grounded, physical, materialistic, organized, and deliberate than fire sign people. Air sign people—Gemini, Libra, and Aquarius—are mentally oriented communicators. Water signs—Cancer, Scorpio, and Pisces—are emotional, sensitive, and creative.

Think of what each element does to the others: water puts out fire or evaporates under heat. Air fans the flames or blows them out. Earth smothers fire, drifts and erodes with too much wind, and becomes mud or fertile soil with water. Those are often perfect analogies for the relationships between people of different sun-sign elements. This astrochemistry was one of the first ways man described his relationships. Fortunately, no one is entirely "air" or "water." We all have a bit, or a lot, of each element in our horoscopes. It is this unique mix that defines each astrological personality.

Within each element, there are three qualities that describe types of behavior associated with the sign. Those of cardinal signs are activists, go-getters. These four signs—Aries, Cancer, Libra, and Capricorn—begin each season. Fixed signs, which happen in the middle of the season, are associated with builders and stabilizers. You'll find that Taurus, Leo, Scorpio, and Aquarius are usually gifted with concentration, stamina, and focus. Mutable signs—Gemini, Virgo, Sagittarius, and Pisces—fall at the end of each season and thus are considered catalysts for change. People born under mutable signs are flexible and adaptable.

The polarity of a sign is either its positive or negative "charge." It can be masculine, active, positive, and yang, like air or fire signs, or it can be feminine, reactive, negative, and yin, like the water and earth signs. The polarities alternate, moving energy around the zodiac like the poles of a battery.

Finally, we consider the sign's place in the order of the zodiac. This is vital to the balance of all the forces and the transmission of energy moving through the signs. You may have noticed that your sign is quite different from your neighboring sign on either side. Yet each seems to grow out of its predecessor like links in a chain and transmits a synthesis of energy gathered along the "chain" to the following sign, beginning with the fire-powered positive charge of Aries.

How the Signs Add Up

SIGN	ELEMENT	QUALITY	POLARITY	PLACE
Aries	fire	cardinal	masculine	first
Taurus	earth	fixed	feminine	second
Gemini	air	mutable	masculine	third
Cancer	water	cardinal	feminine	fourth
Leo	fire	fixed	masculine	fifth
Virgo	earth	mutable	feminine	sixth
Libra	air	cardinal	masculine	seventh
Scorpio	water	fixed	feminine	eighth
Sagittarius	fire	mutable	masculine	ninth
Capricorn	earth	cardinal	feminine	tenth
Aquarius	air	fixed	masculine	eleventh
Pisces	water	mutable	feminine	twelfth

Each Sign Has a Special Planet

Each sign has a "ruling" planet that is most compatible with its energies. Mars adds its fiery assertive characteristics to Aries. The sensual beauty and comfort-loving side of Venus rules Taurus, whereas the idealistic side of Venus rules Libra. Quick-moving Mercury rules two mutable signs, Gemini and Virgo. Its mental agility belongs to Gemini while its analytical side is best expressed in Virgo. The changeable emotional moon is associated with Cancer, while the outgoing Leo personality is ruled by the sun. Scorpio originally shared Mars, but when Pluto was discovered in the last century, its powerful magnetic energies were deemed more suitable to the intense vibrations of the fixed water sign Scorpio. Though Pluto has, as of this writing, been downgraded, it is still considered by astrologers to be a powerful force in the horoscope. Disciplined Capricorn is ruled by Saturn, and expansive Sagittarius by Jupiter. Unpredictable Aquarius is ruled by Uranus and creative, imaginative Pisces by Neptune. In a horoscope, if a planet is placed in the sign it rules, it is sure to be especially powerful.

The Layout of a Horoscope Chart

A horoscope chart is a map of the heavens at a given moment in time. It looks like a wheel with twelve spokes. In between each of the "spokes" is a section called a *house*.

Each house deals with a different area of life and is influenced by a special sign and a planet. Astrologers look at the houses to tell in what area of life an event is happening or about to happen.

The house is governed by the sign passing over the spoke (or cusp of the house) at that particular moment. Though the first house is naturally associated with Aries and Mars, it would also have an additional Capricorn influence if that sign was passing over the house cusp at the time the chart was cast. The sequence of the houses starts with the first house located at the left center spoke (or the number 9 position, if you were reading a clock). The houses are then read *counterclockwise* around the chart, with the fourth house at the bottom of the chart, the tenth house at the top or twelve o'clock position.

Where do the planets belong? Around the horoscope, planets are placed within the houses according to their location at the time of the chart. That is why it is so important to have an accurate time; with no specific time, the planets have no specific location in the houses and one cannot determine which area of life they will apply to. Since the signs move across the houses as the earth turns, planets in a house will naturally intensify the importance of that house. The house that contains the sun is naturally one of the most prominent.

The First House: Self

The sign passing over the first house at the time of your birth is known as your ascendant, or rising sign. The first house is the house of "firsts"—the first impression you make, how you initiate matters, the image you choose to project. This is where you advertise yourself, where you project your personality. Planets that fall here will intensify the way you come across to others. It is the home of Aries and the planet Mars.

The Second House: The Material You

This house is where you experience the material world, what you value. Here are your attitudes about money, possessions, and finances, as well as your earning and spending capacity. On a deeper level, this house reveals your sense of self-worth, the inner values that draw wealth in various forms. It is the natural home of Taurus and the planet Venus.

The Third House: Your Thinking Process

This house describes how you communicate with others, how you reach out to others nearby and interact with the immediate environment. It shows how your thinking process works and the way you express your thoughts. Are you articulate or tongue-tied? Can you think on your feet? This house also shows your first relationships, your experiences with brothers and sisters, as well as how you deal with people close to you, such as your neighbors or pals. It's where you take short trips, write letters, or use the telephone. It shows how your mind works in terms of left-brain logical and analytical functions. It is the home of Gemini and the planet Mercury.

The Fourth House: Your Home Life

The fourth house shows the foundation of life, the psychological underpinnings. Located at the bottom of the chart, this house shows how you are nurtured and made to feel secure—your roots! It shows your early home environment and the circumstances at the end of your life (your final "home"), as well as the place you call home now. Astrologers look here for information about the parental nurturers in your life. It is the home of Cancer and the moon.

The Fifth House: Your Self-Expression

The Leo house is where the creative potential develops. Here you express yourself and procreate, in the sense that children are outgrowths of your creative ability. But this house most represents your inner childlike self, who delights in play. If your inner security has been established by the time you reach this house, you are now free to have fun, romance, and love affairs and to give of yourself. This is also the place astrologers look for playful love affairs, flirtations, and brief romantic encounters (rather than long-term commitments). It is the home of Leo and the sun.

The Sixth House: Care and Maintenance

The sixth house has been called the "care and maintenance" department. This house shows how you take care of your body and organize yourself to perform efficiently in the world. Here is where you get things done, where you look after others and fulfill service duties, such as taking care of pets. Here is what you do to survive on a day-to-day basis. The sixth house demands order in your life; otherwise there would be chaos. The house is your "job" (as opposed to your career, which is the domain of the tenth house), your diet, and your health and fitness regimens. It is the home of Virgo and the planet Mercury.

The Seventh House: Your Relationships

This house shows your attitude toward your partners and those with whom you enter commitments, contracts, or agreements. Here is the way you relate to others, as well as your close, intimate, one-on-one relationships (including open enemies—those you "face off" with). Open hostilities, lawsuits, divorces, and marriages happen here. If the first house represents the "I," the seventh or opposite house is the "not I"—the complementary partner you attract by the way you come across. If you are having trouble with partnerships, consider what you are attracting by the energies of your first and seventh house. It is the home of Libra and the planet Venus.

The Eighth House: Your Power House

The eighth house refers to how you merge with something or someone, and how you handle power and control. This is one of the most mysterious and powerful houses, where your energy transforms itself from "I" to "we." As you give up power and control by uniting with something or someone, two kinds of energies merge and become something greater, leading to a regeneration of the self on a higher level. Here are your attitudes toward sex, shared resources, and taxes (what you share with the government). Because this house involves what belongs to others, you face issues of control and power struggles, or undergo a deep psychological transformation as you bond with another. Here you transcend yourself through dreams, drugs, and occult or psychic experiences that reflect the collective unconscious. It is the home of Scorpio and the planet Pluto.

The Ninth House: Your Worldview

The ninth house shows your search for wisdom and higher knowledge: your belief system. As the third house represents the "lower mind," its opposite on the wheel, the ninth house, is the "higher mind," the abstract, intuitive, spiritual mind that asks "big" questions, like "Why we are here?" After the third house has explored what was close at hand, the ninth stretches out to broaden you mentally with higher education and travel. Here you stretch spiritually with religious activity. Since you are concerned with how everything is related, you tend to push boundaries and take risks. Here is where you express your ideas in a book or thesis, where you pontificate, philosophize, or preach. It is the home of Sagittarius and the planet Jupiter.

The Tenth House: Your Public Life

The tenth house is associated with your public life and high-profile activities. Located directly overhead at the "high noon" position on the horoscope wheel, this is the most "visible" house in the chart, the one where the world sees you. It deals with your career (but not your routine "job") and your reputation. Here is where you go public, take on responsibilities (as opposed to the fourth house, where you stay home). This will affect the career you choose and your "public relations." This house is also associated with your father figure or the main authority figure in your life. It is the home of Capricorn and the planet Saturn.

The Eleventh House: Your Social Concerns

The eleventh house is where you extend yourself to a group, a goal, or a belief system. This house is where you define what you really want: the kinds of friends you have, your political affiliations, and the kind of groups you identify with as an equal. Here is where you become concerned with "what other people think" or where you rebel against social conventions. It's where you become a socially conscious humanitarian or a partying social butterfly. It's where you look to others to stimulate you and discover your kinship to the rest of humanity. The sign on this house can help you understand what you gain and lose from friendships. It is the home of Aquarius and the planet Uranus.

The Twelfth House:
Where You Become Selfless

Old-fashioned astrologers used to put a rather negative spin on this house, calling it the "house of self-undoing." When we "undo ourselves," we surrender control, boundaries, limits, and rules. The twelfth house is where the boundaries between yourself and others become blurred and you become selfless. But instead of being self-undoing, the twelfth house can be a place of great creativity and talent. It is the place where you can tap into the collective unconscious, where your imagination is limitless.

In your trip around the zodiac, you've gone from the "I" of self-assertion in the first house to the final house, which symbolizes the dissolution that happens before rebirth. The twelfth house is where accumulated experiences are processed in the unconscious. Spiritually oriented astrologers look to this house for evidence of past lives and karma. Places where we go for solitude or to do spiritual or reparatory work belong here, such as retreats, religious institutions, or hospitals. Here is also where we withdraw from society voluntarily or involuntarily, and where we are put in prison because of antisocial activity. Selfless giving through charitable acts is part of this house, as is helpless receiving or dependence on charity.

In your daily life, the twelfth house reveals your deepest intimacies, your best-kept secrets, especially those you hide from yourself and repress deep in the unconscious. It is where we surrender a sense of a separate self to a deep feeling of wholeness, such as selfless service in religion or any activity that involves merging with the greater whole. Many sports stars have important planets in the twelfth house, which enable them to play in the zone, finding an inner, almost mystical, strength that transcends their limits. The twelfth house is the home of Pisces and the planet Neptune.

Which Are the Most Powerful Houses?

Houses are stronger or weaker depending on how many planets are inhabiting them. If there are many planets in a given house, it follows that the activities of that house will be especially important in your life. If the planet that rules the house is also located there, this too adds power to the house. The most powerful houses are the first, fourth, seventh, and tenth. These are the houses on "the angles" of a horoscope.

CHAPTER 4

The Moon: Your Inner Light

In some astrology-conscious lands, the moon is given as much importance in a horoscope as the sun. Astrologers often refer to these two bodies as the "lights," an appropriate description, since the sun and moon are not planets, but a star and a satellite. But it is also true that these two bodies shed the most "light" on a horoscope reading.

As the sun shines *out* in a horoscope, revealing the personality, the moon shines *in*. The sign the moon was transiting at the time of your birth reveals much about the inner you, secrets like what you really care about, what makes you feel comfortable and secure. It represents the receptive, reflective, female, nurturing self. It also reflects the one who nurtured you, the mother or mother figure in your chart. In a man's chart, the moon position describes his receptive, emotional, yin side, as well as the woman in his life who will have the deepest effect, usually his mother. (Venus reveals the kind of woman who will attract him physically.)

The moon is more at home in some signs than in others. It rules maternal Cancer and is exalted in Taurus—both comforting, home-loving signs where the natural emotional energies of the moon are easily and productively expressed. But when the moon is in the opposite signs—Capricorn and Scorpio—it leaves the comfortable nest and deals with emotional issues of power and achievement in the outside world. If you were born with the moon in one of these signs, you may find your emotional role in life more challenging.

To determine your moon sign, it is worthwhile to have an accurate horoscope cast, either by an astrologer, a computer program, or one of the online astrology sites that offer free charts. Since detailed moon tables are too extensive for this book, check through the following listing to find the moon sign that feels most familiar.

Moon in Aries

This placement makes you both independent and ardent. You are an idealist, and you tend to fall in and out of love easily. You love a challenge but could cool once your quarry is captured. Your emotional reactions are fast and fiery, quickly expressed and quickly forgotten. You may not think before expressing your feelings. It's not easy to hide how you feel. Channeling all your emotional energy could be one of your big challenges.

Celebrity example: Angelina Jolie

Moon in Taurus

You are a sentimental soul who is very fond of the good life and gravitates toward solid, secure relationships. You like displays of affection and creature comforts—all the tangible trappings of a cozy, safe, calm atmosphere. You are sensual and steady emotionally, but very stubborn, possessive, and determined. You can't be pushed and tend to dislike changes. You should make an effort to broaden your horizons and to take a risk sometimes. You may become very attached to your home turf, your garden, and your possessions. You may also be a collector of objects that are meaningful to you.

Celebrity example: Prince Charles

Moon in Gemini

You crave mental stimulation and variety in life, which you usually get via a varied social life, the excitement of flirtation, or multiple professional involvements. You may marry more than once and have a rather chaotic emotional life due to your difficulty with commitment and settling down, as well as your need to be constantly on the go. (Be sure to find a partner who is as outgoing as you are.) You will have to learn at some point to focus your energies because you tend to be somewhat fragmented—to do two things at once, to have two homes, or even to have two lovers. If you can find a creative way to express your many-faceted nature, you'll be ahead of the game.

Celebrity example: Jim Carrey

Moon in Cancer

This is the most powerful lunar position, which is sure to make a deep imprint on your character. Your needs are very much associated with your reaction to the needs of others. You are very sensitive, caring, and self-protective, though some of you may mask this with a hard shell, like the moon-sensitive crab. This placement also gives an excellent memory, keen intuition, and an uncanny ability to perceive the needs of others. All of the lunar phases will affect you, especially full moons and eclipses, so you would do well to mark them on your calendar. Because you're happiest at home, you may work at home or turn your office into a second home, where you can nurture and comfort people. (You may tend to mother the world.) With natural psychic, intuitive ability, you might be drawn to occult work in some way. Or you may get professionally involved with providing food and shelter to others.

Celebrity example: Tom Cruise

Moon in Leo

This warm, passionate moon takes everything to heart. You are attracted to all that is noble, generous, and aristocratic in life (and you may be a bit of a snob). You have an innate ability to take command emotionally, but you do need strong support, loyalty, and loud applause from those you love. You are possessive of your loved ones and your turf and will roar if anyone threatens to take over your territory.

Celebrity example: Paul McCartney

Moon in Virgo

You are rather cool until you decide if others measure up. But once someone or something meets your high standards, you hold up your end of the arrangement perfectly. You may, in fact, drive yourself too hard to attain some notion of perfection. Try to be a bit easier on yourself and others. Don't always act the censor! You love to be the teacher; you are drawn to situations where you can change others for the better, but sometimes you must learn to accept others for what they are—enjoy what you have!

Celebrity example: John F. Kennedy

Moon in Libra

Like other air-sign moons, you think before you feel. Therefore, you may not immediately recognize the emotional needs of others. However, you are relationship-oriented and may find it difficult to be alone or to do things alone. After you have learned emotional balance by leaning on yourself first, you can have excellent partnerships. It is best for you to avoid extremes, which set your scales swinging and can make your love life precarious. You thrive in a rather conservative, traditional, romantic relationship, where you receive attention and flattery—but not possessiveness—from your partner. You'll be your most charming in an elegant, harmonious atmosphere.

Celebrity example: Leonardo DiCaprio

Moon in Scorpio

This is a moon that enjoys and responds to intense, passionate feelings. You may go to extremes and have a very dramatic emotional life, full of ardor, suspicion, jealousy, and obsession. It would be much healthier to channel your need for power and control into meaningful work. This is a good position for anyone in the fields of medicine, police work, research, the occult, psychoanalysis, or intuitive work, because life-and-death situations don't faze you. However, you do take personal disappointments very hard.

Celebrity example: Elizabeth Taylor

Moon in Sagittarius

You take life's ups and downs with good humor and the proverbial grain of salt. You'll love 'em and leave 'em or take off on a great adventure at a moment's notice. "Born free" could be your slogan. Attracted by the exotic, you have mental and physical wanderlust. You may be too much in search of new mental and spiritual stimulation to ever settle down.

   Celebrity example: Donald Trump

Moon in Capricorn

Are you ever accused of being too cool and calculating? You have an earthy side, but you take prestige and position very seriously. Your strong drive to succeed extends to your romantic life, where you will be devoted to improving your lifestyle and rising to the top. A structured situation where you can advance methodically makes you feel wonderfully secure. You may be attracted to someone older or very much younger or from a different social world. It may be difficult to look at the lighter side of emotional relationships. Though this moon is placed in the sign to your detriment, the good news is that you tend to be very dutiful and responsible to those you care for.

   Celebrity example: Brad Pitt

Moon in Aquarius

You are a people collector with many friends of all backgrounds. You are happiest surrounded by people, and you may feel uneasy when left alone. Though you usually stay friends with lovers, intense emotions and demanding one-on-one relationships turn you off. You don't like anything to be too rigid or scheduled. Though tolerant and understanding, you can be emotionally unpredictable; you may opt for an unconventional love life. With plenty of space, you will be able to sustain relationships with liberal, freedom-loving types.

   Celebrity example: Princess Diana

Moon in Pisces

You are very responsive and empathetic to others, especially if they have problems or are the underdog. (Be on guard against attracting too many people with sob stories.) You'll be happiest if you can express your creative imagination in the arts or in the spiritual or healing professions. Because you may tend to escape in fantasies or overreact to the moods of others, you need an emotional anchor to help you keep a firm foothold in reality. Steer clear of too much escapism (especially in alcohol) or reclusiveness. Places near water soothe your moods. Working in a field that gives you emotional variety will also help you be productive.

Celebrity example: Elvis Presley

CHAPTER 5

The Planets: The Power of Ten

If you know a person's sun sign, you can learn some very useful generic information, but when you know the placement of all ten planets (eight planets plus the sun and moon), you've got a much more accurate profile of the person's character. Then the subject of the horoscope becomes a unique individual, as well as a member of a certain sun sign. You'll discover what makes him angry (Mars), pleased (Venus), or fearful (Saturn).

The planets are the doers of the horoscope, each representing a basic force in life. The sign and house where the planet is located indicate how and where its force will operate. For a moment, think of the horoscope as real estate. Prime property is close to the rising sign or at the top of the chart. If two or more planets are grouped together in one sign, they usually operate like a team, playing off each other, rather than expressing their energy singularly. But a loner, a planet that stands far away from the others, is usually outstanding and often calls the shots.

The sign of a planet also has a powerful influence. In some signs, the planet's energies are very much at home and can easily express themselves. In others, the planet has to work harder and is slightly out of sorts. The sign that most corresponds to the planet's energies is said to be ruled by that planet and obviously is the best place for that planet to be. The next best place is a sign where it is exalted, or especially harmonious. On the other hand, there are places in the horoscope where a planet has to stretch itself to play its role, such as the sign opposite a planet's rulership, which embodies the opposite area of life, and the sign opposite its exaltation. However, a planet that must work harder can also be more complete, because it must grow to meet the challenges of living in a more difficult sign. Like world leaders who've had to struggle for greatness, this planet may actually develop strength and character.

Here's a list of the best places for each planet to be. Note that, as new planets were discovered in the last century, they replaced the traditional rulers of signs which best complemented their energies.

ARIES—Mars
TAURUS—Venus, in its most sensual form
GEMINI—Mercury, in its communicative role
CANCER—the moon
LEO—the sun
VIRGO—also Mercury, this time in its more critical capacity
LIBRA—also Venus, in its more aesthetic, judgmental form
SCORPIO—Pluto, co-ruled by Mars
SAGITTARIUS—Jupiter
CAPRICORN—Saturn
AQUARIUS—Uranus, replacing Saturn, its original ruler
PISCES—Neptune, replacing Jupiter, its original ruler

Those who have many planets in exalted signs are lucky indeed, for here is where the planet can accomplish the most and be its most influential and creative.

SUN—exalted in Aries, where its energy creates action
MOON—exalted in Taurus, where instincts and reactions operate on a highly creative level
MERCURY—exalted in Aquarius, where it can reach analytical heights
VENUS—exalted in Pisces, a sign whose sensitivity encourages love and creativity
MARS—exalted in Capricorn, a sign that puts energy to work productively
JUPITER—exalted in Cancer, where it encourages nurturing and growth
SATURN—at home in Libra, where it steadies the scales of justice and promotes balanced, responsible judgment

URANUS—powerful in Scorpio, where it promotes transformation

NEPTUNE—especially favored in Cancer, where it gains the security to transcend to a higher state

PLUTO—exalted in Pisces, where it dissolves the old cycle, to make way for transition to the new

The Personal Planets: Mercury, Venus, and Mars

These planets work in your immediate personal life.

Mercury affects how you communicate and how your mental processes work. Are you a quick study who grasps information rapidly, or do you learn more slowly and thoroughly? How is your concentration? Can you express yourself easily? Are you a good writer? All these questions can be answered by your Mercury placement.

Venus shows what you react to. What turns you on? What appeals to you aesthetically? Are you charming to others? Are you attractive to look at? Your taste, your refinement, your sense of balance and proportion are all Venus-ruled.

Mars is your outgoing energy, your drive and ambition. Do you reach out for new adventures? Are you assertive? Are you motivated? Self-confident? Hot-tempered? How you channel your energy and drive is revealed by your Mars placement.

Mercury Shows How Your Mind Works

Since Mercury never travels far from the sun, read Mercury in your sun sign, and then the signs preceding and following it. Then decide which reflects the way you think.

Mercury in Aries

Your mind is very active and assertive. It approaches a plan aggressively. You never hesitate to say what you think, never shy away from a battle. In fact, you may relish a verbal confrontation. Tact is not your strong point, so you may have to learn not to trip over your tongue.

Mercury in Taurus

This is a much more cautious Mercury. Though you may be a slow learner, you have good concentration and mental stamina. You want to make your ideas really happen. You'll attack a problem methodically and consider every angle thoroughly, never jumping to conclusions. You'll stick with a subject until you master it.

Mercury in Gemini

You are a wonderful communicator with great facility for expressing yourself both verbally and in writing. You love gathering all kinds of information. You probably finish other people's sentences and express yourself with eloquent hand gestures. You can talk to anybody anytime and probably have phone and E-mail bills to prove it. You read anything from sci-fi to Shakespeare and might need an extra room just for your book collection. Though you learn fast, you may lack focus and discipline. Watch a tendency to jump from subject to subject.

Mercury in Cancer

You rely on intuition more than logic. Your mental processes are usually colored by your emotions, so you may seem shy or hesitant to voice your opinions. However, this placement gives you the advantage of great imagination and empathy in the way you communicate with others.

Mercury in Leo

You are enthusiastic and very dramatic in the way you express yourself. You like to hold the attention of groups and could be a great public speaker. Your mind thinks big, so you'd prefer to deal with the overall picture rather than with the details.

Mercury in Virgo

This is one of the best places for Mercury. It should give you critical ability, attention to details, and thorough analysis. Your mind focuses on the practical side of things. This type of thinking is very well suited to being a teacher or editor.

Mercury in Libra

You're either a born diplomat who smooths over ruffled feathers or a talented debater. Many lawyers have this placement. However, since you're forever weighing the pros and cons of a situation, you may vacillate when making decisions.

Mercury in Scorpio

This is an investigative mind that stops at nothing to get the answers. You may have a sarcastic, stinging wit, a gift for the cutting remark. There's always a grain of truth to your verbal sallies, thanks to your penetrating insight.

Mercury in Sagittarius

You are a super salesman with a tendency to expound. Though you are very broad-minded, you can be dogmatic when it comes to telling others what's good for them. You won't hesitate to tell the truth as you see it, so watch a tendency toward tactlessness. On the plus side, you have a great sense of humor. This position of Mercury is often considered by astrologers to be at a disadvantage because Sagittarius opposes Gemini, the sign Mercury rules, and squares off with Virgo, another Mercury-ruled sign. What often happens is that Mercury in Sagittarius oversteps its bounds and loses sight of the facts in a situation. Do a reality check before making promises that you may not be able to deliver.

Mercury in Capricorn

This placement endows good mental discipline. You have a love of learning and a very orderly approach to your subjects. You will patiently plod through the facts and figures until you have mastered the tasks. You grasp structured situations easily, but may be short on creativity.

Mercury in Aquarius

An independent, original thinker, you'll have more cutting-edge ideas than the average person. You'll be quick to check out any unusual opportunities. Your opinions are so well-researched and grounded that once your mind is made up, it is difficult to change.

Mercury in Pisces

You have the psychic intuitive mind of a natural poet. Learn to make use of your creative imagination. You may think in terms of helping others, but check a tendency to be vague and forgetful of details.

Venus Is the Popularity Planet

Venus tells how you relate to others and to your environment. It shows where you receive pleasure and what you love to do. Find your Venus placement on the chart in this book by looking for the year of your birth in the left-hand column. Then follow the line of that year across the page until you reach the time period of your birthday. The sign heading that column will be your Venus. If you were born on a day when Venus was changing signs, check the signs preceding or following that day to determine if that feels more like your Venus nature.

Venus in Aries

You can't stand to be bored, confined, or ordered around. But a good challenge, maybe even a rousing row, turns you on. Confess—don't you pick a fight now and then just to get someone stirred up? You're attracted by the chase, not the catch, which could cause some problems in your love life, if the object of your affection becomes too attainable. You like to wear red and can spot a trend before anyone else.

Venus in Taurus

All your senses work in high gear. You love to be surrounded by glorious tastes, smells, textures, sounds, and visuals—austerity is not for you. Neither is being rushed. You like time to enjoy your pleasures. Soothing surroundings with plenty of creature comforts are your cup of tea. You like to feel secure in your nest, with no sudden jolts or surprises. You like familiar objects—in fact, you may hate to let anything or anyone go.

Venus in Gemini

You are a lively, sparkling personality who thrives in a situation that affords a constant variety and a frequent change of scenery. A varied social life is important to you, with plenty of mental stimulation and a chance to engage in some light flirtation. Commitment may be difficult, because playing the field is so much fun.

Venus in Cancer

An atmosphere where you feel protected, coddled, and mothered is best for you. You love to be surrounded by children in a cozy, homelike situation. You are attracted to those who are tender and nurturing, who make you feel secure and well provided for. You may be quite secretive about your emotional life or attracted to clandestine relationships.

Venus in Leo

First-class attention in large doses turns you on, and so does the glitter of real gold and the flash of mirrors. You like to feel like a star at all times, surrounded by your admiring audience. The side effect is that you may be attracted to flatterers and tinsel, while the real gold requires some digging.

Venus in Virgo

Everything neatly in its place? On the surface, you are attracted to an atmosphere where everything is in perfect order, but underneath are some basic, earthy urges. You are attracted to those who appeal to your need to teach, be of service, or play out a Pygmalion fantasy. You are at your best when you are busy doing something useful.

Venus in Libra

Elegance and harmony are your key words. You can't abide an atmosphere of contention. Your taste tends toward the classic, with light harmonies of color—nothing clashing, trendy, or outrageous. You love doing things with a partner and should be careful to pick one who is decisive, but patient enough to let you weigh the pros and cons. And steer clear of argumentative types.

Venus in Scorpio

Mysteries intrigue you—in fact, anything that is too open and aboveboard is a bit of a bore. You surely have a stack of whodunits by the bed, along with an erotic magazine or two. You like to solve puzzles. You may also be fascinated with the occult, crime, or scientific research. Intense, all-or-nothing situations add spice to your life, and you love to ferret out the secrets of others. But you could get burned by your flair for living dangerously. The color black, spicy food, dark wood furniture, and heady perfume put you in the right mood.

Venus in Sagittarius

If you are not actually a world traveler, your surroundings are sure to reflect your love of faraway places. You like a casual outdoor atmosphere and a dog or two to pet. There should be plenty of room for athletic equipment and suitcases. You're attracted to kindred souls who love to travel and who share your freedom-loving philosophy of life. Athletics and spiritual or New Age pursuits could be other interests.

Venus in Capricorn

No fly-by-night relationships for you! You want substance in life, and you are attracted to whatever will help you get where you are going. Status objects turn you on. And so do those who have a serious, responsible, businesslike approach, or who remind you of a beloved parent. It is characteristic of this placement to be attracted to someone of a different generation. Antiques, traditional clothing, and dignified behavior are becoming to you.

Venus in Aquarius

This Venus wants to make friends, to be "cool." You like to be in a group, particularly one pushing a worthy cause. You feel quite at home surrounded by people, and could even court fame, yet all the while, you tend to remain detached from intense commitment. Original ideas and unpredictable people fascinate you. You prefer spontaneity and delightful surprises, rather than a well-planned schedule of events.

Venus in Pisces

This Venus loves to give of yourself, and you find plenty of takers. Stray animals and people appeal to your heart and your pocketbook, but be careful to look at their motives realistically once in a while. You are extremely vulnerable to sob stories of all kinds. Fantasy, the arts (especially film, dance, and theater), and psychic or spiritual activities also speak to you.

Mars: The Action Hero

Mars is the mover and shaker in your life. It shows how you pursue your goals, whether you have energy to burn or proceed in a slow, steady pace. It will also show how you get angry. Do you explode, or do a slow burn, or hold everything inside and then get revenge later?

To find your Mars, turn to the chart on pages 82–94. Then find your birth year in the left-hand column and find the line headed by the month of your birth. There you will find an abbreviation of your Mars sign. If the description of your Mars sign doesn't ring true, read the description of the signs preceding and following it. You might have been born on a day when Mars was changing signs, in which case your Mars might fall into the adjacent sign.

Mars in Aries

In the sign it rules, Mars shows its brilliant fiery nature. You have an explosive temper and can be quite impatient. On the other hand, you have tremendous courage, energy, and drive. You'll let nothing stand in your way as you race to be first! Obstacles are met head-on and broken through by force. However, problems that require patience and persistence to solve can have you exploding in rage. You're a great starter, but not necessarily around for the finish.

Mars in Taurus

Slow, steady, concentrated energy gives you the power to last until the finish line. You've great stamina, and you never give up. Your tactic is to wear away obstacles with your persistence. Often you come out a winner because you've had the patience to hang in there. When angered, you do a slow burn.

Mars in Gemini

You can't sit still for long. This Mars craves variety. You often have two or more things going on at once—it's all an amusing game to you. Your life can get very complicated, but that only adds spice and stimulation. What drives you into a nervous, hyper state? Boredom, sameness, routine, and confinement. You can do wonderful things with your hands, and you have a way with words.

Mars in Cancer

You rarely attack head-on. Instead, you'll keep things to yourself, make plans in secret, and always cover your actions. This might be interpreted by some as manipulative, but you are only being self-protective. You get furious when anyone knows too much about you. But you do like to know all about others. Your mothering and feeding instincts can be put to good use, if you work in the food, hotel, or child-care-related businesses. You may have to overcome your fragile sense of security, which prompts you not to take risks and to get physically upset when criticized. Don't take things so personally!

Mars in Leo

You have a very dominant personality that takes center stage—modesty is not one of your traits, nor is taking a back seat. You prefer giving the orders and have been known to make a dramatic scene if they are not obeyed. Properly used, this Mars confers leadership ability, endurance, and courage.

Mars in Virgo

You are the fault-finder of the zodiac, who notices every detail. Mistakes of any kind make you very nervous. You may worry, even if everything is going smoothly. You may not express your anger directly, but you sure can nag. You have definite likes and dislikes, and you are sure you can do the job better than anyone else. You are certainly more industrious and detail-oriented than other signs. Your Mars energy is often most positively expressed in some kind of teaching role.

Mars in Libra

This Mars will have a passion for beauty, justice, and art. Generally, you will avoid confrontations at all costs. You prefer to spend your energy finding diplomatic solutions or weighing pros and cons. Your other techniques are passive aggression or exercising your well-known charm to get people to do what you want.

Mars in Scorpio

This is a powerful placement, so intense that it demands careful channeling into worthwhile activities. Otherwise, you could become obsessed with your sexuality or might use your need for power and control to manipulate others. You are strong-willed, shrewd, and very private about your affairs, and you'll usually have a secret agenda behind your actions. Your great stamina, focus, and discipline would be excellent assets for careers in the military or medical fields, especially research or surgery. When angry, you don't get mad—you get even!

Mars in Sagittarius

This expansive Mars often propels people into sales, travel, athletics or philosophy. Your energies function well when you are on the move. You have a hot temper and are inclined to say what you think before you consider the consequences. You shoot for high goals—and talk endlessly about them—but you may be weak on groundwork. This Mars needs a solid foundation. Watch a tendency to take unnecessary risks.

Mars in Capricorn

This is an ambitious Mars with an excellent sense of timing. You have an eye for those who can be of use to you, and you may dismiss people ruthlessly when you're angry. But you drive yourself hard and deliver full value. This is a good placement for an executive. You'll aim for status and a high material position in life, and keep climbing despite the odds. A great Mars to have!

Mars in Aquarius

This is the most rebellious Mars. You seem to have a drive to assert yourself against the status quo. You may enjoy provoking people, shocking them out of traditional views. Or this placement could express itself in an offbeat sex life. Somehow you often find yourself in unconventional situations. You enjoy being a leader of an active group, which pursues forward-looking studies, politics, or goals.

Mars in Pisces

This Mars is a good actor who knows just how to appeal to the sympathies of others. You create and project wonderful fantasies or use your sensitive antennae to crusade for those less fortunate. You get what you want through creating a veil of illusion and glamour. This is a good Mars for someone in the creative and imaginative fields—a dancer, a performer, a photographer, or an actor. Many famous film stars have this placement. Watch a tendency to manipulate by making others feel sorry for you.

Jupiter Is the Optimist

This big, bright, swirling mass of gases is associated with abundance, prosperity, and the kind of windfall you get without too much hard work. You're optimistic under Jupiter's influence, when anything seems possible. You'll travel, expand your mind with higher education, and publish to share your knowledge widely. On the other hand, Jupiter's influence is neither discriminating nor disciplined. It represents the principle of growth without judgment. Therefore, if not kept in check, it could result in extravagance, weight gain, laziness, and carelessness.

Be sure to look up your Jupiter in the tables in this book. When the current position of Jupiter is favorable, you may get that lucky break. This is a great time to try new things, take risks, travel, or get more education. Opportunities seem to open up easily, so take advantage of them.

Once a year, Jupiter changes signs. That means you are due for an expansive time every twelve years, when Jupiter travels through your sun sign. You'll also have periods every four years when Jupiter is in the same element as your sun sign.

Jupiter in Aries

You are the soul of enthusiasm and optimism. Your luckiest times are when you are getting started on an exciting project or selling an ideal that you really believe in. You may have to watch a tendency to be arrogant with those who do not share your enthusiasm. You follow your impulses, often ignoring budget or other commonsense limitations. To produce real, solid benefits, you'll need patience and the will to follow through wherever this Jupiter falls in your horoscope.

Jupiter in Taurus

You'll spend money on beautiful material things, especially those that come from nature—items made of rare woods, natural fabrics, or precious gems, for instance. You can't have too much comfort or too many sensual pleasures. Watch a tendency to overindulge in good food, or to overpamper yourself with nothing but the best. Spartan living is not for you! You may be especially lucky in matters of real estate.

Jupiter in Gemini

You are the great talker of the zodiac, and you may be a great writer too. But restlessness could be your weak point. You jump around and talk too much; you could be a jack-of-all-trades. Keeping a secret is especially difficult, so you'll also have to watch a tendency to spill the beans. Since you love to be at the center of a beehive of activity, you'll have a vibrant social life. Your best opportunities will come through your talent for language: speaking, writing, communicating, and selling.

Jupiter in Cancer

You are luckiest in situations where you can find emotional closeness or deal with basic security needs, such as food, nurturing, or shelter. You may be a great collector, and you may simply love to accumulate things—you are the one who stashes things away for a rainy day. You probably have a very good memory and love children—in fact, you may have many children to care for. The food, hotel, child-care, and shipping businesses hold good opportunities for you.

Jupiter in Leo

You are a natural showman who loves to live in a larger-than-life way. Yours is a personality full of color that always finds its way into the limelight. You can't have too much attention. Showbiz is a natural place for you, and so is any area where you can play to a crowd. Exercising your flair for drama, your natural playfulness, and your romantic nature brings you good fortune. But watch a tendency to be overextravagant or to monopolize center stage.

Jupiter in Virgo

You actually love those minute details others find boring. To you, they make all the difference between the perfect and the ordinary. You are the fine craftsman who spots every flaw. You expand your awareness by finding the most efficient methods and by being of service to others. Many will be drawn to medical or teaching fields. You'll also have luck in publishing, crafts, nutrition, and service professions. Watch out for a tendency to overwork.

Jupiter in Libra

This is an other-directed Jupiter that develops best with a partner, for the stimulation of others helps you grow. You are also most comfortable in harmonious, beautiful situations, and you work well with artistic people. You have a great sense of fair play and an ability to evaluate the pros and cons of a situation. You usually prefer to play the role of diplomat rather than that of adversary.

Jupiter in Scorpio

You love the feeling of power and control, of taking things to their limit. You can't resist a mystery, and your shrewd, penetrating mind sees right through to the heart of most situations and people. You have luck in work that provides for solutions to matters of life and death. You may be drawn to undercover work, behind-the-scenes intrigue, psychotherapy, the occult, and sex-related ventures. Your challenge will be to develop a sense of moderation and tolerance for other beliefs. You may have luck in handling other people's money—insurance, taxes, and inheritance can bring you a windfall.

Jupiter in Sagittarius

Independent, outgoing, and idealistic, you'll shoot for the stars. This Jupiter compels you to travel far and wide, both physically and mentally, via higher education. You may have luck while traveling in an exotic place. You also have luck with outdoor ventures, exercise, and animals, particularly horses. Since you tend to be very open about your opinions, watch a tendency to be tactless and to exaggerate. Instead, use your wonderful sense of humor to make your point.

Jupiter in Capricorn

Jupiter is much more restrained in Capricorn, the sign of rules and authority. Here, Jupiter can make you overwork and heighten any ambition or sense of duty you may have. You'll expand in areas that advance your position, putting you higher up the social or corporate ladder. You are lucky working within the establishment in a very structured situation, where you can show off your ability to organize and reap rewards for your hard work.

Jupiter in Aquarius

This is another freedom-loving Jupiter, with great tolerance and originality. You are at your best when you are working for a humanitarian cause and in the company of many supporters. This is a good Jupiter for a political career. You'll relate to all kinds of people on all social levels. You have an abundance of original ideas, but you are best off away from routine and any situation that imposes rigid rules. You need mental stimulation!

Jupiter in Pisces

You are a giver whose feelings and pocketbook are easily touched by others, so choose your companions with care. You could be the original sucker for a hard-luck story. Better find a worthy hospital or charity to appreciate your selfless support. You have a great creative imagination and may attract good fortune in fields related to oil, perfume, pharmaceuticals, petroleum, dance, footwear, and alcohol. But beware not to overindulge in alcohol—focus on a creative outlet instead.

Saturn Puts on the Brakes

Jupiter speeds you up with lucky breaks, and then along comes Saturn to slow you down with the disciplinary brakes. It is the planet that can help you achieve lasting goals. Saturn has unfairly been called a malefic planet, one of the bad guys of the zodiac. On the contrary, Saturn is one of our best friends—the kind who tells you what you need to hear, even if it's not good news. Under a Saturn transit, we grow up, take responsibility for our lives, and emerge from whatever test this planet has in store as far wiser, more capable, and mature human beings. After all, it is when we are under pressure that we grow stronger.

When Saturn hits a critical point in your horoscope, you can count on an experience that will make you slow up, pull back, and reexamine your life. It is a call to eliminate what is not working and to shape up. By the end of its twenty-eight-year trip around the zodiac, Saturn will have tested you in all areas of your life. The major tests happen in seven-year cycles, when Saturn passes over the angles of your chart—your rising sign, the top of your chart or midheaven, your descendant, and the nadir or bottom of your chart. This is when the real life-changing experiences happen. But you are also in for a testing period whenever Saturn passes a planet in your chart or stresses that planet from a distance. Therefore, it is useful to check your planetary positions with the timetable of Saturn to prepare in advance, or at least to brace yourself.

When Saturn returns to its location at the time of your birth, at approximately age twenty-eight, you'll have your first Saturn return. At this time, a person usually takes stock or settles down to find his mission in life and assumes full adult duties and responsibilities.

Another way Saturn helps us is to reveal the karmic lessons from previous lives and give us the chance to overcome them. So look at Saturn's challenges as much-needed opportunities for self-improvement. Under a Jupiter influence, you'll have more fun, but Saturn gives you solid, long-lasting results.

Look up your natal Saturn in the tables in this book for clues on where you need work.

Saturn in Aries

Saturn here puts the brakes on Aries's natural drive and enthusiasm. There is often an angry side to this placement. You don't let anyone push you around and you know what's best for yourself. Following orders is not your strong point, nor is diplomacy. You tend to be quick to go on the offensive in relationships, attacking first, before anyone attacks you. Because no one quite lives up to your standards, you often wind up doing everything yourself. You'll have to learn to cooperate and tone down any self-centeredness. Pat Buchanan has this Saturn.

Saturn in Taurus

A big issue is getting control of the cash flow. There will be lean periods that can be frightening, but you have the patience and endurance to stick them out and the methodical drive to prosper in the end. Learn to take a philosophical attitude like Ben Franklin, who also had this placement, and who said, "A penny saved is a penny earned."

Saturn in Gemini

You are a serious student of life, who may have difficulty communicating or sharing your knowledge. You may be shy, speak slowly, or have fears about communicating, like Eleanor Roosevelt. You dwell in the realms of science, theory, or abstract analysis, even when you are dealing with the emotions, like Sigmund Freud, who also had this placement.

Saturn in Cancer

Your tests come with establishing a secure emotional base. In doing so, you may have to deal with some very basic fears centering on your early home environment. Most of your Saturn tests will have emotional roots in those early-childhood experiences. You may have difficulty remaining objective in terms of what you try to achieve, so it will be especially important for you to deal with negative feelings such as guilt, paranoia, jealousy, resentment, and suspicion. Galileo and Michelangelo also navigated these murky waters.

Saturn in Leo

This is an authoritarian Saturn—a strict, demanding parent who may deny the pleasure principle in your zeal to see that rules are followed. Though you may feel guilty about taking the spotlight, you are very ambitious and loyal. You have to watch a tendency toward rigidity, also toward overwork and holding back affection. Joseph Kennedy and Billy Graham share this placement.

Saturn in Virgo

This is a cautious, exacting Saturn, intensely hard on yourself. Most of all, you give yourself the roughest time with your constant worries about every little detail, often making yourself sick. You may have difficulties setting priorities and getting the job done. Your tests will come in learning tolerance and understanding of others. Charles de Gaulle, Mae West, and Nathaniel Hawthorne had this meticulous Saturn.

Saturn in Libra

Saturn is exalted here, which makes this planet an ally. You may choose very serious, older partners in life, perhaps stemming from a fear of dependency. You need to learn to stand solidly on your own before you commit to another. Since you are extremely cautious, you deliberate every involvement—with good reason. It is best that you find an occupation that makes good use of your sense of duty and honor. Steer clear of fly-by-night situations. Both Khrushchev and Mao Tse-tung had this placement.

Saturn in Scorpio

You have great staying power. This Saturn tests you in situations involving the control of others. You may feel drawn to some kind of intrigue or undercover work, like J. Edgar Hoover. Or there may be an air of mystery surrounding your life and death, like Marilyn Monroe and Robert Kennedy who both had this placement. There are lessons to be learned from your sexual involvements. Often sex is used for manipulation or is somehow out of the ordinary. The Roman emperor Caligula and the transsexual Christine Jorgensen are extreme cases.

Saturn in Sagittarius

Your challenges and lessons will come from tests of your spiritual and philosophical values, as happened to Martin Luther King Jr. and Gandhi. You are high-minded and sincere with this reflective, moral placement. Uncompromising in your ethical standards, you could become a benevolent despot.

Saturn in Capricorn

With the help of Saturn at maximum strength, your judgment will improve with age. And, like Spencer Tracy's screen image, you'll be the gray-haired hero with a strong sense of responsibility. You advance in life slowly but steadily, always with a strong hand at the helm and an eye for the advantageous situation. Like Pat Robertson, you're likely to stand for conservative values. Negatively, you may be a loner, prone to periods of melancholy.

Saturn in Aquarius

Your tests come from relationships with groups. Do you care too much about what others think? Do you feel like an outsider, like Greta Garbo? You may fear being different from others and therefore slight your own unique, forward-looking gifts. Or like Lord Byron and Howard Hughes, you may take the opposite tack and rebel in the extreme. You can apply discipline to accomplish great humanitarian goals, as Albert Schweitzer did.

Saturn in Pisces

Your fear of the unknown and the irrational may lead you to the safety and protection of an institution. You may go on the run like Jesse James to avoid looking too deeply inside. Or you might go in the opposite, more positive direction and develop a disciplined psychoanalytic approach, which puts you more in control of your feelings. Some of you will take refuge in work with hospitals, charities, or religious institutions. Queen Victoria, who had this placement, symbolized an era when institutions of all kinds were sustained. Discipline applied to artistic work, especially poetry and dance, or spiritual work, such as yoga or meditation, might be helpful.

How Uranus, Neptune, and Pluto Influence Your Generation

These three planets remain in signs such a long time that a whole generation bears the imprint of the sign. Mass movements, great sweeping changes, fads that characterize a generation, and even the issues of the conflicts and wars of the time are influenced by these outer three planets. When one of these distant planets changes signs, there is a definite shift in the atmosphere, the feeling of the end of an era.

Since these planets are so far away from the sun—too distant to be seen by the naked eye—they pick up signals from the universe at large. These planetary receivers literally link the sun with distant energies, and then perform a similar function in your horoscope by linking your central character with intuitive, spiritual, transformative forces from the cosmos. Each planet has a special domain and will reflect this in the area of your chart where it falls.

Uranus Is the Surprise Ingredient

Uranus is the surprise ingredient that sets you and your generation apart. There is nothing ordinary about this quirky green planet that seems to be traveling on its side, surrounded by a swarm of moons. Is it any wonder that astrologers assigned it to Aquarius, the most eccentric and gregarious sign? Uranus seems to wend its way around the sun, marching to its own tune.

Significantly, Uranus follows Saturn, the planet of limitations and structures. Often we get caught up in the structures we have created to give ourselves a sense of security. However, if we lose contact with our spiritual roots in the process, Uranus is likely to jolt us out of our comfortable rut and wake us up.

Uranus energy is electrical, happening in sudden flashes. It is not influenced by karma or past events, nor does it regard tradition, sex, or sentiment. Uranus's key words are surprise and awakening. Suddenly, there's that flash of inspiration, that bright idea, or that totally new approach that revolutionizes whatever scheme you were undertaking. A Uranus event takes you by surprise, for better or for worse. The Uranus place in your life is where you awaken and become your own person, leaving the structures of Saturn behind. And it is probably the most unconventional place in your chart.

Look up the sign of Uranus at the time of your birth and see where you follow your own tune.

Uranus in Aries

Birth Dates:
   March 31, 1927–November 4, 1927
   January 13, 1928–June 6, 1934
   October 10, 1934–March 28, 1935

Your generation is original, creative, and pioneering. It developed the computer, the airplane, and the cyclotron. You let nothing hold you back from exploring the unknown, and you have a powerful mixture of fire and electricity behind you. Women of your generation were among the first to be liberated. You were the unforgettable style setters. You have a surprise in store for everyone. As with Yoko Ono, Grace Kelly, and Jacqueline Onassis, your life may be jolted by sudden and violent changes.

Uranus in Taurus

Birth Dates:
   June 6, 1934–October 10, 1934
   March 28, 1935–August 7, 1941
   October 5, 1941–May 15, 1942

The great territorial shakeups of World War II began during your generation. You're independent; you're probably self-employed or you would like to be. You have original ideas about making money, and you brace yourself for sudden changes of fortune. This Uranus can cause shake-ups, particularly in finances, but it can also make you a born entrepreneur, like Martha Stewart.

Uranus in Gemini

Birth Dates:
  August 7, 1941–October 5, 1941
  May 15, 1942–August 30, 1948
  November 12, 1948–June 10, 1949
  You were the first children to be influenced by television, and in your adult years, your generation stocks up on answering machines, cell phones, computers, and fax machines—any new way you can communicate. You have an inquiring mind, but your interests may be rather short-lived. This Uranus can be easily fragmented if there is no structure and focus.

Uranus in Cancer

Birth Dates:
  August 30–November 12, 1948
  June 10, 1949–August 24, 1955
  January 28, 1956–June 10, 1956
  This generation came at a time when divorce was becoming commonplace, so your home image is unconventional. You may have an unusual relationship with your parents, or come from a broken home or an unconventional one. You'll have unorthodox ideas about parenting, intimacy, food, and shelter. You may also be interested in dreams, psychic phenomena, and memory work.

Uranus in Leo

Birth Dates:
  August 24, 1955–January 28, 1956
  June 10, 1956–November 1, 1961
  January 10, 1962–August 10, 1962
  This generation understood how to use electronic media. Many of your group are now leaders in the high-tech industries, and you also understand how to use the new media to promote yourself. Like Isadora Duncan, you may have a very eccentric kind of charisma and a life that is sparked by unusual love affairs. Your children may have traits that are out of the ordinary. Where this planet falls in your chart, you'll have

a love of freedom, be a bit of an egomaniac, and show the full force of your personality in a unique way, like tennis great Martina Navratilova.

Uranus in Virgo

Birth Dates:
    November 1, 1961–January 10, 1962
    August 10, 1962–September 28, 1968
    May 20, 1969–June 24, 1969
You'll have highly individual work methods, and many will be finding newer, more practical ways to use computers. Like Einstein, who had this placement, you'll break the rules brilliantly. Your generation came at a time of student rebellions, the civil rights movement, and the general acceptance of health foods. Chances are, you're concerned about pollution and cleaning up the environment. You may also be involved with nontraditional healing methods.

Uranus in Libra

Birth Dates:
    September 28, 1968–May 20, 1969
    June 24, 1969–November 21, 1974
    May 1, 1975–September 8, 1975
Your generation will be always changing partners. Born during the era of women's liberation, you may have come from a broken home and may have no clear image of what a marriage entails. There will be many sudden splits and experiments before you settle down. Your generation will be much involved in legal and political reforms and in changing artistic and fashion looks.

Uranus in Scorpio

Birth Dates:
    November 21, 1974–May 1, 1975
    September 8, 1975–February 17, 1981
    March 20, 1981–November 16, 1981
Interest in transformation, meditation, and life after death

signaled the beginning of New Age consciousness. Your generation recognizes no boundaries, no limits, and no external controls. You'll have new attitudes toward death and dying, psychic phenomena, and the occult. Like Mae West and Casanova, you'll shock 'em sexually.

Uranus in Sagittarius

Birth Dates:
> February 17, 1981–March 20, 1981
> November 16, 1981–February 15, 1988
> May 27, 1988–December 2, 1988

Could this generation be the first to travel in outer space? The new generation with this placement included Charles Lindbergh and a time when the first zeppelins and the Wright Brothers were conquering the skies. Uranus here forecasts great discoveries, mind expansion, and long-distance travel. Like Galileo and Martin Luther, those born in these years will generate new theories about the cosmos and man's relation to it.

Uranus in Capricorn

Birth Dates:
> December 20, 1904–January 30, 1912
> September 4, 1912–November 12, 1912
> February 15, 1988–May 27, 1988
> December 2, 1988–April 1, 1995
> June 9, 1995–January 12, 1996

This generation, now reaching adulthood, will challenge traditions. In these years, we got organized with the help of technology put to practical use. The Internet was born after the great economic boom of the 1990s. Great leaders who were movers and shakers of history, like Julius Caesar and Henry VIII, were born under this placement.

Uranus in Aquarius

Birth Dates:
> January 30, 1912–September 4, 1912
> November 12, 1912–April 1, 1919

August 16, 1919–January 22, 1920
April 1, 1995–June 9, 1995
January 12, 1996–March 10, 2003
September 15, 2003–December 30, 2003

Uranus in Aquarius is the strongest placement for this planet. Recently, we've had the opportunity to witness the full force of its power of innovation, as well as its sudden wake-up calls and insistence on humanitarian values. This was a time of high-tech development, when home computers became as ubiquitous as television. It was a time of globalization, surprise attacks (9/11), and underdeveloped countries demanding attention. The last generation with this placement produced great innovative minds, such as Leonard Bernstein and Orson Welles. The next will become another radical breakthrough generation, much concerned with global issues that involve all humanity.

Uranus in Pisces

Birth Dates:
April 1, 1919–August 16, 1919
January 22, 1920–March 31, 1927
November 4, 1927–January 12, 1928
March 10, 2003–September 15, 2003
December 30, 2003–May 28, 2010

Uranus is now in Pisces, ushering in a new generation. In the past century, Uranus in Pisces focused attention on the rise of electronic entertainment—radio and the cinema—and the secretiveness of Prohibition. This produced a generation of idealists exemplified by Judy Garland's theme, "Somewhere over the Rainbow." Uranus in Pisces also hints at stealth activities, at hospital and prison reform, at high-tech drugs and medical experiments, at shake-ups in the petroleum industry and new locations for Pisces-ruled off-shore drilling. Issues regarding the water and oil supply, water-related storm damage (Hurricane Katrina), sudden hurricanes, droughts, and floods demand our attention.

Neptune Is the Magic Solvent

Neptune is often maligned as the planet of illusions that dissolves reality, enabling you to escape the material world. Under Neptune's influence, you see what you want to see. But Neptune also encourages you to create. It embodies glamour, subtlety, mystery, and mysticism, and governs anything that takes you beyond the mundane world, including out-of-body experiences.

Neptune breaks through and transcends your ordinary perceptions to take you to another level, where you experience either confusion or ecstasy. Its force can pull you off course only if you allow this to happen. Those who use Neptune wisely can translate their daydreams into poetry, theater, design, or inspired moves in the business world, avoiding the tricky con artist side of this planet.

Find your Neptune listed below:

Neptune in Cancer

Birth Dates:
    July 19, 1901–December 25, 1901
    May 21, 1902–September 23, 1914
    December 14, 1914–July 19, 1915
    March 19, 1916–May 2, 1916
Dreams of the homeland, idealistic patriotism, and glamorization of the nurturing assets of women characterized this time. You who were born here have unusual psychic ability and deep insights into basic needs of others.

Neptune in Leo

Birth Dates:
    September 23, 1914–December 14, 1914
    July 19, 1915–March 19, 1916
    May 2, 1916–September 21, 1928
    February 19, 1929–July 24, 1929
Neptune in Leo brought us the glamour and high living of the 1920s and the big spenders of that time. Neptune temptations of gambling, seduction, theater, and lavish entertaining

distracted from the realities of the age. Those born in that generation also made great advances in the arts.

Neptune in Virgo

Birth Dates:
    September 21, 1928–February 19, 1929
    July 24, 1929–October 3, 1942
    April 17, 1943–August 2, 1943
    Neptune in Virgo encompassed the 1930s, the Great Depression, and the beginning of World War II, when a new order was born. This was a time of facing what didn't work. Many were unemployed and found solace at the movies, watching the great Virgo star Greta Garbo or the escapist dance films of Busby Berkeley. New public services were born. Those with Neptune in Virgo later spread the gospel of health and fitness. This generation's devotion to spending hours at the office inspired the word *workaholic*.

Neptune in Libra

Birth Dates:
    October 3, 1942–April 17, 1943
    August 2, 1943–December 24, 1955
    March 12, 1956–October 19, 1956
    June 15, 1957–August 6, 1957
    This was the time of World War II, and the immediate postwar period, when the world regained balance and returned to relative stability. Neptune in Libra was the romantic generation who would later be concerned with relating. As this generation matured, there was a new trend toward marriage and commitment. Racial and sexual equality became important issues, as they redesigned traditional roles to suit modern times.

Neptune in Scorpio

Birth Dates:
    December 24, 1955–March 12, 1956
    October 19, 1956–June 15, 1957
    August 6, 1957–January 4, 1970

May 3, 1970–November 6, 1970

Neptune in Scorpio brought in a generation that would become interested in transformative power. Born in an era that glamorized sex, drugs, rock and roll, and Eastern religion, they matured in a more sobering time of AIDS, cocaine abuse, and New Age spirituality. As they evolve, they will become active in healing the planet from the results of the abuse of power.

Neptune in Sagittarius

Birth Dates:
January 4, 1970–May 3, 1970
November 6, 1970–January 19, 1984
June 23, 1984–November 21, 1984

Neptune in Sagittarius was the time when space travel became a reality. The Neptune influence glamorized new approaches to mysticism, religion, and mind expansion. This generation will take a new approach to spiritual life, with emphasis on visions, mysticism, and clairvoyance.

Neptune in Capricorn

Birth Dates:
January 19, 1984–June 23, 1984
November 21, 1984–January 29, 1998

Neptune in Capricorn brought a time when delusions about material power were glamorized in the mideighties and nineties. There was a boom in the stock market, and the Internet era spawned young tycoons who later lost all their wealth. It was also a time when the psychic and occult worlds spawned a new category of business enterprise, and sold services on television.

Neptune in Aquarius

Birth Dates:
January 29, 1998–April 4, 2011

This should continue to be a time of breakthroughs. Here the creative influence of Neptune reaches a universal audience. This is a time of dissolving barriers and globalization—when we truly become one world. During this transit of high-tech Aquarius, new kinds of entertainment media reach across cultural differences. However, the transit of Neptune has also raised boundary issues between cultures, especially in Middle Eastern countries with Neptune-ruled oil fields. As Neptune raises issues of social and political structures not being as solid as they seem, this could continue to produce rebellion and chaos in the environment. However, by using imagination (Neptune) in partnership with a global view (Aquarius), we could reach creative solutions.

Those born with this placement should be true citizens of the world, with a remarkable creative ability to transcend social and cultural barriers.

Pluto Can Transform You

Though Pluto is a tiny, mysterious body in space, its influence is great. When Pluto zaps a strategic point in your horoscope, your life changes dramatically.

Little Pluto is the power behind the scenes; it affects you at deep levels of consciousness, causing events to come to the surface that will transform you and your generation. Nothing escapes, or is sacred, with this probing planet. Its purpose is to wipe out the past so something new can happen.

The Pluto place in your horoscope is where you have invisible power (Mars governs the visible power), where you can transform, heal, and affect the unconscious needs of the masses. Pluto tells lots about how your generation projects power and what makes it seem cool to others. And when Pluto changes signs, there is a whole new concept of what's cool. Pluto's strange elliptical orbit occasionally runs inside the orbit of neighboring Neptune. Because of its eccentric path, the length of time Pluto stays in any given sign can vary from thirteen to thirty-two years. It covered only seven signs in the last century.

Pluto in Gemini

Late 1800s–May 26, 1914

This was a time of mass suggestion and breakthroughs in communications, when many brilliant writers, such as Ernest Hemingway and F. Scott Fitzgerald, were born. Henry Miller, D. H. Lawrence, and James Joyce scandalized society by using explicit sexual images and language in their literature. "Muckraking" journalists exposed corruption. Pluto-ruled Scorpio president Theodore Roosevelt said, "Speak softly, but carry a big stick." This generation had an intense need to communicate and made major breakthroughs in knowledge. A compulsive restlessness and a thirst for a variety of experiences characterize many of this generation.

Pluto in Cancer

Birth Dates:

May 26, 1914–June 14, 1939

Dictators and mass media arose to wield emotional power over the masses. Women's rights were a popular issue. Deep sentimental feelings, acquisitiveness, and possessiveness characterized these times and people. Most of the great stars of the Hollywood era who embodied the American image were born during this period: Grace Kelly, Esther Williams, Frank Sinatra, and Lana Turner, to name a few.

Pluto in Leo

Birth Dates:

June 14, 1939–August 19, 1957

The performing arts played on the emotions of the masses. Mick Jagger, John Lennon, and rock and roll were born at this time. So were baby boomers like Bill and Hillary Clinton. Those born here tend to be self-centered, powerful, and boisterous. This generation does its own thing, for better or for worse. They are quick to embrace self-transformation in the form of antiaging and plastic surgery techniques, to stay forever young and stay relevant in society.

Pluto in Virgo

Birth Dates:
August 19, 1957–October 5, 1971
April 17, 1972–July 30, 1972

This is the yuppie generation that sparked a mass movement toward fitness, health, and career. It is a much more sober, serious, and driven generation than the fun-loving Pluto in Leo. During this time, machines were invented to process detail work efficiently. Inventions took a practical turn with answering machines, fax machines, car phones, and home-office equipment—all making the workplace far more efficient.

Pluto in Libra

Birth Dates:
October 5, 1971–April 17, 1972
July 30, 1972–November 5, 1983
May 18, 1984–August 27, 1984

A mellower generation, people born at this time are concerned with partnerships, working together, and finding diplomatic solutions to problems. Marriage is important to this generation, and they will define it by combining traditional values with equal partnership. This was a time of women's liberation, gay rights, the ERA, and legal battles over abortion—all of which transformed our ideas about relationships.

Pluto in Scorpio

Birth Dates:
November 5, 1983–May 18, 1984
August 27, 1984–January 17, 1995

Pluto was in its ruling sign for a comparatively short period of time. However, this was a time of record achievements, destructive sexually transmitted diseases, nuclear power controversies, and explosive political issues. Pluto destroys in order to create new understanding—the phoenix rising from the ashes—which should be some consolation for those of you who felt Pluto's force before 1995. Sexual shockers were par for the course during these intense years, when black clothing, transvestites, body piercing, tattoos, and sexually explicit advertising pushed the boundaries of good taste.

Pluto in Sagittarius

Birth Dates:
  January 17, 1995–April 20, 1995
  November 10, 1995–January 27, 2008
  June 13, 2008–November 26, 2008
During the most recent Pluto transit, we were pushed to expand our horizons and find deeper spiritual meaning in life.

Pluto's opposition with Saturn in 2001 brought an enormous conflict between traditional societies and the forces of change. It signaled a time when religious convictions exerted power in our political life as well.

Since Sagittarius is associated with travel, Pluto, the planet of extremes, made space travel a reality for wealthy adventurers, who paid for the privilege of travel on space shuttles. Globalization transformed business and traditional societies as outsourcing became the norm.

New dimensions in electronic publishing, concern with animal rights and the environment, and an increasing emphasis on extreme forms of religion were other signs of Pluto in Sagittarius. Charismatic religious leaders asserted themselves and questions of the boundaries between church and state arose. There were also sexual scandals associated with the church, which transformed the religious power structure.

Pluto in Capricorn

Birth Dates:
  January 25, 2008–June 13, 2008
  November 26, 2008–January 20, 2024
As Pluto in Jupiter-ruled Sagittarius signaled a time of expansion and globalization, Pluto's entry into Saturn-ruled Capricorn in 2008 signaled a time of adjustment, of facing reality and limitations, then finding pragmatic solutions. It will be a time when a new structure is imposed, when we become concerned with what actually works.

As Capricorn is associated with corporations and also with

responsibility and duty, look for dramatic changes in business practices, hopefully with more attention paid to ethical and social responsibility as well as the bottom line. Big business will have enormous power during this transit, perhaps handling what governments have been unable to accomplish. There will be an emphasis on trimming down, perhaps a new belt-tightening regime. And, since Capricorn is the sign of Father Time, there will be a new emphasis on the aging of the population. The generation born now is sure to be a more practical and realistic one than that of their older Pluto in Sagittarius siblings.

VENUS SIGNS 1901–2010

	Aries	Taurus	Gemini	Cancer	Leo	Virgo
1901	3/29–4/22	4/22–5/17	5/17–6/10	6/10–7/5	7/5–7/29	7/29–8/23
1902	5/7–6/3	6/3–6/30	6/30–7/25	7/25–8/19	8/19–9/13	9/13–10/7
1903	2/28–3/24	3/24–4/18	4/18–5/13	5/13–6/9	6/9–7/7	7/7–8/17
						9/6–11/8
1904	3/13–5/7	5/7–6/1	6/1–6/25	6/25–7/19	7/19–8/13	8/13–9/6
1905	2/3–3/6	3/6–4/9	7/8–8/6	8/6–9/1	9/1–9/27	9/27–10/21
	4/9–5/28	5/28–7/8				
1906	3/1–4/7	4/7–5/2	5/2–5/26	5/26–6/20	6/20–7/16	7/16–8/11
1907	4/27–5/22	5/22–6/16	6/16–7/11	7/11–8/4	8/4–8/29	8/29–9/22
1908	2/14–3/10	3/10–4/5	4/5–5/5	5/5–9/8	9/8–10/8	10/8–11/3
1909	3/29–4/22	4/22–5/16	5/16–6/10	6/10–7/4	7/4–7/29	7/29–8/23
1910	5/7–6/3	6/4–6/29	6/30–7/24	7/25–8/18	8/19–9/12	9/13–10/6
1911	2/28–3/23	3/24–4/17	4/18–5/12	5/13–6/8	6/9–7/7	7/8–11/18
1912	4/13–5/6	5/7–5/31	6/1–6/24	6/24–7/18	7/19–8/12	8/13–9/5
1913	2/3–3/6	3/7–5/1	7/8–8/5	8/6–8/31	9/1–9/26	9/27–10/20
	5/2–5/30	5/31–7/7				
1914	3/14–4/6	4/7–5/1	5/2–5/25	5/26–6/19	6/20–7/15	7/16–8/10
1915	4/27–5/21	5/22–6/15	6/16–7/10	7/11–8/3	8/4–8/28	8/29–9/21
1916	2/14–3/9	3/10–4/5	4/6–5/5	5/6–9/8	9/9–10/7	10/8–11/2
1917	3/29–4/21	4/22–5/15	5/16–6/9	6/10–7/3	7/4–7/28	7/29–8/21
1918	5/7–6/2	6/3–6/28	6/29–7/24	7/25–8/18	8/19–9/11	9/12–10/5
1919	2/27–3/22	3/23–4/16	4/17–5/12	5/13–6/7	6/8–7/7	7/8–11/8
1920	4/12–5/6	5/7–5/30	5/31–6/23	6/24–7/18	7/19–8/11	8/12–9/4
1921	2/3–3/6	3/7–4/25	7/8–8/5	8/6–8/31	9/1–9/25	9/26–10/20
	4/26–6/1	6/2–7/7				
1922	3/13–4/6	4/7–4/30	5/1–5/25	5/26–6/19	6/20–7/14	7/15–8/9
1923	4/27–5/21	5/22–6/14	6/15–7/9	7/10–8/3	8/4–8/27	8/28–9/20
1924	2/13–3/8	3/9–4/4	4/5–5/5	5/6–9/8	9/9–10/7	10/8–11/12
1925	3/28–4/20	4/21–5/15	5/16–6/8	6/9–7/3	7/4–7/27	7/28–8/21
1926	5/7–6/2	6/3–6/28	6/29–7/23	7/24–8/17	8/18–9/11	9/12–10/5
1927	2/27–3/22	3/23–4/16	4/17–5/11	5/12–6/7	6/8–7/7	7/8–11/9

Libra	Scorpio	Sagittarius	Capricorn	Aquarius	Pisces
8/23–9/17	9/17–10/12	10/12–1/16	1/16–2/9 11/7–12/5	2/9–3/5 12/5–1/11	3/5–3/29
10/7–10/31	10/31–11/24	11/24–12/18	12/18–1/11	2/6–4/4	1/11–2/6 4/4–5/7
8/17–9/6 11/8–12/9	12/9–1/5			1/11–2/4	2/4–2/28
9/6–9/30	9/30–10/25	1/5–1/30 10/25–11/18	1/30–2/24 11/18–12/13	2/24–3/19 12/13–1/7	3/19–4/13
10/21–11/14	11/14–12/8	12/8–1/1/06			1/7–2/3
8/11–9/7	9/7–10/9 12/15–12/25	10/9–12/15 12/25–2/6	1/1–1/25	1/25–2/18	2/18–3/14
9/22–10/16	10/16–11/9	11/9–12/3	2/6–3/6 12/3–12/27	3/6–4/2 12/27–1/20	4/2–4/27
11/3–11/28	11/28–12/22	12/22–1/15			1/20–2/4
8/23–9/17	9/17–10/12	10/12–11/17	1/15–2/9 11/17–12/5	2/9–3/5 12/5–1/15	3/5–3/29
10/7–10/30	10/31–11/23	11/24–12/17	12/18–12/31	1/1–1/15 1/29–4/4	1/16–1/28 4/5–5/6
11/19–12/8	12/9–12/31		1/1–1/10	1/11–2/2	2/3–2/27
9/6–9/30	1/1–1/4 10/1–10/24	1/5–1/29 10/25–11/17	1/30–2/23 11/18–12/12	2/24–3/18 12/13–12/31	3/19–4/12
10/21–11/13	11/14–12/7	12/8–12/31		1/1–1/6	1/7–2/2
8/11–9/6	9/7–10/9 12/6–12/30	10/10–12/5 12/31	1/1–1/24	1/25–2/17	2/18–3/13
9/22–10/15	10/16–11/8	1/1–2/6 11/9–12/2	2/7–3/6 12/3–12/26	3/7–4/1 12/27–12/31	4/2–4/26
11/3–11/27	11/28–12/21	12/22–12/31		1/1–1/19	1/20–2/13
8/22–9/16	9/17–10/11	1/1–1/14 10/12–11/6	1/15–2/7 11/7–12/5	2/8–3/4 12/6–12/31	3/5–3/28
10/6–10/29	10/30–11/22	11/23–12/16	12/17–12/31	1/1–4/5	4/6–5/6
11/9–12/8	12/9–12/31		1/1–1/9	1/10–2/2	2/3–2/26
9/5–9/30	1/1–1/3 9/31–10/23	1/4–1/28 10/24–11/17	1/29–2/22 11/18–12/11	2/23–3/18 12/12–12/31	3/19–4/11
10/21–11/13	11/14–12/7	12/8–12/31		1/1–1/6	1/7–2/2
8/10–9/6	9/7–10/10 11/29–12/31	10/11–11/28	1/1–1/24	1/25–2/16	2/17–3/12
9/21–10/14	1/1 10/15–11/7	1/2–2/6 11/8–12/1	2/7–3/5 12/2–12/25	3/6–3/31 12/26–12/31	4/1–4/26
11/13–11/26	11/27–12/21	12/22–12/31		1/1–1/19	1/20–2/12
8/22–9/15	9/16–10/11	1/1–1/14 10/12–11/6	1/15–2/7 11/7–12/5	2/8–3/3 12/6–12/31	3/4–3/27
10/6–10/29	10/30–11/22	11/23–12/16	12/17–12/31	1/1–4/5	4/6–5/6
11/10–12/8	12/9–12/31	1/1–1/7	1/8	1/9–2/1	2/2–2/26

VENUS SIGNS 1901–2010

	Aries	Taurus	Gemini	Cancer	Leo	Virgo
1928	4/12–5/5	5/6–5/29	5/30–6/23	6/24–7/17	7/18–8/11	8/12–9/4
1929	2/3–3/7	3/8–4/19	7/8–8/4	8/5–8/30	8/31–9/25	9/26–10/19
	4/20–6/2	6/3–7/7				
1930	3/13–4/5	4/6–4/30	5/1–5/24	5/25–6/18	6/19–7/14	7/15–8/9
1931	4/26–5/20	5/21–6/13	6/14–7/8	7/9–8/2	8/3–8/26	8/27–9/19
1932	2/12–3/8	3/9–4/3	4/4–5/5	5/6–7/12	9/9–10/6	10/7–11/1
			7/13–7/27	7/28–9/8		
1933	3/27–4/19	4/20–5/28	5/29–6/8	6/9–7/2	7/3–7/26	7/27–8/20
1934	5/6–6/1	6/2–6/27	6/28–7/22	7/23–8/16	8/17–9/10	9/11–10/4
1935	2/26–3/21	3/22–4/15	4/16–5/10	5/11–6/6	6/7–7/6	7/7–11/8
1936	4/11–5/4	5/5–5/28	5/29–6/22	6/23–7/16	7/17–8/10	8/11–9/4
1937	2/2–3/8	3/9–4/13	7/7–8/3	8/4–8/29	8/30–9/24	9/25–10/18
	4/14–6/3	6/4–7/6				
1938	3/12–4/4	4/5–4/28	4/29–5/23	5/24–6/18	6/19–7/13	7/14–8/8
1939	4/25–5/19	5/20–6/13	6/14–7/8	7/9–8/1	8/2–8/25	8/26–9/19
1940	2/12–3/7	3/8–4/3	4/4–5/5	5/6–7/4	9/9–10/5	10/6–10/31
			7/5–7/31	8/1–9/8		
1941	3/27–4/19	4/20–5/13	5/14–6/6	6/7–7/1	7/2–7/26	7/27–8/20
1942	5/6–6/1	6/2–6/26	6/27–7/22	7/23–8/16	8/17–9/9	9/10–10/3
1943	2/25–3/20	3/21–4/14	4/15–5/10	5/11–6/6	6/7–7/6	7/7–11/8
1944	4/10–5/3	5/4–5/28	5/29–6/21	6/22–7/16	7/17–8/9	8/10–9/2
1945	2/2–3/10	3/11–4/6	7/7–8/3	8/4–8/29	8/30–9/23	9/24–10/18
	4/7–6/3	6/4–7/6				
1946	3/11–4/4	4/5–4/28	4/29–5/23	5/24–6/17	6/18–7/12	7/13–8/8
1947	4/25–5/19	5/20–6/12	6/13–7/7	7/8–8/1	8/2–8/25	8/26–9/18
1948	2/11–3/7	3/8–4/3	4/4–5/6	5/7–6/28	9/8–10/5	10/6–10/31
			6/29–8/2	8/3–9/7		
1949	3/26–4/19	4/20–5/13	5/14–6/6	6/7–6/30	7/1–7/25	7/26–8/19
1950	5/5–5/31	6/1–6/26	6/27–7/21	7/22–8/15	8/16–9/9	9/10–10/3
1951	2/25–3/21	3/22–4/15	4/16–5/10	5/11–6/6	6/7–7/7	7/8–11/9
1952	4/10–5/4	5/5–5/28	5/29–6/21	6/22–7/16	7/17–8/9	8/10–9/3
1953	2/2–3/3	3/4–3/31	7/8–8/3	8/4–8/29	8/30–9/24	9/25–10/18
	4/1–6/5	6/6–7/7				

Libra	Scorpio	Sagittarius	Capricorn	Aquarius	Pisces
9/5–9/28	1/1–1/3	1/4–1/28	1/29–2/22	2/23–3/17	3/18–4/11
	9/29–10/23	10/24–11/16	11/17–12/11	12/12–12/31	
10/20–11/12	11/13–12/6	12/7–12/30	12/31	1/1–1/5	1/6–2/2
8/10–9/6	9/7–10/11	10/12–11/21	1/1–1/23	1/24–2/16	2/17–3/12
	11/22–12/31				
9/20–10/13	1/1–1/3	1/4–2/6	2/7–3/4	3/5–3/31	4/1–4/25
	10/14–11/6	11/7–11/30	12/1–12/24	12/25–12/31	
11/2–11/25	11/26–12/20	12/21–12/31		1/1–1/18	1/19–2/11
8/21–9/14	9/15–10/10	1/1–1/13	1/14–2/6	2/7–3/2	3/3–3/26
		10/11–11/5	11/6–12/4	12/5–12/31	
10/5–10/28	10/29–11/21	11/22–12/15	12/16–12/31	1/1–4/5	4/6–5/5
11/9–12/7	12/8–12/31		1/1–1/7	1/8–1/31	2/1–2/25
9/5–9/27	1/1–1/2	1/3–1/27	1/28–2/21	2/22–3/16	3/17–4/10
	9/28–10/22	10/23–11/15	11/16–12/10	12/11–12/31	
10/19–11/11	11/12–12/5	12/6–12/29	12/30–12/31	1/1–1/5	1/6–2/1
8/9–9/6	9/7–10/13	10/14–11/14	1/1–1/22	1/23–2/15	2/16–3/11
	11/15–12/31				
9/20–10/13	1/1–1/3	1/4–2/5	2/6–3/4	3/5–3/30	3/31–4/24
	10/14–11/6	11/7–11/30	12/1–12/24	12/25–12/31	
11/1–11/25	11/26–12/19	12/20–12/31		1/1–1/18	1/19–2/11
8/21–9/14	9/15–10/9	1/1–1/12	1/13–2/5	2/6–3/1	3/2–3/26
		10/10–11/5	11/6–12/4	12/5–12/31	
10/4–10/27	10/28–11/20	11/21–12/14	12/15–12/31	1/1–4/5	4/6–5/5
11/9–12/7	12/8–12/31		1/1–1/7	1/8–1/31	2/1–2/24
9/3–9/27	1/1–1/2	1/3–1/27	1/28–2/20	2/21–3/16	3/17–4/9
	9/28–10/21	10/22–11/15	11/16–12/10	12/11–12/31	
10/19–11/11	11/12–12/5	12/6–12/29	12/30–12/31	1/1–1/4	1/5–2/1
8/9–9/6	9/7–10/15	10/16–11/7	1/1–1/21	1/22–2/14	2/15–3/10
	11/8–12/31				
9/19–10/12	1/1–1/4	1/5–2/5	2/6–3/4	3/5–3/29	3/30–4/24
	10/13–11/5	11/6–11/29	11/30–12/23	12/24–12/31	
11/1–11/25	11/26–12/19	12/20–12/31		1/1–1/17	1/18–2/10
8/20–9/14	9/15–10/9	1/1–1/12	1/13–2/5	2/6–3/1	3/2–3/25
		10/10–11/5	11/6–12/5	12/6–12/31	
10/4–10/27	10/28–11/20	11/21–12/13	12/14–12/31	1/1–4/5	4/6–5/4
11/10–12/7	12/8–12/31		1/1–1/7	1/8–1/31	2/1–2/24
9/4–9/27	1/1–1/2	1/3–1/27	1/28–2/20	2/21–3/16	3/17–4/9
	9/28–10/21	10/22–11/15	11/16–12/10	12/11–12/31	
10/19–11/11	11/12–12/5	12/6–12/29	12/30–12/31	1/1–1/5	1/6–2/1

VENUS SIGNS 1901–2010

	Aries	Taurus	Gemini	Cancer	Leo	Virgo
1954	3/12–4/4	4/5–4/28	4/29–5/23	5/24–6/17	6/18–7/13	7/14–8/8
1955	4/25–5/19	5/20–6/13	6/14–7/7	7/8–8/1	8/2–8/25	8/26–9/18
1956	2/12–3/7	3/8–4/4	4/5–5/7 6/24–8/4	5/8–6/23 8/5–9/8	9/9–10/5	10/6–10/31
1957	3/26–4/19	4/20–5/13	5/14–6/6	6/7–7/1	7/2–7/26	7/27–8/19
1958	5/6–5/31	6/1–6/26	6/27–7/22	7/23–8/15	8/16–9/9	9/10–10/3
1959	2/25–3/20	3/21–4/14	4/15–5/10	5/11–6/6	6/7–7/8 9/21–9/24	7/9–9/20 9/25–11/9
1960	4/10–5/3	5/4–5/28	5/29–6/21	6/22–7/15	7/16–8/9	8/10–9/2
1961	2/3–6/5	6/6–7/7	7/8–8/3	8/4–8/29	8/30–9/23	9/24–10/17
1962	3/11–4/3	4/4–4/28	4/29–5/22	5/23–6/17	6/18–7/12	7/13–8/8
1963	4/24–5/18	5/19–6/12	6/13–7/7	7/8–7/31	8/1–8/25	8/26–9/18
1964	2/11–3/7	3/8–4/4	4/5–5/9 6/18–8/5	5/10–6/17 8/6–9/8	9/9–10/5	10/6–10/31
1965	3/26–4/18	4/19–5/12	5/13–6/6	6/7–6/30	7/1–7/25	7/26–8/19
1966	5/6–5/31	6/1–6/26	6/27–7/21	7/22–8/15	8/16–9/8	9/9–10/2
1967	2/24–3/20	3/21–4/14	4/15–5/10	5/11–6/6	6/7–7/8 9/10–10/1	7/9–9/9 10/2–11/9
1968	4/9–5/3	5/4–5/27	5/28–6/20	6/21–7/15	7/16–8/8	8/9–9/2
1969	2/3–6/6	6/7–7/6	7/7–8/3	8/4–8/28	8/29–9/22	9/23–10/17
1970	3/11–4/3	4/4–4/27	4/28–5/22	5/23–6/16	6/17–7/12	7/13–8/8
1971	4/24–5/18	5/19–6/12	6/13–7/6	7/7–7/31	8/1–8/24	8/25–9/17
1972	2/11–3/7	3/8–4/3	4/4–5/10 6/12–8/6	5/11–6/11 8/7–9/8	9/9–10/5	10/6–10/30
1973	3/25–4/18	4/18–5/12	5/13–6/5	6/6–6/29	7/1–7/25	7/26–8/19
1974	5/5–5/31	6/1–6/25	6/26–7/21	7/22–8/14	8/15–9/8	9/9–10/2
1975	2/24–3/20	3/21–4/13	4/14–5/9	5/10–6/6	6/7–7/9 9/3–10/4	7/10–9/2 10/5–11/9
1976	4/8–5/2	5/2–5/27	5/27–6/20	6/20–7/14	7/14–8/8	8/8–9/1
1977	2/2–6/6	6/6–7/6	7/6–8/2	8/2–8/28	8/28–9/22	9/22–10/17
1978	3/9–4/2	4/2–4/27	4/27–5/22	5/22–6/16	6/16–7/12	7/12–8/6
1979	4/23–5/18	5/18–6/11	6/11–7/6	7/6–7/30	7/30–8/24	8/24–9/17
1980	2/9–3/6	3/6–4/3	4/3–5/12 6/5–8/6	5/12–6/5 8/6–9/7	9/7–10/4	10/4–10/30
1981	3/24–4/17	4/17–5/11	5/11–6/5	6/5–6/29	6/29–7/24	7/24–8/18

Libra	Scorpio	Sagittarius	Capricorn	Aquarius	Pisces
8/9–9/6	9/7–10/22	10/23–10/27	1/1–1/22	1/23–2/15	2/16–3/11
	10/28–12/31				
9/19–10/13	1/1–1/6	1/7–2/5	2/6–3/4	3/5–3/30	3/31–4/24
	10/14–11/5	11/6–11/30	12/1–12/24	12/25–12/31	
11/1–11/25	11/26–12/19	12/20–12/31		1/1–1/17	1/18–2/11
8/20–9/14	9/15–10/9	1/1–1/12	1/13–2/5	2/6–3/1	3/2–3/25
		10/10–11/5	11/6–12/6	12/7–12/31	
10/4–10/27	10/28–11/20	11/21–12/14	12/15–12/31	1/1–4/6	4/7–5/5
11/10–12/7	12/8–12/31		1/1–1/7	1/8–1/31	2/1–2/24
9/3–9/26	1/1–1/2	1/3–1/27	1/28–2/20	2/21–3/15	3/16–4/9
	9/27–10/21	10/22–11/15	11/16–12/10	12/11–12/31	
10/18–11/11	11/12–12/4	12/5–12/28	12/29–12/31	1/1–1/5	1/6–2/2
8/9–9/6	9/7–12/31		1/1–1/21	1/22–2/14	2/15–3/10
9/19–10/12	1/1–1/6	1/7–2/5	2/6–3/4	3/5–3/29	3/30–4/23
	10/13–11/5	11/6–11/29	11/30–12/23	12/24–12/31	
11/1–11/24	11/25–12/19	12/20–12/31		1/1–1/16	1/17–2/10
8/20–9/13	9/14–10/9	1/1–1/12	1/13–2/5	2/6–3/1	3/2–3/25
		10/10–11/5	11/6–12/7	12/8–12/31	
10/3–10/26	10/27–11/19	11/20–12/13	2/7–2/25	1/1–2/6	4/7–5/5
			12/14–12/31	2/26–4/6	
11/10–12/7	12/8–12/31		1/1–1/6	1/7–1/30	1/31–2/23
9/3–9/26	1/1	1/2–1/26	1/27–2/20	2/21–3/15	3/16–4/8
	9/27–10/21	10/22–11/14	11/15–12/9	12/10–12/31	
10/18–11/10	11/11–12/4	12/5–12/28	12/29–12/31	1/1–1/4	1/5–2/2
8/9–9/7	9/8–12/31		1/1–1/21	1/22–2/14	2/15–3/10
9/18–10/11	1/1–1/7	1/8–2/5	2/6–3/4	3/5–3/29	3/30–4/23
	10/12–11/5	11/6–11/29	11/30–12/23	12/24–12/31	
10/31–11/24	11/25–12/18	12/19–12/31		1/1–1/16	1/17–2/10
8/20–9/13	9/14–10/8	1/1–1/12	1/13–2/4	2/5–2/28	3/1–3/24
		10/9–11/5	11/6–12/7	12/8–12/31	
10/3–10/26	10/27–11/19	11/20–12/13	12/14–12/31	3/1–4/6	4/7–5/5
			1/30–2/28	1/1–1/29	
11/10–12/7	12/8–12/31		1/1–1/6	1/7–1/30	1/31–2/23
9/1–9/26	9/26–10/20	1/1–1/26	1/26–2/19	2/19–3/15	3/15–4/8
10/17–11/10	11/10–12/4	12/4–12/27	12/27–1/20/78		1/4–2/2
8/6–9/7	9/7–1/7			1/20–2/13	2/13–3/9
9/17–10/11	10/11–11/4	1/7–2/5	2/5–3/3	3/3–3/29.	3/29–4/23
		11/4–11/28	11/28–12/22	12/22–1/16/80	
10/30–11/24	11/24–12/18	12/18–1/11/81			1/16–2/9
8/18–9/12	9/12–10/9	10/9–11/5	1/11–2/4	2/4–2/28	2/28–3/24
			11/5–12/8	12/8–1/23/82	

VENUS SIGNS 1901–2010

	Aries	Taurus	Gemini	Cancer	Leo	Virgo
1982	5/4–5/30	5/30–6/25	6/25–7/20	7/20–8/14	8/14–9/7	9/7–10/2
1983	2/22–3/19	3/19–4/13	4/13–5/9	5/9–6/6	6/6–7/10	7/10–8/27
					8/27–10/5	10/5–11/9
1984	4/7–5/2	5/2–5/26	5/26–6/20	6/20–7/14	7/14–8/7	8/7–9/1
1985	2/2–6/6	6/7–7/6	7/6–8/2	8/2–8/28	8/28–9/22	9/22–10/16
1986	3/9–4/2	4/2–4/26	4/26–5/21	5/21–6/15	6/15–7/11	7/11–8/7
1987	4/22–5/17	5/17–6/11	6/11–7/5	7/5–7/30	7/30–8/23	8/23–9/16
1988	2/9–3/6	3/6–4/3	4/3–5/17	5/17–5/27	9/7–10/4	10/4–10/29
			5/27–8/6	8/28–9/22	9/22–10/16	
1989	3/23–4/16	4/16–5/11	5/11–6/4	6/4–6/29	6/29–7/24	7/24–8/18
1990	5/4–5/30	5/30–6/25	6/25–7/20	7/20–8/13	8/13–9/7	9/7–10/1
1991	2/22–3/18	3/18–4/13	4/13–5/9	5/9–6/6	6/6–7/11	7/11–8/21
					8/21–10/6	10/6–11/9
1992	4/7–5/1	5/1–5/26	5/26–6/19	6/19–7/13	7/13–8/7	8/7–8/31
1993	2/2–6/6	6/6–7/6	7/6–8/1	8/1–8/27	8/27–9/21	9/21–10/16
1994	3/8–4/1	4/1–4/26	4/26–5/21	5/21–6/15	6/15–7/11	7/11–8/7
1995	4/22–5/16	5/16–6/10	6/10–7/5	7/5–7/29	7/29–8/23	8/23–9/16
1996	2/9–3/6	3/6–4/3	4/3–8/7	8/7–9/7	9/7–10/4	10/4–10/29
1997	3/23–4/16	4/16–5/10	5/10–6/4	6/4–6/28	6/28–7/23	7/23–8/17
1998	5/3–5/29	5/29–6/24	6/24–7/19	7/19–8/13	8/13–9/6	9/6–9/30
1999	2/21–3/18	3/18–4/12	4/12–5/8	5/8–6/5	6/5–7/12	7/12–8/15
					8/15–10/7	10/7–11/9
2000	4/6–5/1	5/1–5/25	5/25–6/13	6/13–7/13	7/13–8/6	8/6–8/31
2001	2/2–6/6	6/6–7/5	7/5–8/1	8/1–8/26	8/26–9/20	9/20–10/15
2002	3/7–4/1	4/1–4/25	4/25–5/20	5/20–6/14	6/14–7/10	7/10–8/7
2003	4/21–5/16	5/16–6/9	6/9–7/4	7/4–7/29	7/29–8/22	8/22–9/15
2004	2/8–3/5	3/5–4/3	4/3–8/7	8/7–9/6	9/6–10/3	10/3–10/28
2005	3/22–4/15	4/15–5/10	5/10–6/3	6/3–6/28	6/28–7/23	7/23–8/17
2006	5/3–5/29	5/29–6/24	6/24–7/19	7/19–8/12	8/12–9/6	9/6–9/30
2007	2/21–3/16	3/17–4/10	4/11–5/7	5/8–6/4	6/5–7/13	7/14–8/7
					8/8–10/6	10/7–11/7
2008	4/6–4/30	5/1–5/24	5/25–6/17	6/18–7/11	7/12–8/4	8/5–8/29
2009	2/2–4/11	6/6–7/5	7/5–7/31	731/–8/26	8/26–9/20	9/20–10/14
	4/24–6/6					
2010	3/7–3/31	3/31–4/25	4/25–5/20	5/20–6/14	6/14–7/10	7/10–8/7

Libra	Scorpio	Sagittarius	Capricorn	Aquarius	Pisces
10/2–10/26	10/26–11/18	11/18–12/12	1/23–3/2 12/12–1/5/83	3/2–4/6	4/6–5/4
11/9–12/6	12/6–1/1/84			1/5–1/29	1/29–2/22
9/1–9/25	9/25–10/20	1/1–1/25 10/20–11/13	1/25–2/19 11/13–12/9	2/19–3/14 12/10–1/4	3/14–4/7
10/16–11/9	11/9–12/3	12/3–12/27	12/28–1/19		1/4–2/2
8/7–9/7	9/7–1/7			1/20–2/13	2/13–3/9
9/16–10/10	10/10–11/3	1/7–2/5 11/3–11/28	2/5–3/3 11/28–12/22	3/3–3/28 12/22–1/15	3/28–4/22
10/29–11/23	11/23–12/17	12/17–1/10			1/15–2/9
8/18–9/12	9/12–10/8	10/8–11/5	1/10–2/3 11/15–12/10	2/3–2/27 12/10–1/16/90	2/27–3/23
10/1–10/25	10/25–11/18	11/18–12/12	1/16–3/3 12/12–1/5	3/3–4/6	4/6–5/4
11/9–12/6	12/6–12/31	12/31–1/25/92		1/5–1/29	1/29–2/22
8/31–9/25	9/25–10/19	10/19–11/13	1/25–2/18 11/13–12/8	2/18–3/13 12/8–1/3/93	3/13–4/7
10/16–11/9	11/9–12/2	12/2–12/26	12/26–1/19		1/3–2/2
8/7–9/7	9/7–1/7			1/19–2/12	2/12–3/8
9/16–10/10	10/10–11/13	1/7–2/4 11/3–11/27	2/4–3/2 11/27–12/21	3/2–3/28 12/21–1/15	3/28–4/22
10/29–11/23	11/23–12/17	12/17–1/10/97			1/15–2/9
8/17–9/12	9/12–10/8	10/8–11/5	1/10–2/3 11/5–12/12	2/3–2/27 12/12–1/9	2/27–3/23
9/30–10/24	10/24–11/17	11/17–12/11	1/9–3/4	3/4–4/6	4/6–5/3
11/9–12/5	12/5–12/31	12/31–1/24		1/4–1/28	1/28–2/21
8/31–9/24	9/24–10/19	10/19–11/13	1/24–2/18 11/13–12/8	2/18–3/12 12/8	3/13–4/6
10/15–11/8	11/8–12/2	12/2–12/26	12/26/01– 1/18/02	12/8/00–1/3/01	1/3–2/2
8/7–9/7	9/7–1/7/03		12/26/01–1/18	1/18–2/11	2/11–3/7
9/15–10/9	10/9–11/2	1/7–2/4 11/2–11/26	2/4–3/2 11/26–12/21	3/2–3/27 12/21–1/14/04	3/27–4/21
10/28–11/22	11/22–12/16	12/16–1/9/05		1/1–1/14	1/14–2/8
8/17–9/11	9/11–10/8	10/8–11/15	1/9–2/2 11/5–12/15	2/2–2/26 12/15–1/1/06	2/26–3/22
9/30–10/24	10/24–11/17	11/17–12/11	1/1–3/5	3/5–4/6	4/6–5/3
11/8–12/4	12/5–12/29	12/30–1/24/08		1/3–1/26	1/27–2/20
8/6–9/7	9/7–1/7			1/20–2/13	2/13–3/9
8/30–9/22	9/23–10/17	10/18–11/11	1/24–2/16 11/12–12/6	2/17–3/11 12/7–1/2/09	3/12–4/5
10/14–11/7	11/7–12/1	12/1–12/25	12/25–1/18/10	12/7/08– 1/31/09	1/3–2/2 4/11–4/24
8/7–9/8	9/8–11/8			1/18/10– 2/11/10	2/11–3/7
11/8–11/30	11/30–1/7/11			2/11/10	

How to Use the Mars, Jupiter, and Saturn Tables

Find the year of your birth on the left side of each column. The dates when the planet entered each sign are listed on the right side of each column. (Signs are abbreviated to three letters.) Your birthday should fall on or between each date listed, and your planetary placement should correspond to the earlier sign of that period.

All planet changes are calculated for the Greenwich Mean Time zone.

MARS SIGNS 1901–2010

1901	MAR	1	Leo		OCT	1	Vir
	MAY	11	Vir		NOV	20	Lib
	JUL	13	Lib	1905	JAN	13	Scp
	AUG	31	Scp		AUG	21	Sag
	OCT	14	Sag		OCT	8	Cap
	NOV	24	Cap		NOV	18	Aqu
1902	JAN	1	Aqu		DEC	27	Pic
	FEB	8	Pic	1906	FEB	4	Ari
	MAR	19	Ari		MAR	17	Tau
	APR	27	Tau		APR	28	Gem
	JUN	7	Gem		JUN	11	Can
	JUL	20	Can		JUL	27	Leo
	SEP	4	Leo		SEP	12	Vir
	OCT	23	Vir		OCT	30	Lib
	DEC	20	Lib		DEC	17	Scp
1903	APR	19	Vir	1907	FEB	5	Sag
	MAY	30	Lib		APR	1	Cap
	AUG	6	Scp		OCT	13	Aqu
	SEP	22	Sag		NOV	29	Pic
	NOV	3	Cap	1908	JAN	11	Ari
	DEC	12	Aqu		FEB	23	Tau
1904	JAN	19	Pic		APR	7	Gem
	FEB	27	Ari		MAY	22	Can
	APR	6	Tau		JUL	8	Leo
	MAY	18	Gem		AUG	24	Vir
	JUN	30	Can		OCT	10	Lib
	AUG	15	Leo		NOV	25	Scp

1909	JAN	10	Sag		MAR	9	Pic
	FEB	24	Cap		APR	16	Ari
	APR	9	Aqu		MAY	26	Tau
	MAY	25	Pic		JUL	6	Gem
	JUL	21	Ari		AUG	19	Can
	SEP	26	Pic		OCT	7	Leo
	NOV	20	Ari	1916	MAY	28	Vir
1910	JAN	23	Tau		JUL	23	Lib
	MAR	14	Gem		SEP	8	Scp
	MAY	1	Can		OCT	22	Sag
	JUN	19	Leo		DEC	1	Cap
	AUG	6	Vir	1917	JAN	9	Aqu
	SEP	22	Lib		FEB	16	Pic
	NOV	6	Scp		MAR	26	Ari
	DEC	20	Sag		MAY	4	Tau
1911	JAN	31	Cap		JUN	14	Gem
	MAR	14	Aqu		JUL	28	Can
	APR	23	Pic		SEP	12	Leo
	JUN	2	Ari		NOV	2	Vir
	JUL	15	Tau	1918	JAN	11	Lib
	SEP	5	Gem		FEB	25	Vir
	NOV	30	Tau		JUN	23	Lib
1912	JAN	30	Gem		AUG	17	Scp
	APR	5	Can		OCT	1	Sag
	MAY	28	Leo		NOV	11	Cap
	JUL	17	Vir		DEC	20	Aqu
	SEP	2	Lib	1919	JAN	27	Pic
	OCT	18	Scp		MAR	6	Ari
	NOV	30	Sag		APR	15	Tau
1913	JAN	10	Cap		MAY	26	Gem
	FEB	19	Aqu		JUL	8	Can
	MAR	30	Pic		AUG	23	Leo
	MAY	8	Ari		OCT	10	Vir
	JUN	17	Tau		NOV	30	Lib
	JUL	29	Gem	1920	JAN	31	Scp
	SEP	15	Can		APR	23	Lib
1914	MAY	1	Leo		JUL	10	Scp
	JUN	26	Vir		SEP	4	Sag
	AUG	14	Lib		OCT	18	Cap
	SEP	29	Scp		NOV	27	Aqu
	NOV	11	Sag	1921	JAN	5	Pic
	DEC	22	Cap		FEB	13	Ari
1915	JAN	30	Aqu		MAR	25	Tau

	MAY	6	Gem		OCT	26	Scp
	JUN	18	Can		DEC	8	Sag
	AUG	3	Leo	1928	JAN	19	Cap
	SEP	19	Vir		FEB	28	Aqu
	NOV	6	Lib		APR	7	Pic
	DEC	26	Scp		MAY	16	Ari
1922	FEB	18	Sag		JUN	26	Tau
	SEP	13	Cap		AUG	9	Gem
	OCT	30	Aqu		OCT	3	Can
	DEC	11	Pic		DEC	20	Gem
1923	JAN	21	Ari	1929	MAR	10	Can
	MAR	4	Tau		MAY	13	Leo
	APR	16	Gem		JUL	4	Vir
	MAY	30	Can		AUG	21	Lib
	JUL	16	Leo		OCT	6	Scp
	SEP	1	Vir		NOV	18	Sag
	OCT	18	Lib		DEC	29	Cap
	DEC	4	Scp	1930	FEB	6	Aqu
1924	JAN	19	Sag		MAR	17	Pic
	MAR	6	Cap		APR	24	Ari
	APR	24	Aqu		JUN	3	Tau
	JUN	24	Pic		JUL	14	Gem
	AUG	24	Aqu		AUG	28	Can
	OCT	19	Pic		OCT	20	Leo
	DEC	19	Ari	1931	FEB	16	Can
1925	FEB	5	Tau		MAR	30	Leo
	MAR	24	Gem		JUN	10	Vir
	MAY	9	Can		AUG	1	Lib
	JUN	26	Leo		SEP	17	Scp
	AUG	12	Vir		OCT	30	Sag
	SEP	28	Lib		DEC	10	Cap
	NOV	13	Scp	1932	JAN	18	Aqu
	DEC	28	Sag		FEB	25	Pic
1926	FEB	9	Cap		APR	3	Ari
	MAR	23	Aqu		MAY	12	Tau
	MAY	3	Pic		JUN	22	Gem
	JUN	15	Ari		AUG	4	Can
	AUG	1	Tau		SEP	20	Leo
1927	FEB	22	Gem		NOV	13	Vir
	APR	17	Can	1933	JUL	6	Lib
	JUN	6	Leo		AUG	26	Scp
	JUL	25	Vir		OCT	9	Sag
	SEP	10	Lib		NOV	19	Cap

	DEC	28	Aqu		FEB	17	Tau
1934	FEB	4	Pic		APR	1	Gem
	MAR	14	Ari		MAY	17	Can
	APR	22	Tau		JUL	3	Leo
	JUN	2	Gem		AUG	19	Vir
	JUL	15	Can		OCT	5	Lib
	AUG	30	Leo		NOV	20	Scp
	OCT	18	Vir	1941	JAN	4	Sag
	DEC	11	Lib		FEB	17	Cap
1935	JUL	29	Scp		APR	2	Aqu
	SEP	16	Sag		MAY	16	Pic
	OCT	28	Cap		JUL	2	Ari
	DEC	7	Aqu	1942	JAN	11	Tau
1936	JAN	14	Pic		MAR	7	Gem
	FEB	22	Ari		APR	26	Can
	APR	1	Tau		JUN	14	Leo
	MAY	13	Gem		AUG	1	Vir
	JUN	25	Can		SEP	17	Lib
	AUG	10	Leo		NOV	1	Scp
	SEP	26	Vir		DEC	15	Sag
	NOV	14	Lib	1943	JAN	26	Cap
1937	JAN	5	Scp		MAR	8	Aqu
	MAR	13	Sag		APR	17	Pic
	MAY	14	Scp		MAY	27	Ari
	AUG	8	Sag		JUL	7	Tau
	SEP	30	Cap		AUG	23	Gem
	NOV	11	Aqu	1944	MAR	28	Can
	DEC	21	Pic		MAY	22	Leo
1938	JAN	30	Ari		JUL	12	Vir
	MAR	12	Tau		AUG	29	Lib
	APR	23	Gem		OCT	13	Scp
	JUN	7	Can		NOV	25	Sag
	JUL	22	Leo	1945	JAN	5	Cap
	SEP	7	Vir		FEB	14	Aqu
	OCT	25	Lib		MAR	25	Pic
	DEC	11	Scp		MAY	2	Ari
1939	JAN	29	Sag		JUN	11	Tau
	MAR	21	Cap		JUL	23	Gem
	MAY	25	Aqu		SEP	7	Can
	JUL	21	Cap		NOV	11	Leo
	SEP	24	Aqu		DEC	26	Can
	NOV	19	Pic	1946	APR	22	Leo
1940	JAN	4	Ari		JUN	20	Vir

	AUG	9	Lib		OCT	12	Cap
	SEP	24	Scp		NOV	21	Aqu
	NOV	6	Sag		DEC	30	Pic
	DEC	17	Cap	1953	FEB	8	Ari
1947	JAN	25	Aqu		MAR	20	Tau
	MAR	4	Pic		MAY	1	Gem
	APR	11	Ari		JUN	14	Can
	MAY	21	Tau		JUL	29	Leo
	JUL	1	Gem		SEP	14	Vir
	AUG	13	Can		NOV	1	Lib
	OCT	1	Leo		DEC	20	Scp
	DEC	1	Vir	1954	FEB	9	Sag
1948	FEB	12	Leo		APR	12	Cap
	MAY	18	Vir		JUL	3	Sag
	JUL	17	Lib		AUG	24	Cap
	SEP	3	Scp		OCT	21	Aqu
	OCT	17	Sag		DEC	4	Pic
	NOV	26	Cap	1955	JAN	15	Ari
1949	JAN	4	Aqu		FEB	26	Tau
	FEB	11	Pic		APR	10	Gem
	MAR	21	Ari		MAY	26	Can
	APR	30	Tau		JUL	11	Leo
	JUN	10	Gem		AUG	27	Vir
	JUL	23	Can		OCT	13	Lib
	SEP	7	Leo		NOV	29	Scp
	OCT	27	Vir	1956	JAN	14	Sag
	DEC	26	Lib		FEB	28	Cap
1950	MAR	28	Vir		APR	14	Aqu
	JUN	11	Lib		JUN	3	Pic
	AUG	10	Scp		DEC	6	Ari
	SEP	25	Sag	1957	JAN	28	Tau
	NOV	6	Cap		MAR	17	Gem
	DEC	15	Aqu		MAY	4	Can
1951	JAN	22	Pic		JUN	21	Leo
	MAR	1	Ari		AUG	8	Vir
	APR	10	Tau		SEP	24	Lib
	MAY	21	Gem		NOV	8	Scp
	JUL	3	Can		DEC	23	Sag
	AUG	18	Leo	1958	FEB	3	Cap
	OCT	5	Vir		MAR	17	Aqu
	NOV	24	Lib		APR	27	Pic
1952	JAN	20	Scp		JUN	7	Ari
	AUG	27	Sag		JUL	21	Tau

	SEP	21	Gem		NOV	6	Vir
	OCT	29	Tau	1965	JUN	29	Lib
1959	FEB	10	Gem		AUG	20	Scp
	APR	10	Can		OCT	4	Sag
	JUN	1	Leo		NOV	14	Cap
	JUL	20	Vir		DEC	23	Aqu
	SEP	5	Lib	1966	JAN	30	Pic
	OCT	21	Scp		MAR	9	Ari
	DEC	3	Sag		APR	17	Tau
1960	JAN	14	Cap		MAY	28	Gem
	FEB	23	Aqu		JUL	11	Can
	APR	2	Pic		AUG	25	Leo
	MAY	11	Ari		OCT	12	Vir
	JUN	20	Tau		DEC	4	Lib
	AUG	2	Gem	1967	FEB	12	Scp
	SEP	21	Can		MAR	31	Lib
1961	FEB	5	Gem		JUL	19	Scp
	FEB	7	Can		SEP	10	Sag
	MAY	6	Leo		OCT	23	Cap
	JUN	28	Vir		DEC	1	Aqu
	AUG	17	Lib	1968	JAN	9	Pic
	OCT	1	Scp		FEB	17	Ari
	NOV	13	Sag		MAR	27	Tau
	DEC	24	Cap		MAY	8	Gem
1962	FEB	1	Aqu		JUN	21	Can
	MAR	12	Pic		AUG	5	Leo
	APR	19	Ari		SEP	21	Vir
	MAY	28	Tau		NOV	9	Lib
	JUL	9	Gem		DEC	29	Scp
	AUG	22	Can	1969	FEB	25	Sag
	OCT	11	Leo		SEP	21	Cap
1963	JUN	3	Vir		NOV	4	Aqu
	JUL	27	Lib		DEC	15	Pic
	SEP	12	Scp	1970	JAN	24	Ari
	OCT	25	Sag		MAR	7	Tau
	DEC	5	Cap		APR	18	Gem
1964	JAN	13	Aqu		JUN	2	Can
	FEB	20	Pic		JUL	18	Leo
	MAR	29	Ari		SEP	3	Vir
	MAY	7	Tau		OCT	20	Lib
	JUN	17	Gem		DEC	6	Scp
	JUL	30	Can	1971	JAN	23	Sag
	SEP	15	Leo		MAR	12	Cap

	MAY	3	Aqu		JUN	6	Tau
	NOV	6	Pic		JUL	17	Gem
	DEC	26	Ari		SEP	1	Can
1972	FEB	10	Tau		OCT	26	Leo
	MAR	27	Gem	1978	JAN	26	Can
	MAY	12	Can		APR	10	Leo
	JUN	28	Leo		JUN	14	Vir
	AUG	15	Vir		AUG	4	Lib
	SEP	30	Lib		SEP	19	Scp
	NOV	15	Scp		NOV	2	Sag
	DEC	30	Sag		DEC	12	Cap
1973	FEB	12	Cap	1979	JAN	20	Aqu
	MAR	26	Aqu		FEB	27	Pic
	MAY	8	Pic		APR	7	Ari
	JUN	20	Ari		MAY	16	Tau
	AUG	12	Tau		JUN	26	Gem
	OCT	29	Ari		AUG	8	Can
	DEC	24	Tau		SEP	24	Leo
1974	FEB	27	Gem		NOV	19	Vir
	APR	20	Can	1980	MAR	11	Leo
	JUN	9	Leo		MAY	4	Vir
	JUL	27	Vir		JUL	10	Lib
	SEP	12	Lib		AUG	29	Scp
	OCT	28	Scp		OCT	12	Sag
	DEC	10	Sag		NOV	22	Cap
1975	JAN	21	Cap		DEC	30	Aqu
	MAR	3	Aqu	1981	FEB	6	Pic
	APR	11	Pic		MAR	17	Ari
	MAY	21	Ari		APR	25	Tau
	JUL	1	Tau		JUN	5	Gem
	AUG	14	Gem		JUL	18	Can
	OCT	17	Can		SEP	2	Leo
	NOV	25	Gem		OCT	21	Vir
1976	MAR	18	Can		DEC	16	Lib
	MAY	16	Leo	1982	AUG	3	Scp
	JUL	6	Vir		SEP	20	Sag
	AUG	24	Lib		OCT	31	Cap
	OCT	8	Scp		DEC	10	Aqu
	NOV	20	Sag	1983	JAN	17	Pic
1977	JAN	1	Cap		FEB	25	Ari
	FEB	9	Aqu		APR	5	Tau
	MAR	20	Pic		MAY	16	Gem
	APR	27	Ari		JUN	29	Can

	AUG	13	Leo	1990	JAN	29	Cap
	SEP	30	Vir		MAR	11	Aqu
	NOV	18	Lib		APR	20	Pic
1984	JAN	11	Scp		MAY	31	Ari
	AUG	17	Sag		JUL	12	Tau
	OCT	5	Cap		AUG	31	Gem
	NOV	15	Aqu		DEC	14	Tau
	DEC	25	Pic	1991	JAN	21	Gem
1985	FEB	2	Ari		APR	3	Can
	MAR	15	Tau		MAY	26	Leo
	APR	26	Gem		JUL	15	Vir
	JUN	9	Can		SEP	1	Lib
	JUL	25	Leo		OCT	16	Scp
	SEP	10	Vir		NOV	29	Sag
	OCT	27	Lib	1992	JAN	9	Cap
	DEC	14	Scp		FEB	18	Aqu
1986	FEB	2	Sag		MAR	28	Pic
	MAR	28	Cap		MAY	5	Ari
	OCT	9	Aqu		JUN	14	Tau
	NOV	26	Pic		JUL	26	Gem
1987	JAN	8	Ari		SEP	12	Can
	FEB	20	Tau	1993	APR	27	Leo
	APR	5	Gem		JUN	23	Vir
	MAY	21	Can		AUG	12	Lib
	JUL	6	Leo		SEP	27	Scp
	AUG	22	Vir		NOV	9	Sag
	OCT	8	Lib		DEC	20	Cap
	NOV	24	Scp	1994	JAN	28	Aqu
1988	JAN	8	Sag		MAR	7	Pic
	FEB	22	Cap		APR	14	Ari
	APR	6	Aqu		MAY	23	Tau
	MAY	22	Pic		JUL	3	Gem
	JUL	13	Ari		AUG	16	Can
	OCT	23	Pic		OCT	4	Leo
	NOV	1	Ari		DEC	12	Vir
1989	JAN	19	Tau	1995	JAN	22	Leo
	MAR	11	Gem		MAY	25	Vir
	APR	29	Can		JUL	21	Lib
	JUN	16	Leo		SEP	7	Scp
	AUG	3	Vir		OCT	20	Sag
	SEP	19	Lib		NOV	30	Cap
	NOV	4	Scp	1996	JAN	8	Aqu
	DEC	18	Sag		FEB	15	Pic

	MAR	24	Ari	MAY	28	Can
	MAY	2	Tau	JUL	13	Leo
	JUN	12	Gem	AUG	29	Vir
	JUL	25	Can	OCT	15	Lib
	SEP	9	Leo	DEC	1	Scp
	OCT	30	Vir	2003 JAN	17	Sag
1997	JAN	3	Lib	MAR	4	Cap
	MAR	8	Vir	APR	21	Aqu
	JUN	19	Lib	JUN	17	Pic
	AUG	14	Scp	DEC	16	Ari
	SEP	28	Sag	2004 FEB	3	Tau
	NOV	9	Cap	MAR	21	Gem
	DEC	18	Aqu	MAY	7	Can
1998	JAN	25	Pic	JUN	23	Leo
	MAR	4	Ari	AUG	10	Vir
	APR	13	Tau	SEP	26	Lib
	MAY	24	Gem	NOV	11	Sep
	JUL	6	Can	DEC	25	Sag
	AUG	20	Leo	2005 FEB	6	Cap
	OCT	7	Vir	MAR	20	Aqu
	NOV	27	Lib	MAY	1	Pic
1999	JAN	26	Scp	JUN	12	Ari
	MAY	5	Lib	JUL	28	Tau
	JUL	5	Scp	2006 FEB	17	Gem
	SEP	2	Sag	APR	14	Can
	OCT	17	Cap	JUN	3	Leo
	NOV	26	Aqu	JUL	22	Vir
2000	JAN	4	Pic	SEP	8	Lib
	FEB	12	Ari	OCT	23	Scp
	MAR	23	Tau	DEC	6	Sag
	MAY	3	Gem	2007 JAN	16	Cap
	JUN	16	Can	FEB	25	Aqu
	AUG	1	Leo	APR	6	Pic
	SEP	17	Vir	MAY	15	Ari
	NOV	4	Lib	JUNE	24	Tau
	DEC	23	Scp	AUG	7	Gem
2001	FEB	14	Sag	SEP	28	Can
	SEP	8	Cap	DEC	31	Gem*
	OCT	27	Aqu	2008 MAR	4	Can
	DEC	8	Pic	MAY	9	Leo
2002	JAN	18	Ari	JUL	1	Vir
	MAR	1	Tau	AUG	19	Lib
	APR	13	Gem	OCT	3	Scp

	NOV	16	Sag		AUG	25	Can
	DEC	27	Cap		OCT	16	Leo
2009	FEB	4	Aqu	2010	JUN	7	Vir
	MAR	14	Pic		JUL	29	Lib
	APR	22	Ari		SEP	14	Scp
	MAY	31	Tau		OCT	28	Sag
	JUL	11	Gem		DEC	7	Cap

JUPITER SIGNS 1901–2010

1901	JAN	19	Cap	1927	JAN	18	Pic
1902	FEB	6	Aqu		JUN	6	Ari
1903	FEB	20	Pic		SEP	11	Pic
1904	MAR	1	Ari	1928	JAN	23	Ari
	AUG	8	Tau		JUN	4	Tau
	AUG	31	Ari	1929	JUN	12	Gem
1905	MAR	7	Tau	1930	JUN	26	Can
	JUL	21	Gem	1931	JUL	17	Leo
	DEC	4	Tau	1932	AUG	11	Vir
1906	MAR	9	Gem	1933	SEP	10	Lib
	JUL	30	Can	1934	OCT	11	Scp
1907	AUG	18	Leo	1935	NOV	9	Sag
1908	SEP	12	Vir	1936	DEC	2	Cap
1909	OCT	11	Lib	1937	DEC	20	Aqu
1910	NOV	11	Scp	1938	MAY	14	Pic
1911	DEC	10	Sag		JUL	30	Aqu
1913	JAN	2	Cap		DEC	29	Pic
1914	JAN	21	Aqu	1939	MAY	11	Ari
1915	FEB	4	Pic		OCT	30	Pic
1916	FEB	12	Ari		DEC	20	Ari
	JUN	26	Tau	1940	MAY	16	Tau
	OCT	26	Ari	1941	MAY	26	Gem
1917	FEB	12	Tau	1942	JUN	10	Can
	JUN	29	Gem	1943	JUN	30	Leo
1918	JUL	13	Can	1944	JUL	26	Vir
1919	AUG	2	Leo	1945	AUG	25	Lib
1920	AUG	27	Vir	1946	SEP	25	Scp
1921	SEP	25	Lib	1947	OCT	24	Sag
1922	OCT	26	Scp	1948	NOV	15	Cap
1923	NOV	24	Sag	1949	APR	12	Aqu
1924	DEC	18	Cap		JUN	27	Cap
1926	JAN	6	Aqu		NOV	30	Aqu

1950	APR	15	Pic
	SEP	15	Aqu
	DEC	1	Pic
1951	APR	21	Ari
1952	APR	28	Tau
1953	MAY	9	Gem
1954	MAY	24	Can
1955	JUN	13	Leo
	NOV	17	Vir
1956	JAN	18	Leo
	JUL	7	Vir
	DEC	13	Lib
1957	FEB	19	Vir
	AUG	7	Lib
1958	JAN	13	Scp
	MAR	20	Lib
	SEP	7	Scp
1959	FEB	10	Sag
	APR	24	Scp
	OCT	5	Sag
1960	MAR	1	Cap
	JUN	10	Sag
	OCT	26	Cap
1961	MAR	15	Aqu
	AUG	12	Cap
	NOV	4	Aqu
1962	MAR	25	Pic
1963	APR	4	Ari
1964	APR	12	Tau
1965	APR	22	Gem
	SEP	21	Can
	NOV	17	Gem
1966	MAY	5	Can
	SEP	27	Leo
1967	JAN	16	Can
	MAY	23	Leo
	OCT	19	Vir
1968	FEB	27	Leo
	JUN	15	Vir
	NOV	15	Lib
1969	MAR	30	Vir
	JUL	15	Lib
	DEC	16	Scp

1970	APR	30	Lib
	AUG	15	Scp
1971	JAN	14	Sag
	JUN	5	Scp
	SEP	11	Sag
1972	FEB	6	Cap
	JUL	24	Sag
	SEP	25	Cap
1973	FEB	23	Aqu
1974	MAR	8	Pic
1975	MAR	18	Ari
1976	MAR	26	Tau
	AUG	23	Gem
	OCT	16	Tau
1977	APR	3	Gem
	AUG	20	Can
	DEC	30	Gem
1978	APR	12	Can
	SEP	5	Leo
1979	FEB	28	Can
	APR	20	Leo
	SEP	29	Vir
1980	OCT	27	Lib
1981	NOV	27	Scp
1982	DEC	26	Sag
1984	JAN	19	Cap
1985	FEB	6	Aqu
1986	FEB	20	Pic
1987	MAR	2	Ari
1988	MAR	8	Tau
	JUL	22	Gem
	NOV	30	Tau
1989	MAR	11	Gem
	JUL	30	Can
1990	AUG	18	Leo
1991	SEP	12	Vir
1992	OCT	10	Lib
1993	NOV	9	Scp
1994	DEC	9	Sag
1996	JAN	3	Cap
1997	JAN	21	Aqu
1998	FEB	4	Pic
1999	FEB	13	Ari

	JUN	28	Tau					
	OCT	23	Ari	2005	OCT	26	Scp	
2000	FEB	14	Tau	2006	NOV	24	Sag	
	JUN	30	Gem	2007	DEC	17	Cap	
2001	JUL	14	Can	2009	JAN	5	Aqu	
2002	AUG	1	Leo	2010	JAN	18	Pis	
2003	AUG	27	Vir		JUN	6	Ari	
2004	SEP	24	Lib		SEP	9	Pis	

SATURN SIGNS 1903–2010

1903	JAN	19	Aqu		OCT	18	Pic
1905	APR	13	Pic	1938	JAN	14	Ari
	AUG	17	Aqu	1939	JUL	6	Tau
1906	JAN	8	Pic		SEP	22	Ari
1908	MAR	19	Ari	1940	MAR	20	Tau
1910	MAY	17	Tau	1942	MAY	8	Gem
	DEC	14	Ari	1944	JUN	20	Can
1911	JAN	20	Tau	1946	AUG	2	Leo
1912	JUL	7	Gem	1948	SEP	19	Vir
	NOV	30	Tau	1949	APR	3	Leo
1913	MAR	26	Gem		MAY	29	Vir
1914	AUG	24	Can	1950	NOV	20	Lib
	DEC	7	Gem	1951	MAR	7	Vir
1915	MAY	11	Can		AUG	13	Lib
1916	OCT	17	Leo	1953	OCT	22	Scp
	DEC	7	Can	1956	JAN	12	Sag
1917	JUN	24	Leo		MAY	14	Scp
1919	AUG	12	Vir		OCT	10	Sag
1921	OCT	7	Lib	1959	JAN	5	Cap
1923	DEC	20	Scp	1962	JAN	3	Aqu
1924	APR	6	Lib	1964	MAR	24	Pic
	SEP	13	Scp		SEP	16	Aqu
1926	DEC	2	Sag		DEC	16	Pic
1929	MAR	15	Cap	1967	MAR	3	Ari
	MAY	5	Sag	1969	APR	29	Tau
	NOV	30	Cap	1971	JUN	18	Gem
1932	FEB	24	Aqu	1972	JAN	10	Tau
	AUG	13	Cap		FEB	21	Gem
	NOV	20	Aqu	1973	AUG	1	Can
1935	FEB	14	Pic	1974	JAN	7	Gem
1937	APR	25	Ari		APR	18	Can

1975	SEP	17	Leo		JUN	30	Aqu
1976	JAN	14	Can	1994	JAN	28	Pic
	JUN	5	Leo	1996	APR	7	Ari
1977	NOV	17	Vir	1998	JUN	9	Tau
1978	JAN	5	Leo		OCT	25	Ari
	JUL	26	Vir	1999	MAR	1	Tau
1980	SEP	21	Lib	2000	AUG	10	Gem
1982	NOV	29	Scp		OCT	16	Tau
1983	MAY	6	Lib	2001	APR	21	Gem
	AUG	24	Scp	2003	JUN	3	Can
1985	NOV	17	Sag	2005	JUL	16	Leo
1988	FEB	13	Cap	2007	SEP	2	Vir
	JUN	10	Sag	2009	OCT	29	Lib
	NOV	12	Cap	2010	APR	7	Vir
1991	FEB	6	Aqu		JUL	21	Lib
1993	MAY	21	Pic				

CHAPTER 6

Where It All Happens:
Your Rising Sign

To find out what's happening in a horoscope, you first have to look east. The degree of the zodiac ascending over the eastern horizon at the time you were born, which is called the rising sign or ascendant, marks the beginning of the first house, one of twelve divisions of the horoscope, each of which represents a different area of life. These "houses" contain the planets, the doers in a chart. After the rising sign, the other houses parade around the chart in sequence, with the following sign on the next house cusp. Therefore, the setup of the chart—*what* happens *where*—depends on the rising sign.

Though you can learn much about a person by the signs and interactions of the sun, moon, and planets in the horoscope, without a valid rising sign, the collection of planets has no "homes." One would have no idea which area of life could be influenced by a particular planet. For example, you might know that a person has Mars in Aries, which will describe that person's dynamic fiery energy. But if you also know that the person has a Capricorn rising sign, this Mars will fall in the fourth house of home and family, so you know where that energy will operate.

Due to the earth's rotation, the rising sign changes every two hours, which means that babies born later or earlier on the same day in the same hospital will have most planets in the same signs, but may not have the same rising sign. Therefore, their planets may fall in different houses in the chart. For instance, if Mars is in Gemini and your rising sign is Taurus,

Mars will most likely be active in the second or financial house of your chart. Someone born later in the same day when the rising sign is Virgo would have Mars positioned at the top of the chart, energizing the tenth house of career.

Most astrologers insist on knowing the exact time of a client's birth before they analyze a chart. The more accurate your birth time, the more accurately an astrologer can position the planets in your chart by determining the correct rising sign.

How Your Rising Sign Can Influence Your Sun Sign

Your rising sign has an important relationship with your sun sign. Some will complement the sun sign; others hide it under a totally different mask, as if playing an entirely different role, making it difficult to guess the person's sun sign from outer appearances. This may be the reason why you might not look or act like your sun sign's archetype. For example, a Leo with a conservative Capricorn ascendant would come across as much more serious than a Leo with a fiery Aries or Sagittarius ascendant.

Though the rising sign usually creates the first impression you make, there are exceptions. When the sun sign is reinforced by other planets in the same sign, this might overpower the impression of the rising sign. For instance, a Leo sun plus a Leo Venus and Leo Jupiter would counteract the more conservative image that would otherwise be conveyed by the person's Capricorn ascendant.

Those born early in the morning when the sun was on the horizon will be most likely to project the image of their sun sign. These people are often called a "double Aries" or a "double Virgo" because the same sun sign and ascendant reinforce each other.

Find Your Rising Sign

Look up your rising sign on the chart at the end of this chapter. Since rising signs change every two hours, it is important to know your birth time as close to the minute as possible. Even a few minutes' difference could change the rising sign and therefore the setup of your chart. If you are unsure about the exact time, but know within a few hours, check the following descriptions to see which is most like the personality you project.

Aries Rising: Alpha Energy

You are the most aggressive version of your sun sign, with boundless energy that can be used productively if it's channeled in the right direction. Watch a tendency to overreact emotionally and blow your top. You come across as openly competitive, a positive asset in business or sports. Be on guard against impatience, which could lead to head injuries. Your walk and bearing could have the telltale head-forward Aries posture. You may wear more bright colors, especially red, than others of your sign, or be a redhead. You may also have a tendency to drive your car faster.

Can you see the alpha Aries tendency in Barbra Streisand (a sun sign Taurus) and Bette Midler (a sun sign Sagittarius)?

Taurus Rising: Down-to-Earth

You're slow-moving, with a beautiful (or distinctive) speaking or singing voice. You probably surround yourself with comfort, good food, luxurious surroundings, and other sensual pleasures. You prefer welcoming others into your home to gadding about. You may have a talent for business, especially in trading, appraising, and real estate. A Taurus ascendant gives a well-padded physique that gains weight easily, like Liza Minnelli. This ascendant can also endow females with a curvaceous beauty.

Gemini Rising: A Way with Words

You're naturally sociable, with lighter, more ethereal mannerisms than others of your sign, especially if you're female. You love to communicate with people, and express your ideas easily, like former British prime minister Tony Blair. You may have a talent for writing or public speaking. You thrive on variety, a constantly changing scene, and a lively social life. However, you may relate to others at a deeper level than might be suspected. And you will be far more sympathetic and caring than you project. You will probably travel widely, changing partners and jobs several times (or juggle two at once). Physically, your nerves are quite sensitive. Occasionally, you would benefit from a calm, tranquil atmosphere away from your usual social scene.

Cancer Rising: Nurturing Instincts

You are naturally acquisitive, possessive, private, a money-maker like Bill Gates or Michael Bloomberg. You easily pick up others' needs and feelings—a great gift in business, the arts, and personal relationships. But you must guard against overreacting or taking things too personally, especially during full-moon periods. Find creative outlets for your natural nurturing gifts, such as helping the less fortunate, particularly children. Your insights would be helpful in psychology. Your desire to feed and care for others would be useful in the restaurant, hotel, or child-care industries. You may be especially fond of wearing romantic old clothes, collecting antiques, and dining on exquisite food. Since your body may retain fluids, pay attention to your diet. To relax, escape to places near water.

Leo Rising: Diva Dazzle

You may come across as more poised than you really feel. However, you play it to the hilt, projecting a proud royal presence. A Leo ascendant gives you a natural flair for drama, like Marilyn Monroe, and you might be accused of stealing the spotlight. You'll also project a much more outgoing, optimistic, and sunny personality than others of your sign. You take care to please your public by always projecting star quality, probably tossing a luxuriant mane of hair, sporting a striking hairstyle, or dressing to impress. Females often dazzle with colorful clothing or spectacular jewelry. Since you may have a strong parental nature, you could well become a family matriarch or patriarch, like George H. W. Bush.

Virgo Rising: High Standards

Virgo rising endows you with a practical, analytical outer image. You seem neat, orderly, and more particular than others of your sign. Others in your life may feel they must live up to your high standards. Though at times you may be openly critical, this masks a well-meaning desire to have only the best for loved ones. Your sharp eye for details could be used in the financial world, or your literary skills could draw you to teaching or publishing. The healing arts, health care, and service-oriented professions attract many with a Virgo ascendant. You're likely to take good care of yourself, with great attention to health, diet, and exercise, like Madonna. You might even show some hypochondriac tendencies, like Woody Allen. Physically, you may have a very sensitive digestive system.

Libra Rising: The Charmer

Libra rising gives you a charming, social, and public persona, like John F. Kennedy and Bill Clinton. You tend to avoid confrontations in relationships, preferring to smooth the way or negotiate diplomatically rather than give in to an emotional reaction. Because you are interested in all aspects of a situation, you may be slow to reach decisions. Physically, you'll have good proportions and physical symmetry. You will move with natural grace and balance. You're likely to have pleasing, if not beautiful, facial features, with a winning smile, like Cary Grant. You'll show natural good taste and harmony in your clothes and home decor. Legal, diplomatic, or public relations professions could draw your interest.

Scorpio Rising: Air of Mystery

You project an intriguing air of mystery with this ascendant, as the Scorpio secretiveness and sense of underlying power combine with your sun sign. Like Jacqueline Kennedy Onassis, you convey that there's more to you than meets the eye. You seem like someone who is always in control and who can move comfortably in the world of power. Your physical look comes across as intense. Many of you have remarkable eyes, with a direct, penetrating gaze. But you'll never reveal your private agenda, and you tend to keep your true feelings under wraps (watch a tendency toward paranoia). You may have an interesting romantic history with secret love affairs, like Grace Kelly. Many of you heighten your air of mystery by wearing black. You're happiest near water; you should provide yourself with a seaside retreat.

Sagittarius Rising: The Explorer

You travel with this ascendant. You may also be a more outdoor, sportive type, with an athletic, casual, and outgoing air. Your moods are camouflaged with cheerful optimism or a philosophical attitude. Though you don't hesitate to speak your mind—like Ted Turner, who was called the Mouth of the South—you can also laugh at your troubles or crack a joke more easily than others of your sign. A Sagittarius ascendant can also draw you to the field of higher education or to spiritual life. You'll seem to have less attachment to things and people, and you may explore the globe. Your strong, fast legs are a physical bonus.

Capricorn Rising: Serious Business

This rising sign makes you come across as serious, goal-oriented, disciplined, and careful with cash. You are not one of the zodiac's big spenders, though you might splurge occasionally on items with good investment value. You're the conservative type in dress and environment, and you might come across as quite formal and businesslike, like Rupert Murdoch. You'll function well in a structured or corporate environment where you can climb to the top. (You are always aware of who's the boss.) In your personal life, you could be a loner or a single parent who is father and mother to your children.

Aquarius Rising: One of a Kind

You come across as less concerned about what others think and could even be a bit eccentric. Your appearance is sure to be unique and memorable. You're more at ease with groups of people than others in your sign, and you may be attracted to public life, like Jay Leno. Your appearance may be unique, either unconventional or unimportant to you. Those of you whose sun is in a water sign (Cancer, Scorpio, or Pisces) may exercise your nurturing qualities with a large group, an extended family, or a day-care or community center.

Pisces Rising: Romantic Roles

Your creative, nurturing talents are heightened and so is your ability to project emotional drama. And, like Antonio Banderas, your dreamy eyes and poetic air bring out the protective instinct in others. You could be attracted to the arts, especially theater, dance, film, and photography, or to psychology, spiritual practice, and charity work. You are happiest when you are using your creative ability to help others. Since you are vulnerable to mood swings, it is important for you to find interesting, creative work where you can express your talents and heighten your self-esteem. Accentuate the positive. Be wary of escapist tendencies, particularly involving alcohol or drugs to which you are supersensitive, like Whitney Houston.

RISING SIGNS—A.M. BIRTHS

	1 AM	2 AM	3 AM	4 AM	5 AM	6 AM	7 AM	8 AM	9 AM	10 AM	11 AM	12 NOON
Jan 1	Lib	Sc	Sc	Sc	Sag	Sag	Cap	Cap	Aq	Aq	Pis	Ar
Jan 9	Lib	Sc	Sc	Sag	Sag	Sag	Cap	Cap	Aq	Pis	Ar	Tau
Jan 17	Sc	Sc	Sc	Sag	Sag	Cap	Cap	Aq	Aq	Pis	Ar	Tau
Jan 25	Sc	Sc	Sag	Sag	Sag	Cap	Cap	Aq	Pis	Ar	Tau	Tau
Feb 2	Sc	Sc	Sag	Sag	Cap	Cap	Aq	Pis	Pis	Ar	Tau	Gem
Feb 10	Sc	Sag	Sag	Sag	Cap	Cap	Aq	Pis	Ar	Tau	Tau	Gem
Feb 18	Sc	Sag	Sag	Cap	Cap	Aq	Pis	Pis	Ar	Tau	Gem	Gem
Feb 26	Sag	Sag	Sag	Cap	Aq	Aq	Pis	Ar	Tau	Tau	Gem	Gem
Mar 6	Sag	Sag	Cap	Cap	Aq	Pis	Pis	Ar	Tau	Gem	Gem	Can
Mar 14	Sag	Cap	Cap	Aq	Aq	Pis	Ar	Tau	Tau	Gem	Gem	Can
Mar 22	Sag	Cap	Cap	Aq	Pis	Ar	Ar	Tau	Gem	Gem	Can	Can
Mar 30	Cap	Cap	Aq	Pis	Pis	Ar	Tau	Tau	Gem	Can	Can	Can
Apr 7	Cap	Cap	Aq	Pis	Ar	Ar	Tau	Gem	Gem	Can	Can	Leo
Apr 14	Cap	Aq	Aq	Pis	Ar	Tau	Tau	Gem	Gem	Can	Leo	Leo
Apr 22	Cap	Aq	Pis	Ar	Ar	Tau	Gem	Gem	Gem	Can	Leo	Leo
Apr 30	Aq	Aq	Pis	Ar	Tau	Tau	Gem	Can	Can	Can	Leo	Leo
May 8	Aq	Pis	Ar	Ar	Tau	Gem	Gem	Can	Can	Leo	Leo	Leo
May 16	Aq	Pis	Ar	Tau	Gem	Gem	Can	Can	Leo	Leo	Leo	Vir
May 24	Pis	Ar	Ar	Tau	Gem	Gem	Can	Can	Leo	Leo	Leo	Vir
June 1	Pis	Ar	Tau	Gem	Gem	Can	Can	Can	Leo	Leo	Vir	Vir
June 9	Ar	Ar	Tau	Gem	Gem	Can	Can	Leo	Leo	Leo	Vir	Vir
June 17	Ar	Tau	Gem	Gem	Can	Can	Can	Leo	Leo	Vir	Vir	Vir
June 25	Tau	Tau	Gem	Gem	Can	Can	Leo	Leo	Leo	Vir	Vir	Lib
July 3	Tau	Gem	Gem	Can	Can	Can	Leo	Leo	Vir	Vir	Vir	Lib
July 11	Tau	Gem	Gem	Can	Can	Leo	Leo	Leo	Vir	Vir	Lib	Lib
July 18	Gem	Gem	Can	Can	Can	Leo	Leo	Vir	Vir	Vir	Lib	Lib
July 26	Gem	Gem	Can	Can	Leo	Leo	Vir	Vir	Vir	Lib	Lib	Lib
Aug 3	Gem	Can	Can	Can	Leo	Leo	Vir	Vir	Vir	Lib	Lib	Sc
Aug 11	Gem	Can	Can	Leo	Leo	Leo	Vir	Vir	Lib	Lib	Lib	Sc
Aug 18	Can	Can	Can	Leo	Leo	Vir	Vir	Vir	Lib	Lib	Sc	Sc
Aug 27	Can	Can	Leo	Leo	Leo	Vir	Vir	Lib	Lib	Lib	Sc	Sc
Sept 4	Can	Can	Leo	Leo	Leo	Vir	Vir	Lib	Lib	Lib	Sc	Sc
Sept 12	Can	Leo	Leo	Leo	Vir	Vir	Lib	Lib	Lib	Sc	Sc	Sag
Sept 20	Leo	Leo	Leo	Vir	Vir	Vir	Lib	Lib	Sc	Sc	Sc	Sag
Sept 28	Leo	Leo	Leo	Vir	Vir	Lib	Lib	Lib	Sc	Sc	Sag	Sag
Oct 6	Leo	Leo	Vir	Vir	Vir	Lib	Lib	Sc	Sc	Sc	Sag	Sag
Oct 14	Leo	Vir	Vir	Vir	Lib	Lib	Lib	Sc	Sc	Sag	Sag	Cap
Oct 22	Leo	Vir	Vir	Lib	Lib	Lib	Sc	Sc	Sc	Sag	Sag	Cap
Oct 30	Vir	Vir	Vir	Lib	Lib	Sc	Sc	Sc	Sag	Sag	Cap	Cap
Nov 7	Vir	Vir	Lib	Lib	Lib	Sc	Sc	Sc	Sag	Sag	Cap	Cap
Nov 15	Vir	Vir	Lib	Lib	Sc	Sc	Sc	Sag	Sag	Cap	Cap	Aq
Nov 23	Vir	Lib	Lib	Lib	Sc	Sc	Sag	Sag	Sag	Cap	Cap	Aq
Dec 1	Vir	Lib	Lib	Sc	Sc	Sc	Sag	Sag	Cap	Cap	Aq	Aq
Dec 9	Lib	Lib	Lib	Sc	Sc	Sag	Sag	Sag	Cap	Cap	Aq	Pis
Dec 18	Lib	Lib	Sc	Sc	Sc	Sag	Sag	Cap	Cap	Aq	Aq	Pis
Dec 28	Lib	Lib	Sc	Sc	Sag	Sag	Sag	Cap	Aq	Aq	Pis	Ar

RISING SIGNS—P.M. BIRTHS

	1 PM	2 PM	3 PM	4 PM	5 PM	6 PM	7 PM	8 PM	9 PM	10 PM	11 PM	12 MIDNIGHT
Jan 1	Tau	Gem	Gem	Can	Can	Can	Leo	Leo	Vir	Vir	Vir	Lib
Jan 9	Tau	Gem	Gem	Can	Can	Leo	Leo	Leo	Vir	Vir	Vir	Lib
Jan 17	Gem	Gem	Can	Can	Can	Leo	Leo	Vir	Vir	Vir	Lib	Lib
Jan 25	Gem	Gem	Can	Can	Leo	Leo	Leo	Vir	Vir	Lib	Lib	Lib
Feb 2	Gem	Can	Can	Can	Leo	Leo	Vir	Vir	Vir	Lib	Lib	Sc
Feb 10	Gem	Can	Can	Leo	Leo	Leo	Vir	Vir	Lib	Lib	Lib	Sc
Feb 18	Can	Can	Can	Leo	Leo	Vir	Vir	Vir	Lib	Lib	Sc	Sc
Feb 26	Can	Can	Leo	Leo	Leo	Vir	Vir	Lib	Lib	Lib	Sc	Sc
Mar 6	Can	Leo	Leo	Leo	Vir	Vir	Vir	Lib	Lib	Sc	Sc	Sc
Mar 14	Can	Leo	Leo	Vir	Vir	Vir	Lib	Lib	Lib	Sc	Sc	Sag
Mar 22	Leo	Leo	Leo	Vir	Vir	Lib	Lib	Lib	Sc	Sc	Sc	Sag
Mar 30	Leo	Leo	Vir	Vir	Vir	Lib	Lib	Sc	Sc	Sc	Sag	Sag
Apr 7	Leo	Leo	Vir	Vir	Lib	Lib	Lib	Sc	Sc	Sc	Sag	Sag
Apr 14	Leo	Vir	Vir	Vir	Lib	Lib	Sc	Sc	Sc	Sag	Sag	Cap
Apr 22	Leo	Vir	Vir	Lib	Lib	Lib	Sc	Sc	Sc	Sag	Sag	Cap
Apr 30	Vir	Vir	Vir	Lib	Lib	Sc	Sc	Sc	Sag	Sag	Cap	Cap
May 8	Vir	Vir	Lib	Lib	Lib	Sc	Sc	Sc	Sag	Sag	Cap	Cap
May 16	Vir	Vir	Lib	Lib	Sc	Sc	Sc	Sag	Sag	Cap	Cap	Aq
May 24	Vir	Lib	Lib	Lib	Sc	Sc	Sag	Sag	Sag	Cap	Cap	Aq
June 1	Vir	Lib	Lib	Sc	Sc	Sc	Sag	Sag	Cap	Cap	Aq	Aq
June 9	Lib	Lib	Lib	Sc	Sc	Sag	Sag	Sag	Cap	Cap	Aq	Pis
June 17	Lib	Lib	Sc	Sc	Sc	Sag	Sag	Cap	Cap	Aq	Aq	Pis
June 25	Lib	Lib	Sc	Sc	Sag	Sag	Sag	Cap	Cap	Aq	Pis	Ar
July 3	Lib	Sc	Sc	Sc	Sag	Sag	Cap	Cap	Aq	Aq	Pis	Ar
July 11	Lib	Sc	Sc	Sag	Sag	Sag	Cap	Cap	Aq	Pis	Ar	Tau
July 18	Sc	Sc	Sc	Sag	Sag	Cap	Cap	Aq	Aq	Pis	Ar	Tau
July 26	Sc	Sc	Sag	Sag	Sag	Cap	Cap	Aq	Pis	Ar	Tau	Tau
Aug 3	Sc	Sc	Sag	Sag	Sag	Cap	Cap	Aq	Pis	Ar	Tau	Gem
Aug 11	Sc	Sag	Sag	Sag	Cap	Cap	Aq	Pis	Ar	Tau	Tau	Gem
Aug 18	Sc	Sag	Sag	Cap	Cap	Aq	Pis	Pis	Ar	Tau	Gem	Gem
Aug 27	Sag	Sag	Sag	Cap	Cap	Aq	Pis	Ar	Tau	Tau	Gem	Gem
Sept 4	Sag	Sag	Cap	Cap	Aq	Pis	Pis	Ar	Tau	Gem	Gem	Can
Sept 12	Sag	Sag	Cap	Aq	Aq	Pis	Ar	Tau	Tau	Gem	Gem	Can
Sept 20	Sag	Cap	Cap	Aq	Pis	Pis	Ar	Tau	Gem	Gem	Can	Can
Sept 28	Cap	Cap	Aq	Aq	Pis	Ar	Tau	Tau	Gem	Gem	Can	Can
Oct 6	Cap	Cap	Aq	Pis	Ar	Ar	Tau	Gem	Gem	Can	Can	Leo
Oct 14	Cap	Aq	Aq	Pis	Ar	Tau	Tau	Gem	Gem	Can	Can	Leo
Oct 22	Cap	Aq	Pis	Ar	Ar	Tau	Gem	Gem	Can	Can	Leo	Leo
Oct 30	Aq	Aq	Pis	Ar	Tau	Tau	Gem	Can	Can	Can	Leo	Leo
Nov 7	Aq	Aq	Pis	Ar	Tau	Tau	Gem	Can	Can	Can	Leo	Leo
Nov 15	Aq	Pis	Ar	Tau	Gem	Gem	Can	Can	Can	Leo	Leo	Vir
Nov 23	Pis	Ar	Ar	Tau	Gem	Gem	Can	Can	Can	Leo	Leo	Vir
Dec 1	Pis	Ar	Tau	Gem	Gem	Can	Can	Can	Leo	Leo	Vir	Vir
Dec 9	Ar	Tau	Tau	Gem	Gem	Can	Can	Leo	Leo	Leo	Vir	Vir
Dec 18	Ar	Tau	Gem	Gem	Can	Can	Can	Leo	Leo	Vir	Vir	Vir
Dec 28	Tau	Tau	Gem	Gem	Can	Can	Leo	Leo	Vir	Vir	Vir	Lib

CHAPTER 7

The Keys to Reading Your Horoscope: The Glyphs

Are you ready to take your astrology knowledge to the next level and read your first horoscope chart? If so, you'll encounter a new language of symbols, because horoscope charts are written in glyphs, a centuries-old pictographic language. These little "pictures" are a type of shorthand used by astrologers around the world to indicate the planets and the signs.

There's no way to avoid learning the glyphs, if you want to get deeper into astrology. Whether you download your chart from one of the many Internet sites that offer free charts or you buy one of the many interesting astrology programs, you'll find charts are always written in glyph language. Some software makes it easier for beginners by listing the planets and their signs in English alongside the chart and other programs will pop up an English interpretation as your roll your mouse over the glyph. However, in the long run, it's much easier—and more fun—to learn the glyphs yourself.

There's an extra bonus to learning the glyphs: They contain a kind of visual code, with built-in clues that will tell you not only which sign or planet each represents, but what the symbol means in a deeper, more esoteric sense. Actually the physical act of writing the symbol is a mystical experience in itself, a way to invoke the deeper meaning of the sign or planet through age-old visual elements that have been with us since time began.

Since there are only twelve signs and ten planets (not counting a few asteroids and other space objects some astrologers use), it's a lot easier than learning to read a foreign language. Here's a code cracker for the glyphs, beginning with the glyphs for the planets. To those who already know their glyphs, don't just skim over the chapter. These familiar graphics have hidden meanings you will discover!

The Glyphs for the Planets

The glyphs for the planets are easy to learn. They're simple combinations of the most basic visual elements: the circle, the semicircle or arc, and the cross. However, each component of a glyph has a special meaning in relation to the other parts of the symbol.

The circle, which has no beginning or end, is one of the oldest symbols of spirit or spiritual forces. Early diagrams of the heavens—spiritual territory—are shown in circular form. The never-ending line of the circle is the perfect symbol for eternity. The semicircle or arc is an incomplete circle, symbolizing the receptive, finite soul, which contains spiritual potential in the curving line.

The vertical line of the cross symbolizes movement from heaven to earth. The horizontal line describes temporal movement, here and now, in time and space. Combined in a cross, the vertical and horizontal planes symbolize manifestation in the material world.

The Sun Glyph ☉

The sun is always shown by this powerful solar symbol, a circle with a point in the center. The center point is you, your spiritual center, and the symbol represents your infinite personality incarnating (the point) into the finite cycles of birth and death.

The sun has been represented by a circle or disk since ancient Egyptian times when the solar disk represented the sun god, Ra. Some archaeologists believe the great stone circles found in England were centers of sun worship. This particular version of the symbol was brought into common use in the sixteenth century after German occultist and scholar Cornelius Agrippa (1486–1535) wrote a book called *Die Occulta Philosophia,* which became accepted as the authority in the field. Agrippa collected many of the medieval astrological and magical symbols in this book, which have been used by astrologers since then.

The Moon Glyph ☽

The moon glyph is the most recognizable symbol on a chart, a left-facing arc stylized into the crescent moon. As part of a circle, the arc symbolizes the potential fulfillment of the entire circle, the life force that is still incomplete. Therefore, it is the ideal representation of the reactive, receptive, emotional nature of the moon.

The Mercury Glyph ☿

Mercury contains all three elemental symbols: the crescent, the circle, and the cross in vertical order. This is the "Venus with a hat" glyph (compare with the symbol of Venus). With another stretch of the imagination, can't you see the winged cap of Mercury the messenger? Think of the upturned crescent as antennae that tune in and transmit messages from the sun, reminding you that Mercury is the way you communicate, the way your mind works. The upturned arc is receiving energy into the spirit or solar circle, which will later be translated into action on the material plane, symbolized by the cross. All the elements are equally sized because Mercury is neutral; it doesn't play favorites! This planet symbolizes objective, detached, unemotional thinking.

The Venus Glyph ♀

Here the relationship is between two components: the circle of spirit and the cross of matter. Spirit is elevated over matter, pulling it upward. Venus asks, "What is beautiful? What do you like best? What do you love to have done to you?" Consequently, Venus determines both your ideal of beauty and what feels good sensually. It governs your own allure and power to attract, as well as what attracts and pleases you.

The Mars Glyph ♂

In this glyph, the cross of matter is stylized into an arrowhead pointed up and outward, propelled by the circle of spirit. With a little imagination, you can visualize it as the shield and spear of Mars, the ancient god of war. You can deduce that Mars embodies your spiritual energy projected into the outer world. It's your assertiveness, your initiative, your aggressive drive, what you like to do to others, your temper. If you know someone's Mars, you know whether they'll blow up when angry or do a slow burn. Your task is to use your outgoing Mars energy wisely and well.

The Jupiter Glyph ♃

Jupiter is the basic cross of matter, with a large stylized crescent perched on the left side of the horizontal, temporal plane. You might think of the crescent as an open hand, because one meaning of Jupiter is "luck," what's handed to you. You don't have to work for what you get from Jupiter; it comes to you, if you're open to it.

The Jupiter glyph might also remind you of a jumbo jet plane, with a huge tail fin, about to take off. This is the planet of travel, mental and spiritual, of expanding your horizons via new ideas, new spiritual dimensions, and new places. Jupiter embodies the optimism and enthusiasm of the traveler about to embark on an exciting adventure.

The Saturn Glyph ♄

Flip Jupiter over, and you've got Saturn. This might not be immediately apparent because Saturn is usually stylized into an "h" form like the one shown here. The principle it expresses is the opposite of Jupiter's expansive tendencies. Saturn pulls you back to earth: the receptive arc is pushed down underneath the cross of matter. Before there are any rewards or expansion, the duties and obligations of the material world must be considered. Saturn says, "Stop, wait, finish your chores before you take off!"

Saturn's glyph also resembles the sickle of old "Father Time."

Saturn was first known as Chronos, the Greek god of time, fo time brings all matter to an end. When it was the most distan planet (before the discovery of Uranus), Saturn was believe to be the place where time stopped. After the soul departe from earth, it journeyed back to the outer reaches of the un verse and finally stopped at Saturn, or at "the end of time."

The Uranus Glyph ♅

The glyph for Uranus is often stylized to form a capital *H* a ter Sir William Herschel, who discovered the planet. But th more esoteric version curves the two pillars of the H into cres cent antennae, or "ears," like satellite disks receiving signa from space. These are perched on the horizontal material lin of the cross of matter and pushed from below by the circle c the spirit. To many sci-fi fans, Uranus looks like an orbitin satellite.

Uranus channels the highest energy of all, the white electrica light of the universal spiritual force that holds the cosmos to gether. This pure electrical energy is gathered from all over th universe. Because Uranus energy doesn't follow any ordinar celestial drumbeat, it can't be controlled or predicted (which also true of those who are strongly influenced by this eccentr planet). In the symbol, this energy is manifested through th balance of polarities (the two opposite arms of the glyph) lik the two polarized wires of a lightbulb.

The Neptune Glyph ♆

Neptune's glyph is usually stylized to look like a trident, th weapon of the Roman god Neptune. However, on a more esc teric level, it shows the large upturned crescent of the sol pierced through by the cross of matter. Neptune nails dow or materializes, soul energy, bringing impulses from the sol level into manifestation. That is why Neptune is associate with imagination or "imagining in," making an image of th soul. Neptune works through feelings, sensitivity, and the my tical capacity to bring the divine into the earthly realm.

The Pluto Glyph ♀

Pluto is written two ways. One is a composite of the letters *PL,* the first two letters of the word Pluto and coincidentally the initials of Percival Lowell, one of the planet's discoverers. The other, more esoteric symbol is a small circle above a large open crescent that surmounts the cross of matter. This depicts Pluto's power to regenerate. Imagine a new little spirit emerging from the sheltering cup of the soul. Pluto rules the forces of life and death. After this planet has passed a sensitive point in your chart, you are transformed, reborn in some way.

Sci-fi fans might visualize this glyph as a small satellite (the circle) being launched. It was shortly after Pluto's discovery that we learned how to harness the nuclear forces that made space exploration possible. Pluto rules the transformative power of atomic energy, which totally changed our lives and from which there is no turning back.

The Glyphs for the Signs

On an astrology chart, the glyph for the sign will appear after that of the planet. For example, when you see the moon glyph followed first by a number and then by another glyph representing the sign, this means that the moon was passing over a certain degree of that astrological sign at the time of the chart. On the dividing lines between the houses on your chart, you'll find the symbol for the sign that rules the house.

Because sun sign symbols do not contain the same basic geometric components of the planetary glyphs, we must look elsewhere for clues to their meanings. Many have been passed down from ancient Egyptian and Chaldean civilizations with few modifications. Others have been adapted over the centuries.

In deciphering many of the glyphs, you'll often find that the symbols reveal a dual nature of the sign, which is not always apparent in the usual sun sign descriptions. For instance, the Gemini glyph is similar to the Roman numeral for two, and reveals this sign's longing to discover a twin soul. The Cancer glyph may be interpreted as resembling either the nurturing breasts or the self-protective claws of a crab, both symbols associated with the contrasting qualities of this sign. Libra's glyph embodies the duality of the spirit balanced with material reality. The Sagittarius glyph shows that the aspirant must also carry along the earthly animal nature in his quest. The Capricorn sea goat is another symbol with dual emphasis. The goat climbs high, yet is always pulled back by the deep waters of the unconscious. Aquarius embodies the double wave of mental detachment, balanced by the desire for connection with others, in a friendly way. Finally, the two fishes of Pisces which are forever tied together, show the duality of the soul and the spirit that must be reconciled.

The Aries Glyph ♈

Since the symbol for Aries is the Ram, this glyph is obviously associated with a ram's horns, which characterize one aspect of the Aries personality—an aggressive, me-first, leaping headfirst attitude. But the symbol can be interpreted in other ways as well. Some astrologers liken it to a fountain of energy which Aries people also embody. The first sign of the zodiac bursts on the scene eagerly, ready to go. Another analogy is to the eyebrows and nose of the human head, which Aries rules and the thinking power that is initiated by the brain.

One theory of this symbol links it to the Egyptian god Amun, represented by a ram in ancient times. As Amun-Ra, this god was believed to embody the creator of the universe, the leader of all the other gods. This relates easily to the position of Aries as the leader (or first sign) of the zodiac, which begins at the spring equinox, a time of the year when nature is renewed.

The Taurus Glyph ♉

This is another easy glyph to draw and identify. It takes little imagination to decipher the bull's head with long curving horns. Like its symbol the Bull, the archetypal Taurus is slow to anger but ferocious when provoked, as well as stubborn, steady, and sensual. Another association is the larynx (and hyroid) of the throat area (ruled by Taurus) and the eusta-chian tubes running up to the ears, which coincides with the relationship of Taurus to the voice, song, and music. Many famous singers, musicians, and composers have prominent Taurus influences.

Many ancient religions involved a bull as the central figure in fertility rites or initiations, usually symbolizing the victory of man over his animal nature. Another possible origin is in the sacred bull of Egypt, who embodied the incarnate form of Osiris, god of death and resurrection. In early Christian imagery, the Taurus Bull represented St. Luke.

The Gemini Glyph ♊

The standard glyph immediately calls to mind the Roman numeral for two (II) and the Twins symbol, as it is called, for Gemini. In almost all drawings and images used for this sign, the relationship between two persons is emphasized. Usually one twin will be touching the other, which signifies communication, human contact, the desire to share.

The top line of the Gemini glyph indicates mental communication, while the bottom line indicates shared physical space.

The most famous Gemini legend is that of the twin sons Castor and Pollux, one of whom had a mortal father while the other was the son of Zeus, king of the gods. When it came time for the mortal twin to die, his grief-stricken brother pleaded with Zeus, who agreed to let them spend half the year on earth in mortal form and half in immortal life, with the gods on Mount Olympus. This reflects a basic duality of humankind, which possesses an immortal soul yet is also subject to the limits of mortality.

The Cancer Glyph ♋

Two convenient images relate to the Cancer glyph. It is easiest to decode the curving claws of the Cancer symbol, the Crab. Like the crab's, Cancer's element is water. This sensitive sign also has a hard protective shell to protect its tender interior. The crab must be wily to escape predators, scampering sideways and hiding under rocks. The crab also responds to the cycles of the moon, as do all shellfish. The other image is that of two female breasts, which Cancer rules, showing that this is a sign that nurtures and protects others as well as itself.

In ancient Egypt, Cancer was also represented by the scarab beetle, a symbol of regeneration and eternal life.

The Leo Glyph ♌

Notice that the Leo glyph seems to be an extension of Cancer's glyph, with a significant difference. In the Cancer glyph the lines curve inward protectively. The Leo glyph expresses energy outwardly. And there is no duality in the symbol, the Lion, or in Leo, the sign.

Lions have belonged to the sign of Leo since earliest times. It is not difficult to imagine the king of beasts with his sweeping mane and curling tail from this glyph. The upward sweep of the glyph easily describes the positive energy of Leo: the flourishing tail, the flamboyant qualities. Another analogy, perhaps a stretch of the imagination, is that of a heart leaping up with joy and enthusiasm, also very typical of Leo, which also rules the heart. In early Christian imagery, the Leo Lion represented St. Mark.

The Virgo Glyph ♍

You can read much into this mysterious glyph. For instance, it could represent the initials of "Mary Virgin," or a young woman holding a staff of wheat, or stylized female genitalia, all common interpretations. The M shape might also remind you that Virgo is ruled by Mercury. The cross beneath the symbol reveals the grounded, practical nature of this earth sign.

The earliest zodiacs link Virgo with the Egyptian goddess Isis, who gave birth to the god Horus after her husband Osiris had been killed, in the archetype of a miraculous conception. There are many ancient statues of Isis nursing her baby son which are reminiscent of medieval Virgin and Child motifs. This sign has also been associated with the image of the Holy Grail, when the Virgo symbol was substituted with a chalice.

The Libra Glyph ♎

It is not difficult to read the standard image for Libra, the Scales, into this glyph. There is another meaning, however, that is equally relevant: the setting sun as it descends over the horizon. Libra's natural position on the zodiac wheel is the descendant, or sunset position (as the Aries natural position is the ascendant, or rising sign). Both images relate to Libra's personality. Libra is always weighing pros and cons for a balanced decision. In the sunset image, the sun (male) hovers over the horizontal earth (female) before setting. Libra is the space between these lines, harmonizing yin and yang, spiritual and material, male and female, ideal and real worlds. The glyph has also been linked to the kidneys, which are associated with Libra.

The Scorpio Glyph ♏

With its barbed tail, this glyph is easy to identify as the Scorpion for the sign of Scorpio. It also represents the male sexual parts, over which the sign rules. From the arrowhead, you can draw the conclusion that Mars was once its ruler. Some earlier Egyptian glyphs for Scorpio represent it as an erect serpent, so the Serpent is an alternate symbol.

Another symbol for Scorpio, which is not identifiable in this glyph, is the Eagle. Scorpios can go to extremes, either in soaring like the eagle or self-destructing like the scorpion. In early Christian imagery, which often used zodiacal symbols, the Scorpio Eagle was chosen to symbolize the intense apostle St. John the Evangelist.

The Sagittarius Glyph ♐

This is one of the easiest to spot and draw: an upward pointing arrow lifting up a cross. The arrow is pointing skyward, while the cross represents the four elements of the material world, which the arrow must convey. Elevating materiality into spirituality is an important Sagittarius quality, which explains why this sign is associated with higher learning, religion, philosophy, travel—the aspiring professions. Sagittarius can also send barbed arrows of frankness in the pursuit of truth, so the Archer symbol for Sagittarius is apt. (Sagittarius is also the sign of the supersalesman.)

Sagittarius is symbolically represented by the centaur, a mythological creature who is half man, half horse, aiming his arrow toward the skies. Though Sagittarius is motivated by spiritual aspiration, it also must balance the powerful appetites of the animal nature. The centaur Chiron, a figure in Greek mythology, became a wise teacher who, after many adventures and world travels, was killed by a poisoned arrow.

The Capricorn Glyph ♑

One of the most difficult symbols to draw, this glyph may take some practice. It is a representation of the sea goat: a mythical animal that is a goat with a curving fish's tail. The goat part of Capricorn wants to leave the waters of the emotions and climb to the elevated areas of life. But the fish tail is the unconscious, the deep chaotic psychic level that draws the goat back. Capricorn is often trying to escape the deep, feeling part of life by submerging himself in work, steadily ascending to the top. To some people, the glyph represents a seated figure with a bent knee, a reminder that Capricorn governs the knee area of the body.

An interesting aspect of this glyph is the contrast of the sharp pointed horns—which represent the penetrating shrewd, conscious side of Capricorn—with the swishing tail—which represents its serpentine, unconscious, emotional force. One Capricorn legend, which dates from Roman times, tells of the earthy fertility god, Pan, who tried to save himself from uncontrollable sexual desires by jumping into the Nile. His upper body then turned into a goat, while the lower part became a fish. Later, Jupiter gave him a safe haven as a constellation in the skies.

The Aquarius Glyph ♒

This ancient water symbol can be traced back to an Egyptian hieroglyph representing streams of life force. Symbolized by the Water Bearer, Aquarius is distributor of the waters of life—the magic liquid of regeneration. The two waves can also be linked to the positive and negative charges of the electrical energy that Aquarius rules, a sort of universal wavelength. Aquarius is tuned in intuitively to higher forces via this electrical force. The duality of the glyph could also refer to the dual nature of Aquarius, a sign that runs hot and cold and that is friendly but also detached in the mental world of air signs.

In Greek legends, Aquarius is represented by Ganymede, who was carried to heaven by an eagle in order to become the cupbearer of Zeus and to supervise the annual flooding of the Nile. The sign later became associated with aviation and notions of flight. Like the other fixed signs (Taurus, Scorpio, and Leo), Aquarius is associated with an apostle, in this case St. Matthew.

The Pisces Glyph)(

Here is an abstraction of the familiar image of Pisces, two Fishes swimming in opposite directions yet bound together by a cord. The Fishes represent the spirit—which yearns for the freedom of heaven—and the soul—which remains attached to the desires of the temporal world. During life on earth, the spirit and the soul are bound together. When they complement each other, instead of pulling in opposite directions, they facilitate the Pisces creativity. The ancient version of this glyph, taken from the Egyptians, had no connecting line, which was added in the fourteenth century.

In another interpretation, it is said that the left fish indicates the direction of involution or the beginning of a cycle, while the right fish signifies the direction of evolution, the way to completion of a cycle. It's an appropriate grand finale for Pisces, the last sign of the zodiac.

CHAPTER 8

Join the Astrology Community

Astrology fans love to share their knowledge and socialize. So why not join the community of astrologers online or at a conference? You might be surprised to find an astrology club in your local area. Connecting with other astrology fans and learning more about this fascinating subject has never been easier. In fact the many options available with just a click of your computer are mind-boggling.

You need only type the word *astrology* into any Internet search engine and watch hundreds of listings of astrology-related sites pop up. There are local meetings and international conferences where you can meet and study with other astrologers, and books and tapes to help you learn at home. You could even combine your vacation with an astrological workshop in an exotic locale, such as Bali or Mexico.

To help you sort out the variety of options available, here are our top picks of the Internet and the astrological community at large.

National Council for Geocosmic Research (NCGR)

Whether you'd like to know more about such specialties as financial astrology or techniques for timing events, or if you'd prefer the psychological or mythological approach, you'll meet the top astrologers at conferences sponsored by the National Council for Geocosmic Research. NCGR is dedicated to providing quality education, bringing astrologers and astrology fans together at conferences, and promoting fellowship. Their course structure provides a systematized study of the many facets of astrology. The organization sponsors educational workshops, taped lectures, conferences, and a directory of professional astrologers.

For an annual membership fee, you get their excellent publications and newsletters, plus the opportunity to network with other astrology buffs at local chapter events. At this writing there are chapters in twenty-six states and four countries.

To join NCGR and for the latest information on upcoming events and chapters in your city, consult their Web site: www. geocosmic.org.

American Federation of Astrologers (AFA)

Established in 1938, this is one of the oldest astrological organizations in the United States. AFA offers conferences, conventions, and a correspondence course. If you are looking for a reading, their interesting Web site will refer you to an accredited AFA astrologer.

6535 South Rural Road
Tempe, AZ 85283
Phone: (888) 301-7630 or (480) 838-1751
Fax: (480) 838-8293
Web site: www.astrologers.com

Association for Astrological Networking (AFAN)

Did you know that astrologers are still being harassed for practicing astrology? AFAN provides support and legal information, and works toward improving the public image of astrology. AFAN's network of local astrologers links with the international astrological community. Here are the people who will go to bat for astrology when it is attacked in the media. Everyone who cares about astrology should join!

8306 Wilshire Boulevard
PMB 537
Beverly Hills, CA 90211
Phone: (800) 578-2326
E-mail: info@afan.org
Web site: www.afan.org

International Society for Astrology Research (ISAR)

An international organization of professional astrologers dedicated to encouraging the highest standards of quality in the field of astrology with an emphasis on research. Among ISAR's benefits are quarterly journals, a weekly e-mail news-letter, and a free membership directory.

P.O. Box 38613
Los Angeles, CA 90038
Fax: (805) 933-0301
Web site: www.isarastrology.com

Astrology Magazines

In addition to articles by top astrologers, most have listings of astrology conferences, events, and local happenings.

Horoscope Guide
Kappa Publishing Group
6198 Butler Pike
Suite 200
Blue Bell, PA 19422-2600
Web site: www.kappapublishing.com/astrology

Dell Horoscope
Their Web site features a listing of local astrological meet-ings.

Customer Service
6 Prowitt Street
Norwalk, CT 06855
Phone: (800) 220-7443
Web site: www.dellhoroscope.com

The Mountain Astrologer
A favorite magazine of astrology fans, *The Mountain Astrologer* also has an interesting Web site featuring the latest news from an astrological point of view, plus feature articles from the magazine.

P.O. Box 970
Cedar Ridge, CA 95924
Web site: www.mountainastrologer.com

Astrology College

Kepler College of Astrological Arts and Sciences

A degree-granting college, which is also a center of astrology, has long been the dream of the astrological community and is a giant step forward in providing credibility to the profession. Therefore, the opening of Kepler College in 2000 was a historical event for astrology. It is the only college in the United States authorized to issue BA and MA degrees in astrological studies. Here is where to study with the best scholars, teachers, and communicators in the field. A long-distance study program is available for those interested.

Kepler College also offers online noncredit courses that anyone can take via the Kepler Community Learning Center. Classes range from two days to ten weeks in length, and the cost will vary depending upon the class taken. Students can access an online Web site to enroll in specific classes and interact with other students and instructors.

For more information, contact:

4630 200th Street SW
Suite P
Lynnwood, WA 98036
Phone: (425) 673-4292
Fax: (425) 673-4983
Web site: www.kepler.edu

Our Favorite Web sites

Of the thousands of astrological Web sites that come and go on the Internet, these have stood the test of time and are likely to still be operating when this book is published.

Astrodienst (www.astro.com)

Don't miss this fabulous international site, which has long been one of the best astrology resources on the Internet. It's a great place to view your own astrology chart. The world atlas on this site will give you the accurate longitude and latitude of your birthplace for setting up your horoscope. Then you can print out your free chart in a range of easy-to-read formats. Other attractions: a list of famous people born on your birth date, a feature that helps you choose the best vacation spot, and articles by world-famous astrologers.

AstroDatabank (www.astrodatabank.com)

When the news is breaking, you can bet this site will be the first to get accurate birthdays of the headliners. The late astrologer Lois Rodden was a stickler for factual information and her meticulous research is being continued, much to the benefit of the astrological community. The Web site specializes in charts of current newsmakers, political figures, and international celebrities. You can also participate in discussions and analysis of the charts and see what some of the world's best astrologers have to say about them. Their AstroDatabank program, which you can purchase at the site, provides thousands of birthdays sorted into categories. It's an excellent research tool.

StarIQ (www.stariq.com)

Find out how top astrologers view the latest headlines at the must-see StarIQ site. Many of the best minds in astrology comment on the latest news, stock market ups and downs, and political contenders. You can sign up to receive e-mail forecasts at the most important times keyed to your individual chart. (This is one of the best of the online forecasts.)

Astro-Noetics (www.astro-noetics.com)

For those who are ready to explore astrology's interface with politics, popular culture, and current events, here is a sophisticated site with in-depth articles and personality profiles. Lots of depth and content here for the astrology-savvy surfer.

Astrology Books (www.astroamerica.com)

The Astrology Center of America sells a wide selection of books on all aspects of astrology, from the basics to the most advanced, at this online bookstore. Also available are many hard-to-find and used books.

Astrology Scholars' Sites

See what Robert Hand, one of astrology's great teachers, has to offer on his site at www.robhand.com. A leading expert on the history of astrology, he's on the cutting edge of the latest research.

The Project Hindsight group of astrologers is devoted to restoring the astrology of the Hellenistic period, the primary source for all later Western astrology. There are fascinating articles for astrology fans on this site at www.projecthindsight. com.

Financial Astrology Sites

Financial astrology is a hot specialty, with many tipsters, players, and theorists. There are online columns, newsletters, specialized financial astrology software, and mutual funds run by astrology seers. One of the more respected financial astrologers is Ray Merriman, whose market comments on www.mmacycles.com are a must for those following the bulls and bears.

Explore Your Relationships (www.topsynergy.com)

Ever wondered how you'd get along with Brad Pitt, Halle Berry, or another famous hottie? TopSynergy offers a clever tool called a relationship analyst that will help you use astrology to analyze past, present, or possible future relationships. There's a database of celebrity horoscopes for you to partner with your own as well. It's free for unlimited use.

How to Zoom Around the Sky

If you haven't already discovered the wonders of Google Earth (www.earth.google.com), then you've been missing close-up aerial views of anyplace on the planet from your old hometown to the beaches of Hawaii. Even more fascinating for astrology buffs is the newest feature called Google Sky, a marvel of computer technology that lets you view the sky overhead from anyplace you choose. Want to see the stars over Paris at the moment? A few clicks of your mouse will take you there. Then you can follow the tracks of the sun, moon, and planets or check astronomical information and beautiful Hubble images. Go to the Google Web site to download this free program. Then get ready to take a cosmic tour around the earth and sky.

Listen to the Sounds of Your Sign

Astrology Weekly (www.astrologyweekly.com) is a Web site from Romania, with lots to offer astro surfers. Here you can check all the planetary placements for the week, get free charts, join an international discussion group, and check out charts for countries and world leaders. Of special interest is the chart generator, an easy-to-use feature that will create a natal chart. Just click on *new chart* and enter the year, month, day, time, longitude, and latitude of your birth place. Select the Placidus or Koch house system and click on *show it*. Your chart should come right up on the screen. You can then copy the link to your astrology chart, store it, and later share your chart with friends. If you don't have astrology software, this is a good way to view charts instantly. This site also has some fun ways to pass the time, such as listening to music especially chosen for your sun sign.

Stellar Gifts

If you've ever wondered what to give your astrology buddies, here's the place to find foolproof gifts. How about a mug, mouse pad, or plaque decorated with someone's chart? Would a special person like a pendant personalized with their planets? Check out www.milestonegifts.co.uk for some great ideas for putting those astrology charts to decorative use.

CHAPTER 9

The Best Astrology Software: Take Your Knowledge to the Next Level

Are you ready to begin looking at charts of friends and family? Would you like to call up your favorite celebrity's chart or check the aspects every day on your BlackBerry? Perhaps you'd like to study astrology in depth and would prefer a more comprehensive program that adapts to your needs as you learn. If you haven't discovered the wonders of astrology software, you're missing out!

Astrology technology has advanced to the point where even a computerphobe can call up a Web site on a BlackBerry browser and put a chart on the screen in seconds. It does help to have some basic knowledge of the signs, houses, planets, and especially the glyphs for the planets and the signs. Then you can practice reading charts and relating the planets to the lives of friends, relatives, and daily events, the ideal way to get more involved with astrology.

There's a program for every level of interest at all price points—starting with free. For the dabbler, there are the affordable Winstar Express, Know, and Time Passages. For the serious student, there are Astrology (free), Solar Fire, Kepler, Winstar Plus—software that does every technique on the planet and gives you beautiful chart printouts. If you're a MAC user, you'll be satisfied with the wonderful IO and Time Passages software.

However, since all the programs use the astrology symbols or glyphs, for planets and signs, rather than written words, you should learn the glyphs before you purchase your software. Chapter 7 will help you do just that. Here are some software options for you to explore.

Easy for Beginners

Time Passages

Designed for either a Macintosh or Windows computer, Time Passages is straightforward and easy to use. It allows you to generate charts and interpretation reports for yourself or friends and loved ones at the touch of a button. If you haven't yet learned the astrology symbols, this might be the program for you. Just roll your mouse over any symbols of the planets, signs, or house cusps, and you'll be shown a description in plain English below the chart. Then click on the planet, sign, or house cusp and up pops a detailed interpretation. Couldn't be easier. A new Basic Edition, under fifty dollars at this writing, is bargain priced and ideal for beginners.

Time Passages
(866) 772-7876 (866-77-ASTRO)
Web site: www.astrograph.com

The "Know Thru Astrology" Series

This new series is designed especially for the nonastrologer. There are four programs in the series: KNOW Your Self, KNOW Your Future, KNOW Your Lover, and KNOW Your Child, each priced at an affordable $49.95 (at this writing). Though it is billed as beginner software, the KNOW series offers many sophisticated options, such as a calendar to let you navigate future or past influences, detailed chart interpretations, built-in pop-ups to show you what everything means. You'll need a PC running current Windows versions starting with Windows 98 SE, with 512 Mb RAM, and a hard drive with 170–300 Mb free space.

Matrix Software
126 South Michigan Avenue
Big Rapids, MI 49307
(800) 752-6387
Web site: www.astrologysoftware.com

Growth Opportunities

Astrolabe

Astrolabe is one of the top astrology software resources. Check out the latest version of their powerful Solar Fire software for Windows. It's a breeze to use and will grow with your increasing knowledge of astrology to the most sophisticated levels. This company also markets a variety of programs for all levels of expertise and a wide selection of computer-generated astrology readings. This is a good resource for innovative software as well as applications for older computers.

The Astrolabe Web site is a great place to start your astrology tour of the Internet. Visitors to the site are greeted with a chart of the time you log on. And you can get your chart calculated, also free, with a mini interpretation e-mailed to you.

Astrolabe
Box 1750-R
Brewster, MA 02631
Phone: (800) 843-6682
Web site: www.alabe.com

Matrix Software

You'll find a wide variety of software at student and advanced levels in all price ranges, demo disks, lots of interesting readings. Check out Winstar Express, a powerful but reasonably priced program suitable for all skill levels. The Matrix Web site offers lots of fun activities for Web surfers, such as free readings from the I Ching, the runes, and the tarot. There are many free desktop backgrounds with astrology themes.

Matrix Software
126 South Michigan Avenue
Big Rapids, MI 49307
Phone: (800) 752-6387
Web site: www.astrologysoftware.com

Astro Computing Services (ACS)

Books, software, individual charts, and telephone readings
are offered by this company. Their freebies include astrology
greeting cards and new moon reports. Find technical astrology materials here such as *The American Ephemeris* and PC
atlases. ACS will calculate and send charts to you, a valuable
service if you do not have a computer.

Starcrafts Publishing
334 Calef Hwy.
Epping, NH 03042
Phone: (866) 953-8458
Web site: www.astrocom.com

Air Software

Here you'll find powerful, creative astrology software, plus
current stock market analysis. Financial astrology programs
for stock market traders are a specialty. There are some interesting freebees at this site. Check out the maps of eclipse
paths for any year and a free astrology clock program.

Air Software
115 Caya Avenue
West Hartford, CT 06110
Phone: (800) 659-1247
Web site: www.alphee.com

Kepler: State of the Art

Here's a program that's got everything. Gorgeous graphic images, audio-visual effects, and myriad sophisticated chart options are built into this fascinating software. It's even got an

astrological encyclopedia, plus diagrams and images to help
you understand advanced concepts. This program is pricey
but if you're serious about learning astrology, it's an investment that will grow with you! Check out its features at www.
astrosoftware.com.

Timecycles Research: For Mac Users

Here's where Mac users can find astrology software that's as
sophisticated as it gets. If you have a Mac, you'll love their
beautiful graphic IO Series programs.

Time Cycles Research
P.O. Box 797
Waterford, CT 06385
(800) 827-2240
Web site: www.timecycles.com

Shareware and Freeware:
The Price Is Right!

Halloran Software: A Super Shareware
Program

Check out Halloran Software's Web site, which offers several
levels of Windows astrology software. Beginners should consider their Astrology for Windows shareware program, which
is available in unregistered demo form as a free download and
in registered form for a very reasonable price.

Halloran Software
P.O. Box 75713
Los Angeles, CA 90075
(800) 732-4628
Web site: www.halloran.com

ASTROLOG

If you're computer-savvy, you can't go wrong with Walter Pullen's amazingly complete Astrology program, which is offered absolutely free at the site. The Web address is www.astrolog. org/astrolog.htm.

Astrolog is an ultrasophisticated program with all the features of much more expensive programs. It comes in versions for all formats: DOS, Windows, Mac, and UNIX. It has some cool features, such as a revolving globe and a constellation map. If you are looking for astrology software with all the bells and whistles that doesn't cost big bucks, this program has it all!

Buying a Computer with Astrology in Mind?

The good news is that astrology software is becoming more sophisticated and fun to use. However, if you've inherited an old computer, don't despair. You don't need the fastest processor and all the newest bells and whistles to run perfectly adequate astrology software. It is still possible to find programs for elder systems, including many new exciting programs.

To take full advantage of all the options, it is best to have a system that runs versions of Windows starting with Windows 98 SE. If you're buying a new computer, invest in one with as much RAM as possible, at least 1 GB. A CD drive will be necessary to load programs or an Internet connection, if you prefer to download programs online.

Mac fans who want to run Windows astrology software should invest in dual boot computers that will operate both the Mac and the Windows XP and Vista platforms.

CHAPTER 10

Ask the Expert: A Personal Reading Could Help

In these changing times, preparing ourselves for challenges ahead becomes a top priority as new issues surface in our lives. This could be the ideal time to add an astrologer to your dream team of advisers. Horoscopes can offer general advice to all members of your sign, but a personal reading can deal with what matters most to you. It can help you sort out a problem, find and use the strengths in your horoscope, set you on a more fulfilling career path, give you insight into your romantic life, or help you decide where to relocate. Many people consult astrologers to find the optimum time to schedule an important event, such as a wedding or business meeting.

Another good reason for a reading is to refine your knowledge of astrology by consulting with someone who has years of experience analyzing charts. You might choose an astrologer with a specialty that intrigues you. Armed with the knowledge of your chart that you have acquired so far, you can then learn to interpret subtle nuances or gain insight into your talents and abilities.

How do you choose when there are so many different kinds of readings available, especially since the Internet has brought astrology into the mainstream? Besides individual one-on-one readings with a professional astrologer, there are personal readings by mail, telephone, Internet, and tape. Well-advertised computer-generated reports and celebrity-sponsored readings are sure to attract your attention on commercial Web sites and in magazines. You can even purchase a reading that is incorporated into an expensive handmade fine art book. Then there are astrologers who specialize in specific areas such as finance or medical astrology. And unfortunately, there are many questionable practitioners who range from streetwise Gypsy fortune-tellers to unscrupulous scam artists.

The following basic guidelines can help you sort out your options to find the reading that's right for you.

One-on-One Consultations with a Professional Astrologer

Nothing compares to a one-on-one consultation with a professional astrologer who has analyzed thousands of charts and can pinpoint the potential in yours. During your reading, you can get your specific questions answered and discuss possible paths you might take. There are many astrologers who now combine their skills with training in psychology and are well-suited to help you examine your alternatives.

To give you an accurate reading, an astrologer needs certain information from you: the date, time, and place where you were born. (A horoscope can be cast about anyone or anything that has a specific time and place.) Most astrologers will then enter this information into a computer, which will calculate a chart in seconds, and interpret the resulting chart.

If you don't know your exact birth time, you can usually locate it at the Bureau of Vital Statistics at the city hall of the town or the county seat in the state where you were born. If you still have no success in getting your time of birth, some astrologers can estimate an approximate birth time by using past events in your life to determine the chart. This technique is called rectification.

How to Find an Astrologer

Choose your astrologer with the same care as you would any trusted adviser, such as a doctor, lawyer, or banker. Unfortunately, anyone can claim to be an astrologer—to date, there is no licensing of astrologers or universally established professional criteria. However, there are nationwide organizations of serious, committed astrologers that can help you in your search.

Good places to start your investigation are organizations such as the American Federation of Astrologers (AFA) or the National Council for Geocosmic Research (NCGR), which offer a program of study and certification. If you live near a major city, there is sure to be an active NCGR chapter or astrology club in your area; many are listed in astrology magazines available at your local newsstand. In response to many requests for referrals, both the AFA and the NCGR have directories of professional astrologers listed on their Web sites; these directories include a glossary of terms and an explanation of specialties within the astrological field. Contact the NCGR and AFA headquarters for information. (See also Chapter 8.)

What Happens in a Reading

As a potentially lucrative freelance business, astrology has always attracted self-styled experts who may not have the knowledge or the counseling experience to give a helpful reading. These astrologers can range from the well-meaning amateur to the charlatan or street-corner Gypsy who has for many years given astrology a bad name. Be very wary of astrologers who claim to have occult powers or who make pretentious claims of celebrated clients or miraculous achievements. You can often tell from the initial phone conversation if the astrologer is legitimate. He or she should ask for your birthday time and place and then conduct the conversation in a professional manner. Any astrologer who gives a reading based only on your sun sign is highly suspect.

When you arrive at the reading, the astrologer should be prepared. The consultation should be conducted in a private, quiet place. The astrologer should be interested in your problems of the moment. A good reading is interactive and involves feedback on your part, so if the reading is not relating to your concerns, you should let the astrologer know. You should feel free to ask questions and get clarifications of any technical terms. The more you actively participate, rather than expecting the astrologer to carry the reading or come forth with oracular predictions, the more meaningful your experience will be. An astrologer should help you validate your current experience and be frank about possible negative happenings, but also suggest a positive course of action.

In their approach to a reading, some astrologers may be more literal and others more intuitive. Those who have had counseling training may take a more psychological approach. Though some astrologers may seem to have an almost psychic ability, extrasensory perception or any other parapsychological talent is not essential. A very accurate picture can be drawn from the data in your horoscope chart.

An astrologer may do several charts for each client, including one for the time of birth and a progressed chart, showing the evolution from birth to the present time. According to your individual needs, there are many other possibilities, such as a chart for a different location if you are contemplating a change of place. Relationships between any two people, things, or events can be interpreted with a chart that compares one partner's horoscope with the other's. A composite chart, which uses the midpoint between planets in two individual charts to describe the relationship, is another commonly used device.

An astrologer will be particularly interested in transits, those times when cycling planets activate the planets or sensitive points in your birth chart. These indicate important events in your life.

Many astrologers offer readings recorded on tape or CD, which is another option to consider, especially if the astrologer you choose lives at a distance from you. In this case, you'll be mailed a recorded reading based on your birth chart. This type of reading is more personal than a computer printout and can give you valuable insights, though it is not equivalent to a live dialogue with the astrologer when you can discuss your specific interest and issues of the moment.

The Telephone Reading

Telephone readings come in two varieties: a dial-in taped reading, usually recorded in advance by an astrologer, or a live consultation with an "astrologer" on the other end of the line. The recorded readings are general daily or weekly forecasts, applied to all members of your sign and charged by the minute. The quality depends on the astrologer. Be aware that these readings can run up quite a telephone bill, especially if you get into the habit of calling every day. Be sure that you are aware of the per-minute cost of each call beforehand.

Live telephone readings also vary with the expertise of the astrologer. Ideally, the astrologer at the other end of the line enters your birth data into a computer, which then quickly calculates your chart. This chart will be referred to during the consultation. The advantage of a live telephone reading is that your individual chart is used and you can ask about a specific problem. However, before you invest in any reading, be sure that your astrologer is qualified and that you fully understand in advance how much you will be charged. There should be no unpleasant financial surprises later. The best astrologer is one who is recommended to you by a friend or family member.

Computer-Generated Reports

Companies that offer computer programs (such as ACS, Matrix, and Astrolabe) also offer a variety of computer-generated horoscope readings. These can be quite comprehensive, offering a beautiful printout of the chart plus many pages of detailed information about each planet and aspect of the chart. You can then study it at your convenience. Of course, the interpretations will be general, since there is no personal input from you, and might not cover your immediate concerns. Since computer-generated horoscopes are much lower in cost than live consultations, you might consider them as either a supplement or a preparation for an eventual live reading. You'll then be more familiar with your chart and able to plan specific questions in advance. They also make a terrific gift for astrology fans. In chapter 9, there are listed several companies that offer computerized readings prepared by reputable astrologers.

Whichever option you decide to pursue, may your reading be an empowering one!

CHAPTER 11

Loving Every Sign in the Zodiac

In times of change, we crave the comfort of a loving partner
more than ever. If we don't have love, we want to know how
and where to find it; and if we already have a loving relationship, we want to know how to make it last forever. You can use
astrology to find a lover, understand the one you have, or add
excitement to your current relationship. Here are sun-sign seduction tips for romancing every sign in the zodiac.

Aries: Play Hard to Get

This highly physical sign is walking dynamite with a brief attention span. Don't be too easy to get, ladies. A little challenge, a
lively debate, and a merry chase only heat them up. They want
to see what you're made of. Once you've lured them into your
lair, be a challenge and a bit of a daredevil. Pull out your X-rated
tricks. Don't give your all—let them know there's more where
that came from. Make it exciting; show you're up for adventure.
Wear bright red somewhere interesting. Since Aries rules the
head and face, be sure to focus on these areas in your lovemaking. Use your lips, tongue, breath, and even your eyelashes to
the max. Practice scalp massages and deep kissing techniques.
Aries won't wait, so when you make your move, be sure you're
ready to follow through. No head games or teasing!

To keep you happy, you've got to voice your *own* needs,
because this lover will be focused on *his*. Teach him how to
please, or this could be a one-sided adventure.

Taurus: Appeal to All Their Senses

Taurus wins as the most sensual sign, with the most sexual stamina. This man is earthy and lusty in bed; he can go on all night. This is not a sign to tease. Like a bull, he'll see red, not bed. So make him comfortable, and then bombard all his senses. Good food gets Taurus in the mood. So do the right music, fragrance, revealing clothes, and luxurious bedlinens. Give him a massage with delicious-smelling and -tasting oils; focus on the neck area.

Don't forget to turn off the phone! Taurus hates interruptions. Since they can be very vocal lovers, choose a setting where you won't be disturbed. And don't ever rush; enjoy a long, slow, delicious encounter.

Gemini: Be a Playmate

Playful Gemini loves games, so make your seduction fun. Be their lost twin soul or confidante. Good communication is essential, so share deep secrets and live out fantasies. This sign adores variety. Nothing bores Gemini more than making love the same way all the time, or bringing on the heavy emotions. So trot out all the roles you've been longing to play. Here's the perfect partner. But remember to keep it light and fun. Gemini's turn-on zone is the hands, and this sign gives the best massages. Gadgets that can be activated with a touch amuse Gemini. This sign is great at doing two things at once, like making love while watching an erotic film. Turn the cell phone off unless you want company. On the other hand, Gemini is your sign for superhot phone sex.

Gemini loves a change of scene. So experiment on the floor, in the shower, or on the kitchen table. Borrow a friend's apartment or rent a hotel room for variety.

Cancer: Use the Moon

The key to Cancer is to get this moon child in the mood. Consult the moon—a full moon is best. Wining, dining, old-fashioned courtship, and breakfast in bed are turn-ons. Whatever makes your Cancer feel secure will promote shedding inhibitions in the sack. (Don't try any of your Aries daredevil techniques here!) Cancer prefers familiar, comfortable, homey surroundings. Cancer's turn-on zone is the breasts. Cancer women often have naturally inflated chests. Cancer men may fantasize about a well-endowed playmate. If your breasts are enhanced, show them off. Cancer will want to know all your deepest secrets, so invent a few good ones. But lots of luck delving into *their* innermost thoughts!

Take your Cancer near water. The sight and sound of the sea can be their aphrodisiac. A moonlit beach, a deserted swimming pool, a Jacuzzi, or a bubble bath are good seduction spots. Listen to the rain patter on the roof in a mountain cabin.

Leo: Offer the Royal Treatment

Leo must be the best and hear it from you often. In return, they'll perform for you, telling you just what you want to hear (true or not). They like a lover with style and endurance, and to be swept off their feet and into bed. Leos like to go first-class all the way, so build them up with lots of attention, wining and dining, and special gifts.

Never mention other lovers or make them feel second-best. A sure signal for Leo to look elsewhere is a competitive spouse. Leos take great pride in their bodies, so you should pour on the admiration. A few well-placed mirrors could inspire them. So would a striptease with beautiful lingerie, expensive fragrance on the sheets, and, if female, an occasional luxury hotel room, with champagne and caviar delivered by room service. Leo's erogenous zone is the lower back, so a massage with expensive oils would make your lion purr with pleasure.

Virgo: Let Them Be the Teacher

Virgo's standards are so sky-high that you may feel intimidated at first. The key to pleasing fussy Virgo lovers is to look for the hot fantasy beneath their cool surface. They're really looking for someone to make over. So let Virgo play teacher, and you play the willing student; the doctor-patient routine works as well. Be Eliza Doolittle to his Henry Higgins.

Let Virgo help you improve your life, quit smoking, learn French, and diet. Read an erotic book together, and then practice the techniques. Or study esoteric, erotic exercises from the Far East.

The Virgo erogenous zone is the tummy area, which should be your base of operations. Virgo likes things pristine and clean. Fall onto crisp, immaculate white sheets. Wear a sheer virginal white nightie. Smell shower-fresh with no heavy perfume. Be sure your surroundings pass the hospital test. A shower together afterward (with great-smelling soap) could get the ball rolling again.

Libra: Look Your Best

Libra must be turned on aesthetically. Make sure you look as beautiful as possible, and wear something stylishly seductive but never vulgar. Have a mental affair first, as you flirt and flatter this sign. Then proceed to the physical. Approach Libra like a dance partner, ready to waltz or tango.

Libra must be in the mood for love; otherwise, forget it. Any kind of ugliness is a turnoff. Provide an elegant and harmonious atmosphere, with no loud noise, clashing colors, or uncomfortable beds. Libra is not an especially spontaneous lover, so it is best to spend time warming them up. Libra's back is his erogenous zone, your cue to provide back rubs with scented potions. Once in bed, you can be a bit aggressive sexually. Libra loves strong, decisive moves. Set the scene, know what you want, and let Libra be happy to provide it.

Scorpio: Be an All-or-Nothing Lover

Scorpio is legendary in bed, often called the sex sign of the zodiac. But seducing them is often a power game. Scorpio likes to be in control, even the quiet, unassuming ones. Scorpio loves a mystery, so don't tell all. Keep them guessing about you, offering tantalizing hints along the way. The hint of danger often turns Scorpio on, so you'll find members of this sign experimenting with the exotic and highly erotic forms of sex. Sadomasochism, bondage, or anything that tests the limits of power could be a turn-on for Scorpio.

Invest in some sexy black leather and some powerful music. Clothes that lace, buckle, or zip tempt Scorpio to untie you. Present yourself as a mysterious package just waiting to be unwrapped.

Once in bed, there are no holds barred with Scorpio. They'll find your most pleasurable pressure points, and touch you as you've never been touched before. They are quickly aroused (the genital area belongs to this sign) and are willing to try anything. But they can be possessive. Don't expect your Scorpio to share you with anyone. It's all or nothing for them.

Sagittarius: Be a Happy Wanderer

Sagittarius men are the Don Juans of the zodiac—love-'em-and-leave-'em types who are difficult to pin down. Your seduction strategy is to join them in their many pursuits, and then hook them with love on the road. Sagittarius enjoys sex in venues that suggest movement; planes, SUVs, or boats. But a favorite turn-on place is outdoors, in nature. A deserted hiking path, a field of tall grass, or a remote woodland glade—all give the centaur sexy ideas. Athletic Sagittarius might go for some personal training in an empty gym. Join your Sagittarius for amorous aerobics, meditate together, and explore the tantric forms of sex. Lovemaking after hiking and skiing would be healthy fun.

Sagittarius enjoys lovers from exotic ethnic backgrounds, or lovers met in spiritual pursuits or on college campuses. Sagit arius are great cheerleaders and motivators, and will enjoy feeling that they have inspired you to be all that you can be.

There may be a canine or feline companion sharing your Sagittarius lover's bed with you, so check your allergies. And bring Fido or Felix a toy to keep them occupied.

Capricorn: Take Their Mind off Business

The great news about Capricorn lovers is that they improve with age. They are probably the sexiest seniors. So stick around, if you have a young one. They're lusty in bed (it's not the sign of the goat for nothing), and can be quite raunchy and turned on by X-rated words and deeds. If this is not your thing, let them know. The Capricorn erogenous zone is the knees. Some discreet fondling in public places could be your opener. Capricorn tends to think of sex as part of a game plan for the future. They are well-organized, and might regard lovemaking as relaxation after a long day's work. This sign often combines business with pleasure. So look for a Capricorn where there's a convention, trade show, or work-related conference.

Getting Capricorn's mind off his agenda and onto yours could take some doing. Separate him from his buddies by whispering sexy secrets in his ear. Then convince him you're an asset to his image and a boon to his health. Though he may seem uptight at first, you'll soon discover he's a love animal who makes a wonderful and permanent pet.

Aquarius: Give Them Enough Space

This sign really does not want an all-consuming passion or an all-or-nothing relationship. Aquarius needs space. But once they feel free to experiment with a spontaneous and exciting partner, Aquarius can give you a far-out sexual adventure.

Passion begins in the mind, so a good mental buildup is key. Aquarius is an inventive sign who believes love is a playground without rules. Plan surprise, unpredictable encounters in unusual places. Find ways to make love transcendental, an extraordinary and unique experience. Be ready to try anything Aquarius suggests, if only once. Calves and ankles are the special Aquarius erogenous zone, so perfect your legwork.

Be careful not to be too possessive. Your Aquarius needs lots of space and tolerance for friends (including old lovers) and their many outside interests.

Pisces: Live Their Fantasies

Pisces is the sign of fantasy and imagination. This sign has great theatrical talent. Pisces looks for lovers who will take care of them. Pisces will return the favor! Here is someone who can psych out your deepest desires without mentioning them. Pisces falls for sob stories and is always ready to empathize. It wouldn't hurt to have a small problem for Pisces to help you overcome. It might help if you cry on his shoulder for this sign needs to be needed. Use your imagination when setting the scene for love. A dramatic setting brings out Pisces theatrical talents. Or creatively use the element of water. Rain on the roof, waterfalls, showers, beach houses, water beds, and Jacuzzis could turn up the heat. Experiment with pulsating jets of water. Take midnight skinny-dips in deserted pools.

The Pisces erogenous zone is the feet. This is your cue to give a sensuous foot massage using scented lotions. Let him paint your toes. Beautiful toenails in sexy sandals are a special turn-on.

Your Hottest Love Match

Here's a tip for finding your hottest love match. If your lover's Mars sign makes favorable aspects to your Venus, is in the same element (earth, air, fire, water), or is in the same sign your lover will do what you want done! Mars influences how we act when we make love, while Venus shows what we like one to us. Sometimes fighting and making up is the sexiest fun of all. If you're the type who needs a spark to keep lust alive (you know who you are!), then look for Mars and Venus in different signs of the same quality (fixed or cardinal or mutable). For instance, a fixed sign (Taurus, Leo, Scorpio, Aquarius) paired with another fixed sign can have a sexy tug-of-war before you finally surrender. Two cardinal signs (Aries, Cancer, Libra, Capricorn) set off passionate fireworks when they clash. Mutable signs (Gemini, Virgo, Sagittarius, Pisces) play a fascinating game of cat and mouse, never quite catching each other.

Your Most Seductive Time

The best time for love is when Venus is in your sign, making you the most desirable sign in the zodiac. This only lasts about three weeks (unless Venus is retrograde) so don't waste time! And find out the time this year when Venus is in your sign by consulting the Venus chart at the end of chapter 5.

What's the Sexiest Sign?

It depends on what sign you are. Astrology has traditionally given this honor to Scorpio, the sign associated with the sex organs. However, we are all a combination of different signs and turn-ons). Gemini's communicating ability and manual dexterity could deliver the magic touch. Cancer's tenderness and understanding could bring out your passion more than regal Leo.

Which Is the Most Faithful Sign?

The earth signs of Capricorn, Taurus, and Virgo are usually the most faithful. They tend to be more home- and family-

oriented, and they are usually choosy about their mates. It'
impractical, inconvenient, and probably expensive to pla
around, or so they think.

Who'll Play Around?

The mutable signs of Gemini, Pisces, and Sagittarius wi
the playboy or playgirl sweepstakes. These signs tend to b
changeable, fickle, and easily bored. But they're so much fun

CHAPTER 12

Financial Tips from the Stars

Getting the most bang from our buck will be our personal challenge this year, as we continue to learn to live within our means and balance our budgets. One of the advantages of astrology is that we can know the natural direction of the cosmic forces in advance and make financial plans accordingly.

Over the past few years, we've experienced a dramatic shift from the expansive risk taking of Pluto in Sagittarius to the conservative, thrift-promoting Pluto in Capricorn. This influence should continue for several years. Financially savvy astrologers also look to the movement of Jupiter, the planet of luck and expansion, for growth opportunities. Jupiter gives an extra boost to the sign it is passing through. Jupiter moves through Pisces, a sign that Jupiter especially favors, so Pisces and fellow water signs, Cancer and Scorpio, receive extra-lucky rays. Most of us could benefit from using some Pisces-inspired creativity, insight, and imagination especially in the area of our horoscope where Jupiter will be giving us growth opportunities. Pisces will give us the imaginative ideas; then Jupiter enters Aries briefly over the summer and for a lengthy stay next year, which should give us the courage and pioneering spirit to pursue them.

Aries

You've got a taste for fast money, quick turnover, and edgy investments, with no patience for gradual, long-term gains.

You're an impulse buyer with the nerve for risky tactics that could backfire. On the other hand, you're a pioneer who can see into the future, who dares to take a gamble on a new idea or product that could change the world ... like Sam Walton of the Wal-Mart stores, who changed the way we shop. You need a backup plan in case one of your big ideas burns out. To protect your money, get a backup plan you can follow without thinking about it. Have a percentage of your income automatically put into a savings or retirement account. Then give yourself some extra funds to play with. Your weak point is your impatience; so you're not one to wait out a slow market or watch savings slowly accumulate. When Jupiter moves into Aries temporarily this summer, you'll want to move full steam ahead. However, you may have to reevaluate your goals in the fall. Save your big moves for next year, when Jupiter reenters Aries and you can make real progress.

Taurus

You're a saver who loves to see your cash, as well as your possessions, accumulate. You have no qualms about steadily increasing your fortune. You're a savvy trader and a shrewd investor, in there for long-term gains. You have low toleration for risk; you hate to lose anything. But you do enjoy luxuries and may need to reward yourself frequently. You might pass up an opportunity because it seems too risky, but you should take a chance once in a while. Since you're inspired by Jupiter in Pisces and Aries this year, it's time to support your long-range goals and ideals by exploring socially conscious investments, especially in the clean-energy field and the creative arts. You're especially lucky in real estate or any occupation that requires appraising and trading, as well as earth-centered businesses like organic farming and conservation.

Gemini

With Gemini, the cash can flow in and then out just as quickly. You naturally multi-task, and you are sure to have several projects going at once, as well as several credit cards, which can easily get out of hand. Saving is not one of your strong points—too boring. You fall in and out of love with different ideas; you have probably tried a round of savings techniques. Diversification is your best strategy. Have several different kinds of investments—at least one should be a long-term plan. Set savings goals and then regularly deposit small amounts into your accounts. Follow the lead of Gemini financial adviser Suze Orman and get a good relationship going with your money! With lucky Jupiter accenting your public image, there should be new career opportunities this year. Investigate careers in communications and the media.

Cancer

You can be a natural moneymaker with your peerless intuition. You can spot a winner that everyone else misses. Consider Cancer success stories like those of cosmetics queen Estee Lauder and Roxanne Quimby, of Burt's Bees, who turned her friend's stash of beeswax into a thriving cosmetics business. Who knew? So trust your intuition. You are a saver who always has a backup plan, just in case. Remember to treat and nurture yourself as well as others. Investments in the food industry, restaurants, hotels, shipping, and water-related industries are Cancer territory. You're one of the luckiest signs this year, so keep your antennae tuned for new investment opportunities.

Leo

You love the first-class lifestyle, but may not always have the resources to support it. Finding a way to fund your extravagant tastes is the Leo challenge. Some courses in money management or an expert financial coach could set you on the right track. However, you're also a terrific salesperson, and you're fabulous in high-profile jobs that pay a lot. You're the community tastemaker; you satisfy your appetite for "the best" by working for a quality company that sells luxury goods, splendid real estate, dream vacations, and first-class travel—that way you'll have access to the lifestyle without having to pay for it. This year, Jupiter brings luck through fortunate partnerships and travel.

Virgo

Your sign is a stickler for details, which includes your money management. You like to follow your spending and saving closely; you enjoy planning, budgeting, and price comparison. Your sign usually has no problem sticking to a savings or investment plan. You have a critical eye for quality, and you like to bargain and to shop to get the best value. In fact, Warren Buffet, a Virgo billionaire, is known for value investing. You buy cheap and sell at a profit. Investing in health care, organic products, and food could be profitable for you. With Jupiter in Pisces accenting partnerships, you might want to team up for investing purposes this year.

Libra

Oh, do you ever love to shop! And you often have an irresistible urge to acquire an exquisite object or a designer dress you can't really afford or to splurge on the perfect antique armoire. You don't like to settle for second-rate or bargain buys. Learning to prioritize your spending is especially difficult for your sign, so try to find a good money manager to do it for you. Following a strictly balanced budget is your key to financial success. With Libra's keen eye for quality and good taste, you are a savvy picker at auctions and antiques fairs, so you might be able to turn around your purchase for a profit. With Jupiter accenting the care and maintenance part of your life, this is an excellent year to put your finances in order and balance the budget.

Scorpio

Scorpios prefer to stay in control of their finances at all times. You're sure to have a financial-tracking program on your computer. You're not an impulse buyer, unless you see something that immediately turns you on. Rely on your instincts! Scorpio is the sign of credit cards, taxes, and loans, so you are able to use these tools cleverly. Investing for Scorpio is rarely casual. You'll do extensive research and track your investments by reading the financial pages, annual reports, and profit-loss statements. Investigate the arts, media, and oil and water projects for Jupiter-favored investments this year.

Sagittarius

Sagittarius is a natural gambler, with a high tolerance for risk. It's important for you to learn when to hold 'em, and when to fold 'em, as the song goes, by setting limits on your risk taking and covering your assets. You enjoy the thrill of playing the stock market, where you could win big and lose big. Money itself is rarely the object for Sagittarius—it's the game that counts. Since your sign rarely saves for a rainy day, your best strategy might be a savings plan that transfers a certain amount into a savings account. Regular bill-paying plans are another strategy to keep you on track. Jupiter favors investing in home improvements and family-related businesses this year.

Capricorn

You're one of the strongest money managers in the zodiac, which should serve you well this year when Jupiter, the planet of luck and expansion, is blessing your house of finance. You're a born bargain hunter and clever negotiator—a saver rather than a spender. You are the sign of self-discipline, which works well when it comes to sticking with a budget and living frugally while waiting for resources to accumulate. You are likely to plan carefully for your elder years, profiting from long-term investments. You have a keen sense of value, and you will pick up a bargain and then turn it around at a nice profit. Jupiter favors the communications industry and opportunities in your local area this year.

Aquarius

There should be many chances to speculate on forward-looking ventures this year. The Aquarius trait of unpredictability extends to your financial life, where you surprise us all with your ability to turn something totally unique into a money spinner. Consider your wealthy sign mates Oprah Winfrey and Michael Bloomberg, who have been able to intuit what the public will buy at a given moment. Some of your ideas might sound far-out, but they turn out to be right on the money. Investing in high-tech companies that are on the cutting edge of their field is good for Aquarius. You'll probably intuit which ones will stay the course. You'll feel good about investing in companies that improve the environment, such as new types of fuel, or ones that are related to your favorite cause.

Pisces

Luck is with you this year! The typical Pisces is probably the sign least interested in money management. However, there are many billionaires born under your sign, such as Michael Dell, David Geffen, and Steve Jobs. Generally they have made money from innovative ideas and left the details to others. That might work for you. Find a Scorpio, Capricorn, or Virgo to help you set a profitable course and systematically save (which is not in your nature). Sign up for automatic bill paying so you won't have to think about it. If you keep in mind how much less stressful life will be and how much more you can do when you're not worried about paying bills, you might be motivated enough to stick to a sensible budget. Investment-wise, consider anything to do with water—off-shore drilling, water conservation and purifying, shipping, and seafood. Petroleum is also ruled by your sign, as are institutions related to hospitals.

CHAPTER 13

Children of 2010

Parents of several children may see a marked difference between children born in 2010 and those born more than two years ago, because the cosmic atmosphere has changed, which should imprint the personalities of this year's children.

Astrologers look to the slow-moving outer planets—Uranus, Neptune, and Pluto—to describe a generation. When an outer planet changes signs, this indicates a significant shift in energy, which is the case in 2010. In the first half of the year, Uranus and Jupiter in Pisces continue the visionary and creative influence of that sign, which will be reflected in the children born then. However, Uranus moves briefly into fiery Aries in June, which will be accompanied by Jupiter, the planet of expansion, indicating a very astrologically active summer of 2010. Children born during the warm months will reflect this with more drive and energy. After Uranus retrogrades back into Pisces in mid-August for the remainder of the year, the atmosphere becomes somewhat calmer. Neptune still passing through Aquarius and Pluto in Capricorn should add vision and practicality to the personality of this year's children. This generation will be focused on saving the planet and on making things work in order to clear the path for the future. Saturn in Libra will enter the mixture, teaching them diplomacy in getting along with others.

Astrology can be an especially helpful tool when used to design an environment that enhances and encourages each child's positive qualities. Some parents start before conception, planning the birth of their child as far as possible to harmonize with the signs of other family members. However, each baby has its own schedule, so if yours arrives a week early or late, or elects a different sign than you'd planned, recognize that the new sign may be more in line with the mission your child is here to accomplish. In other words, if you were hoping for a Libra child and he arrives during Virgo, that Virgo energy may be just what is needed to stimulate or complement your family. Remember that there are many astrological elements besides the sun sign that indicate strong family ties. Usually each child will share a particular planetary placement, an emphasis on a particular sign or house, or a certain chart configuration with his parents and other family members. Often there is a significant planetary angle that will define the parent-child relationship, such as family sun signs that form a T-square or a triangle.

One important thing you can do is to be sure the exact moment of birth is recorded. This will be essential in calculating an accurate astrological chart. The following descriptions can be applied to the sun or moon sign (if known) of a child—the sun sign will describe basic personality and the moon sign indicates the child's emotional needs.

The Aries Child

Baby Aries is quite a handful. This energetic child will walk—and run—as soon as possible, and perform daring feats of exploration. Caregivers should be vigilant. Little Aries seems to know no fear (and is especially vulnerable to head injuries). Many Aries children, in their rush to get on with life, seem hyperactive, and they are easily frustrated when they can't get their own way. Violent temper tantrums and dramatic physical displays are par for the course with this child, requiring a time-out mat or naughty chair.

The very young Aries should be monitored carefully, since he is prone to take risks and may injure himself. Aries love to take things apart and may break toys easily, but with encouragement, the child will develop formidable coordination. Aries's bossy tendencies should be molded into leadership qualities, rather than bullying, which should be easy to do with this year's babies. Encourage these children to take out aggressions and frustrations in active, competitive sports, where they usually excel. When young Aries learns to focus energies long enough to master a subject and learns consideration for others, the indomitable Aries spirit will rise to the head of the class.

Aries born in 2010 will be a more subdued version of this sign, but still loaded with energy. The Capricorn effect should make little Aries easier to discipline and more focused on achievement. A natural leader!

The Taurus Child

This is a cuddly, affectionate child who eagerly explores the world of the senses, especially the senses of taste and touch. The Taurus child can be a big eater and will put on weight easily if not encouraged to exercise. Since this child likes comfort and gravitates to beauty, try coaxing little Taurus to exercise to music, or take him or her out of doors, with hikes or long walks. Though Taurus may be a slow learner, this sign has an excellent retentive memory and generally masters a subject thoroughly. Taurus is interested in results and will see each project patiently through to completion, continuing long after others have given up. This year's earth sign planets will give him a wonderful sense of support and accomplishment.

Choose Taurus toys carefully to help develop innate talents. Construction toys, such as blocks or erector sets, appeal to their love of building. Paints or crayons develop their sense of color. Many Taurus have musical talent and love to sing, which is apparent at a young age.

This year's Taurus will want a pet or two, and a few plants of his own. Give little Taurus a small garden, and watch the natural green thumb develop. This child has a strong sense of acquisition and an early grasp of material value. After filling a piggy bank, Taurus graduates to a savings account, before other children have started to learn the value of money.

Little Taurus gets a bonanza of good luck from Jupiter in compatible Pisces, supported by Pluto in Capricorn and Saturn retrograding back into Virgo, a compatible earth sign. These should give little Taurus an especially easygoing disposition and provide many opportunities to live up to his sign's potential.

The Gemini Child

Little Gemini will talk as soon as possible, filling the air with questions and chatter. This is a friendly child who enjoys social contact, seems to require company, and adapts quickly to different surroundings. Geminis have quick minds that easily grasp the use of words, books, and telephones, and will probably learn to talk and read at an earlier age than most. Though they are fast learners, Gemini may have a short attention span, darting from subject to subject. Projects and games that help focus the mind could be used to help them concentrate. Musical instruments, typewriters, and computers help older Gemini children combine mental with manual dexterity. Geminis should be encouraged to finish what they start before they go on to another project. Otherwise, they can become jack-of-all-trade types who have trouble completing anything they do. Their disposition is usually cheerful and witty, making these children popular with their peers and delightful company at home.

This year's Gemini baby is impulsive and full of energy, with a strong Aries influence in his life. He will be highly independent and original, a go-getter. When he grows up, Gemini may change jobs several times before he finds a position that satisfies his need for stimulation and variety.

The Cancer Child

This emotional, sensitive child is especially influenced by patterns set in early life. Young Cancers cling to their first memories as well as their childhood possessions. They thrive in calm emotional waters, with a loving, protective mother, and usually

155

remain close to her (even if their relationship with her was difficult) throughout their lives. Divorce and death—anything that disturbs the safe family unit—are devastating to Cancers, who may need extra support and reassurance during a family crisis.

They sometimes need a firm hand to push the positive, creative side of their personality and discourage them from getting swept away by emotional moods or resorting to emotional manipulation to get their way. If this child is praised and encouraged to find creative expression, Cancers will be able to express their positive side consistently, on a firm, secure foundation.

This year's Cancer baby may run against type, thanks to a meeting of Jupiter and Uranus in hyperactive Aries, which might make him much more outgoing and energetic than usual. He should have natural leadership tendencies, which should be encouraged, and the parents' challenge will be to find positive outlets for his energy.

The Leo Child

Leo children love the limelight and will plot to get the lion's share of attention. These children assert themselves with flair and drama, and can behave like tiny tyrants to get their way. But in general, they have a sunny, positive disposition and are rarely subject to blue moods.

At school, they're the types voted most popular, head cheerleader, or homecoming queen. Leo is sure to be noticed for personality, if not for stunning looks or academic work; the homely Leo will be a class clown, and the unhappy Leo can be the class bully.

Above all, a Leo child cannot tolerate being ignored for long. Drama or performing-arts classes, sports, and school politics are healthy ways for Leo to be a star. But Leos must learn to take lesser roles occasionally, or they will have some painful putdowns in store. Usually, their popularity is well earned; they are hard workers who try to measure up to their own high standards—and usually succeed.

This year's Leo should be a highly active version of the sign, with Saturn in Libra teaching lessons of balance and diplomacy in relationships, while Jupiter and Uranus in Aries amp up the energy level and Pluto in Capricorn demands focus and results. Good use of this energy could produce pioneers, fearless natural leaders who could change the world for the better.

The Virgo Child

The young Virgo can be a quiet, rather serious child, with a quick, intelligent mind. Early on, little Virgo shows far more attention to detail and concern with small things than other children. Little Virgo has a built-in sense of order and a fascination with how things work. It is important for these children to have a place of their own, which they can order as they wish and where they can read or busy themselves with crafts and hobbies. This child's personality can be very sensitive. Little Virgo may get hyper and overreact to seemingly small irritations, which can take the form of stomach upsets or delicate digestive systems. But this child will flourish where there is mental stimulation and a sense of order. Virgos thrive in school, especially in writing or language skills, and they seem truly happy when buried in books. Chances are, young Virgo will learn to read ahead of classmates. Hobbies that involve detail work or that develop fine craftsmanship are especially suited to young Virgos.

Baby Virgo of 2010 is likely to be an early talker, and will show concern for the welfare of others. This child should be a natural communicator and may show an interest in the arts or the legal profession.

The Libra Child

The Libra child learns early about the power of charm and appearance. This is often a very physically appealing child with an enchanting dimpled smile, who is naturally sociable and enjoys the company of both children and adults. It is a rare Libra child who is a discipline problem, but when their behavior is unacceptable, they respond better to calm discussion than displays of emotion, especially if the discussion revolves around fairness. Because young Libras without a strong direction tend to drift with the mood of the group, these children should be encouraged to develop their unique talents and powers of discrimination, so they can later stand on their own.

In school, this child is usually popular and will often have to choose between social invitations and studies. In the teen years, social pressures mount as the young Libra begins to look for a partner. This is the sign of best friends, so Libra's choice of companions can have a strong effect on his future direction. Beautiful Libra girls may be tempted to go steady or have an unwise early marriage. Chances are, both sexes will fall in and out of love several times in their search for the ideal partner.

Little Libra of 2010 is an especially creative, expressive child, who may have strong artistic talents. This child is endowed with much imagination, as well as social skills.

The Scorpio Child

The Scorpio child may seem quiet and shy, but will surprise others with intense feelings and formidable willpower. Scorpio children are single-minded when they want something and intensely passionate about whatever they do. One of a caregiver's tasks is to teach this child to balance activities and emotions, yet at the same time to make the most of his great concentration and intense commitment.

Since young Scorpios do not show their depth of feelings easily, parents will have to learn to read almost imperceptible signs that troubles are brewing beneath the surface. Both Scorpio boys and girls enjoy games of power and control on or off the playground. Scorpio girls may take an early interest in the opposite sex, masquerading as tomboys, while Scorpio boys may be intensely competitive and loners. When her powerful energies are directed into work, sports, or challenging studies, Scorpio is a superachiever, focused on a goal. With trusted friends, young Scorpio is devoted and caring—the proverbial friend through thick and thin, loyal for life.

Scorpio 2010 has a strong emphasis on achievement and success. Uranus and lucky Jupiter in Pisces in their house of creativity should put them on the cutting edge of whichever field they choose.

The Sagittarius Child

This restless, athletic child will be out of the playpen and off on explorative adventures as soon as possible. Little Sagittarius is remarkably well-coordinated, attempting daredevil feats on any wheeled vehicle from scooters to skateboards. These natural athletes need little encouragement to channel their energies into sports. Their cheerful friendly dispositions earn them popularity in school, and once they have found a subject where their talent and imagination can soar, they will do well academically. They love animals, especially horses, and will be sure to have a pet or two, if not a home zoo. When they are old enough to take care of themselves, they'll clamor to be off on adventures of their own, away from home, if possible.

This is a child who loves to travel, who will not get homesick at summer camp, and who may sign up to be a foreign-exchange student or spend summers abroad. Outdoor adventure appeals to little Sagittarius, especially if it involves an active sport, such as skiing, cycling or mountain climbing. Give them enough space and encouragement, and their fiery spirit will propel them to achieve high goals.

Baby Sagittarius of 2010 has a natural generosity of spirit and an optimistic, social nature. Home and family will be especially important to him, though he may have an unconventional family life. He'll have an ability to look past the surface of things to seek out what has lasting value.

The Capricorn Child

These purposeful, goal-oriented children will work to capacity if they feel this will bring results. They're not ones who enjoy work for its own sake—there must be a goal in sight. Authority figures can do much to motivate these children, but once set on an upward path, young Capricorn will mobilize his energy and talent and work harder, and with more perseverance, than any other sign. Capricorn has built-in self-discipline that can achieve remarkable results, even if lacking the flashy personality, quick brainpower, or penetrating insight of others. Once involved, young Capricorn will stick to a task until it is mastered. This child also knows how to use others to his advantage and may well become the team captain or class president.

A wise parent will set realistic goals for the Capricorn child, paving the way for the early thrill of achievement. Youngsters should be encouraged to express their caring, feeling side to others, as well as their natural aptitude for leadership. Capricorn children may be especially fond of grandparents and older relatives, and will enjoy spending time with them and learning from them. It is not uncommon for young Capricorns to have an older mentor or teacher who guides them. With their great respect for authority, Capricorn children will take this influence very much to heart.

The Capricorn born in 2010 should be a good talker, with sharp mental abilities. He is likely to be social and outgoing, with lots of friends and closeness to brothers and sisters.

The Aquarius Child

The Aquarius child has a well-focused, innovative mind that often streaks so far ahead of peers that this child seems like an oddball. Routine studies never hold the restless youngster for long; he or she will look for another, more experimental place to try out his ideas and develop his inventions. Life is a laboratory to the inquiring Aquarius mind. School politics, sports, science, and the arts offer scope for their talents. But if there is no room for expression within approved social limits, Aquarius is sure to rebel. Questioning institutions and religions comes naturally, so these children may find an outlet elsewhere, becoming rebels with a cause. It is better not to force these children to conform, but rather to channel forward-thinking young minds into constructive group activities.

This year's Aquarius will have special financial talent. Luck and talent are his and fame could be in the stars!

The Pisces Child

Give young Pisces praise, applause, and a gentle, but firm, push in the right direction. Lovable Pisces children may be abundantly talented, but may be hesitant to express themselves, because they are quite sensitive and easily hurt. It is a parent's challenge to help them gain self-esteem and self-confidence. However, this same sensitivity makes them trusted friends who'll have many confidants as they develop socially. It also endows many Pisces with spectacular creative talent.

Pisces adores drama and theatrics of all sorts; therefore, encourage them to channel their creativity into art forms rather than indulging in emotional dramas. Understand that they may need more solitude than other children may as they develop their creative ideas. But though daydreaming can be creative, it is important that these natural dreamers not dwell too long in the world of fantasy. Teach them practical coping skills for the real world.

Since Pisces are sensitive physically, parents should help them build strong bodies with proper diet and regular exercise. Young Pisces may gravitate to more individual sports, such as swimming, sailing, and skiing, rather than to team sports. Or they may prefer more artistic physical activities, like dance or ice-skating.

Born givers, these children are often drawn to the underdog (they quickly fall for sob stories) and attract those who might take advantage of their empathic nature. Teach them to choose friends wisely, to set boundaries in relationships, and to protect their emotional vulnerability—invaluable lessons in later life.

With the planet Uranus now in Pisces along with lucky Jupiter, the 2010 baby belongs to a generation of Pisces movers and shakers. This child may have a rebellious streak that rattles the status quo. But this generation also has a visionary nature, which will be much concerned with the welfare of the world at large.

CHAPTER 14

Give the Perfect Gift to Every Sign

So often we're in a quandary about what to give a loved one, someone who has everything, that hard-to-please friend, or a fascinating new person in your life, or about the right present for a wedding, birthday, or hostess gift. Why not let astrology help you make the perfect choice by appealing to each sun sign's personality. When you're giving a gift, you're also making a memory, so it should be a special occasion. The gift that's most appreciated is one that touches the heart, reminds you both of a shared experience, or shows that the giver has really cared enough to consider the recipient's personality.

In general, the water signs (Cancer, Pisces, Scorpio) enjoy romantic, sentimental, and imaginative gifts given in a very personal way. Write your loved one a poem or a song to express your feelings. Assemble an album of photos or mementos of all the good times you've shared. Appeal to their sense of fantasy. Scorpio Richard Burton had the right idea when he gave Pisces Elizabeth Taylor a diamond bracelet hidden in lavender roses (her favorite color).

Fire signs (Aries, Leo, Sagittarius) appreciate a gift presented with lots of flair. Pull out the drama, like the actor who dazzled his Aries sweetheart by presenting her with trash cans overflowing with daisies.

Air signs (Gemini, Libra, Aquarius) love to be surprised with unusual gifts. The Duke of Windsor gave his elegant Gemini duchess, Wallis Windsor, fabulous jewels engraved with love notes and secret messages in their own special code.

Earth signs (Taurus, Virgo, Capricorn) value solid, tangible gifts or ones that appeal to all the senses. Delicious gourmet treats, scented body lotions, the newest CDs, the gift of a massage, or stocks and bonds are sure winners! Capricorn Elvis Presley once received a gold-plated piano from his wife.

Here are some specific ideas for each sign:

Aries

These are the trendsetters of the zodiac, who appreciate the latest thing! For Aries, it's the excitement that counts, so present your gift in a way that will knock their socks off. Aries is associated with the head, so a jaunty hat, hair ornaments, chandelier earrings, sunglasses, and hair-taming devices are good possibilities. Aries love games of any kind that offer a real challenge, like war video games, military themes, or rousing music with a beat. Anything red is a good bet: red flowers, red gems, and red accessories. How about giving Aries a way to let off steam with a gym membership or aerobic-dancing classes? Monogram a robe with a nickname in red.

Taurus

These are touchy-feely people who love things that appeal to all their senses. Find something that sounds, tastes, smells, feels, or looks good. And don't stint on quality or comfort. Taurus know the value of everything and will be aware of the price tag. Taurus foodies will appreciate chef-worthy kitchen gadgets, the latest cookbook, and gourmet treats. Taurus is a great collector. Find out what their passion is and present them with a rare item or a beautiful storage container such as an antique jewelry box. Green-thumb Taurus would love some special plants or flowers, garden tools, beautiful plant containers. Appeal to their sense of touch with fine fabrics—high-thread-count sheets, cashmere, satin, and mohair. One of the animal-loving signs, Taurus might appreciate a retractable leash or soft bed for the dog or cat. Get them a fine wallet or checkbook cover. They'll use it often.

Gemini

Mercury-ruled Gemini appreciates gifts that appeal to their mind. The latest book or novel, a talked-about film, a CD from a hot new singer, or a high-tech gadget might appeal. A beautiful diary or a tape recorder would record their adventures. Since Geminis often do two things at once, a telephone gadget that leaves their hands free would be appreciated. In fact, a new telephone device or superphone would appeal to these great communicators. Gloves, rings, and bracelets accent their expressive hands. Clothes from an interesting new designer appeal to their sense of style. You might try giving Gemini a variety of little gifts in a beautiful box or a Christmas stocking. A tranquil massage at a local spa would calm Gemini's sensitive nerves. Find an interesting way to wrap your gift. Nothing boring, please!

Cancer

Cancer is associated with home and family, so anything to do with food, entertaining at home, and family life is a good bet. Beautiful dishes or serving platters, silver items, fine crystal and linen, gourmet cookware, cooking classes or the latest DVD from a cooking teacher might be appreciated. Cancer designers Vera Wang and Giorgio Armani have perfected the Cancer style and have many home products available, as well as their elegant designer clothing. Naturally, anything to do with the sea is a possibility: pearls, coral, or shell jewelry. Boat and water-sports equipment might work. Consider cruise wear for traveling Cancers. Sentimental Cancer loves antiques and silver frames for family photos. Cancer people are often good photographers, so consider frames, albums, and projectors to showcase their work. Present your gift in a personal way with a special note.

Leo

Think big with Leo and appeal to this sign's sense of drama. Go for the gold (Leo's color) with gold jewelry, designer clothing, or big attention-getting accessories. Follow their signature style, which could be superelegant, like Jacqueline Onassis, or superstar, like Madonna or Jennifer Lopez. This sign is always ready for the red carpet and stays beautifully groomed, so stay within these guidelines when choosing your gift. Feline motifs and animal prints are usually a hit. The latest grooming aids, high-ticket cosmetics, and mirrors reflect their best image. Beautiful hairbrushes tame their manes. Think champagne, high-thread-count linens, and luxurious loungewear or lingerie. Make Leo feel special with a custom portrait or photo shoot with your local star photographer. Be sure to go for spectacular wrapping, with beautiful paper and ribbons. Present your gift with a flourish!

Virgo

Virgo usually has a special subject of interest and would appreciate relevant books, films, lectures, or classes. Choose health-oriented things: gifts to do with fitness and self-improvement. Virgo enjoys brainteasers, crossword puzzles, computer programs, organizers, and digital planners. Fluffy robes, bath products, and special soaps appeal to Virgo's sense of cleanliness. Virgo loves examples of good, practical design: efficient telephones, beautiful briefcases, computer cases, desk accessories. Choose natural fibers and quiet colors when choosing clothes for Virgo. Virgo has high standards, so go for quality when choosing a gift.

Libra

Whatever you give this romantic sign, go for beauty and romance. Libra loves accessories, decorative objects, whatever makes him or his surroundings more aesthetically pleasing. Beautiful flowers in pastel colors are always welcome. Libras are great hosts and hostesses, who might appreciate a gift related to fine dining: serving pieces, linens, glassware, flower vases. Evening or party clothes please since Libra has a gadabout social life. Interesting books, objets d'art, memberships to museums, and tickets to cultural events are good ideas. Fashion or home-decorating magazine subscriptions usually please Libra women. Steer away from anything loud, garish, or extreme. Think pink, one of their special colors, when giving Libra jewelry, clothing, or accessories. It's a very romantic sign, so be sure to remember birthdays, holidays, and anniversaries with a token of affection.

Scorpio

Scorpios love mystery, so bear that in mind when you buy these folks a present. You could take this literally and buy them a good thriller DVD, novel, or video game. Scorpios are power players, so a book about one of their sign might please. Bill Gates, Jack Welch, Condoleezza Rice, and Hillary Clinton are hot Scorpio subjects. Scorpios love black leather, suede, fur, anything to do with the sea, power tools, tiny spy tape recorders, and items with secret compartments or intricate locks. When buying a handbag for Scorpio, go for simple shapes with lots of interior pockets. Sensuous Scorpios appreciate hot lingerie, sexy linens, body lotions, and perfumed candles. Black is the favored color for Scorpio clothing—go for sexy textures like cashmere and satin in simple shapes by designers like Calvin Klein. This sign is fascinated with the occult, so give them an astrology or tarot-card reading, beautiful crystals, or an astrology program for the computer.

Sagittarius

For these outdoor people, consider adventure trips, designer sportswear, gear for their favorite sports. A funny gift or something for their pets pleases Sagittarius. For clothing and accessories, the fashionista of this sign tends to like bright colors and dramatic innovative styles. Otherwise, casual sportswear is a good idea. These travelers usually have a favorite getaway place; give them a travel guide, DVD, novel, or history book that would make their trip more interesting. Luggage is also a good bet. Sleek carry-ons, travel wallets, ticket holders, business-card cases, and wheeled computer bags might please these wanderers. Anything that makes travel more comfortable and pleasant is good for Sagittarius, including a good book to read en route. This sign is the great gambler of the zodiac, so gifts related to their favorite gambling venue would be appreciated.

Capricorn

For this quality-conscious sign, go for a status label from the best store in town. Get Capricorns something good for their image and career. They could be fond of things Spanish, like flamenco or tango music, or of country-and-western music and motifs. In the bookstore, go for biographies of the rich and famous, or advice books to help Capricorn get to the top. Capricorns take their gifts seriously, so steer away from anything too frivolous. Garnet, onyx, or malachite jewelry, Carolina Herrera fragrance and clothing, and beautiful briefcases and wallets are good ideas. Glamorous status tote bags carry business gear in style. Capricorns like golf, tennis, and sports that involve climbing, cycling, or hiking, so presents could be geared to their outdoor interests. Elegant evening accessories would be fine for this sign, which often entertains for business.

Aquarius

Give Aquarius a surprise gift. This sign is never impressed with things that are too predictable. So use your imagination to present the gift in an unusual way or at an unexpected time. With Aquarius, originality counts. When in doubt, give them something to think about, a new electronic gadget, perhaps a small robot, or an advanced computer game. Or something New Age, like an amethyst-crystal cluster. Aquarius like innovative materials with a space-age look. They are the ones with the wraparound glasses, the titanium computer cases. This air sign loves to fly—an airplane ticket always pleases. Books should be on innovative subjects, politics, or adventures of the mind. Aquarius goes for unusual color combinations—especially electric blue or hot pink—and abstract patterns. They like the newest, coolest looks on the cutting edge of fashion and are not afraid to experiment. Think of Paris Hilton's constantly changing looks. Look for an Aquarius gift in an out-of-the-way boutique or local hipster hangout. They'd be touched if you find out Aquarius's special worthy cause and make a donation. Spirit them off to hear their favorite guru.

Pisces

Pisces respond to gifts that have a touch of fantasy, magic, and romance. Look for mystical gifts with a touch of the occult. Romantic music (a customized CD of favorite love songs) and love stories appeal to Pisces sentimentalists. Pisces is associated with perfume and fragrant oils, so help this sign indulge with their favorite scent in many forms. Anything to do with the ocean, fish, and water sports appeals to Pisces. How about a whirlpool, a water-therapy spa treatment, or a sea salt rub. Appeal to this sign with treats for the feet: foot massages, pedcures, ballet tickets, and dance lessons. Cashmere socks and metallic evening sandals are other Pisces pleasers. A romantic dinner overlooking the water is Pisces paradise. A case of fine wine or another favorite liquid is always appreciated. Write a love poem and enclose it with your gift.

CHAPTER 15

Your Pet-Scope for 2010: How to Choose Your Best Friend for Life

With Jupiter, the planet of luck and expansion, in compassionate Pisces, this is a great time to bring joy into your life by adopting an animal friend. At this writing, 63 percent of all American households have at least one pet, according to a recent survey by the American Pet Product Manufacturers Association. And we spend billions of dollars on the care and feeding of our beloved pets. Our pets are counted as part of the family, often sharing our beds and accompanying us on trips.

Whether you choose to adopt an animal from a local shelter or buy a Thoroughbred from a breeder, try for an optimal time of adoption and sun sign of your new friend. If you're rescuing an animal, however, it's difficult to know the sun sign of the animal, but you can adopt on a day when the moon is compatible with yours, which should bless the emotional relationship. Using the moon signs listed in the daily forecasts in this book, choose a day when the moon is in your sign, a sign of the same element, or a compatible element. This means fire and air signs should go for a day when the moon is in fire signs Aries, Leo, Sagittarius or air signs Gemini, Libra, or Aquarius. Water and earth signs should choose a day when the moon is in water signs Cancer, Scorpio, or Pisces or earth signs Taurus, Virgo, or Capricorn. If possible, aim for a new moon, good for beginning a new relationship.

Here are some sign-specific tips for adopting an animal that will be your best friend for life.

Aries: The Rescuer

Aries gets special pleasure from rescuing animals in distress and rehabbing them, so do check your local shelters if you're thinking of adopting an animal. As an active fire sign, you'd be happiest with a lively animal that can accompany you, and you might do well with a rescue animal such as a German shepherd or Labrador retriever. You'd also enjoy training such an animal. Otherwise look for intelligence, alertness, playfulness and obedience in your friend. Since Aries tend to have an active life, look for a sleek, low maintenance coat on your dog or cat. Cat lovers would enjoy the more active breeds such as the Siamese or Abyssinian.

An Aries sun-sign dog or cat would be ideal. Aries animals have a brave, energetic, rather combative nature. They can be mischievous, so the kittens and puppies should be monitored for safety. They'll dare to jump higher, run faster, and chase more animals than their peers. They may require stronger words and more obedience training than other signs. Give them plenty of toys and play active games with them often.

Taurus: The Toucher

Taurus is a touchy-feely sign, and this extends to your animal relationships. Look for a dog or cat that enjoys being petted and groomed, is affectionate, and adapts well to family life. As one of the great animal-loving signs, Taurus is likely to have several pets, so it is important that they all get along together. Give each one its own special safe space to minimize turf wars.

Taurus animals are calm and even tempered, but do not like being teased and could retaliate, so be sure to instruct children in the proper way to handle and play with their pet. Since this sign has strong appetites and tends to put on weight easily, be careful not to overindulge them in caloric treats and table snacks. Sticking to a regular feeding schedule could help eliminate between-meal snacking.

Taurus female animals are excellent mothers and make good breeders. They tend to be clean and less destructive of home furnishings than other animals.

Gemini: The Companion

A bright, quick-witted sign like yours requires an equally interesting and communicative pet. Choose a social animal that adapts well to different environments, since you may travel or have homes in different locations.

Gemini animals can put up with noise, telephones, music, and different people coming and going. They'll want to be part of the action, so place a pillow or roost in a public place. They do not like being left alone, however, so, if you will be away for long periods, find them an animal companion to play with. You might consider adopting two Gemini pets from the same litter.

Animals born under this sign are easy to teach and some enjoy doing tricks or retrieving. They may be more vocal than other animals, especially if they are confined without companionship.

Cancer: The Nurturer

Cancer enjoys a devoted, obedient animal who demonstrates loyalty to its master. An affectionate, home-loving dog or cat who welcomes you and sits on your lap would be ideal. The emotional connection with your pet is most important; therefore, you may depend on your powerful psychic powers when choosing an animal. Wait until you feel that strong bond of psychic communication between you both. The moon sign of the day you adopt is very important for moon-ruled Cancer, so choose a water sign, if possible.

Cancer animals need a feeling of security; they don't like changes of environment or too much chaos at home. If you intend to breed your animal, the Cancer pet makes a wonderful and fertile mother.

Leo: The Prideful Owner

The Leo owner may choose a pet that reminds you of your own physical characteristics, such as similar coloring or build. You'll be proud of your pet, keep the animal groomed to perfection, and choose the most spectacular example of the breed. Noble animals with a regal attitude, beautiful fur, or striking markings are often preferred, such as the Himalayan or red tabby Persian cat, the standard poodle, the chow chow dog. An attention getter is a must.

Under the sign of the King of Beasts, Leo-born animals have proud noble natures. They usually have a cheerful, magnanimous disposition and rule their domains regardless of their breed, holding their heads with pride and walking with great authority. They enjoy grooming, like to show off and be the center of attention. Leo animals are naturals for the show ring, thriving in the spotlight and applause. They'll thrive with plenty of petting, pampering, and admiration.

Virgo: The Caregiver

Virgo owners will be very particular about their pets, paying special attention to requirements for care and maintenance. You need a pet who is clean, obedient, intelligent, yet rather quiet. A highly active, barking or meowing pet that might get on your nerves is a no-no.

Cats are usually very good pets for Virgo. Choose one of the calm breeds, such as a Persian. Though this is a high-maintenance cat, its beauty and personality will be rewarding.

You are compassionate with animals in need, and you might find it rewarding to volunteer at a local shelter or veterinary clinic or to train service dogs.

Virgo animals can be fussy eaters, very particular about their environment. They are gentle and intelligent, and respond to kind words and quiet commands, never harsh treatment.

Virgo is an excellent sign for dogs that are trained to do service work, since they seem to enjoy being useful and are intelligent enough to be easily trained.

Libra: The Beautifier

The Libra owner responds to beauty and elegance in your pet. You require a well-mannered, but social companion, who can be displayed in all of nature's finery. An exotic variety such as a graceful curly-haired Devon Rex cat would be a show-stopper. Libra often prefers the smaller varieties, such as a miniature schnauzer, a mini-greyhound or a teacup poodle.

Pets born under Libra are usually charming, well-mannered gentlemen who love the comforts of home life. They tend to be more careful than other signs, not rushing willfully into potentially dangerous situations. They'll avoid confrontations and harsh sounds, responding to words of love and gentle corrections.

Scorpio: The Powerful

Scorpios enjoy a powerful animal with a strong character. They enjoy training animals in obedience, would do well with service dogs, guard dogs, or police animals. Some Scorpios enjoy the more exotic, edgy pets, such as hairless Sphynx cats or Chinese chin dogs. Scorpios could find rescuing animals in dire circumstances and finding them new homes especially rewarding, as Matthew McConaughey did during Hurricane Katrina.

Animals born under this sign tend to be one-person pets, very strongly attached to their owners and extremely loyal and possessive. They are natural guard animals who will take extreme risks to protect their owners. They are best ruled by love and with consistent behavior training. They need to respect their owners and will return their love with great devotion.

Sagittarius: The Jovial Freedom Lover

Sagittarius is a traveler and one of the great animal lovers of the zodiac. The horse is especially associated with your sign, and you could well be a "horse whisperer." You generally respond most to large, active animals. If a small animal, like a Chihuahua, steals your heart, be sure it's one that travels well or tolerates your absence. Outdoor dogs like hunting dogs, retrievers, and border collies would be good companions on your outdoor adventures.

Sagittarius animals are freedom-loving, jovial, happy-go-lucky types. They may be wanderers, however, so be sure they have the proper identification tags and consider embedded microchip identification. These animals tend to be openly affectionate, companionable, untemperamental. They enjoy socializing and playing with humans and other animals and are especially good with active children.

Capricorn: The Thoroughbred

Capricorn is a discriminating owner, with a great sense of responsibility toward your animal. You will be concerned with maintenance and care, will rarely neglect or overlook any health issues with your pet. You will also discipline your pet wisely, not tolerating any destructive or outrageous antics. You will be attracted to good breeding, good manners, and deep loyalty from your pet.

The Capricorn pet tends to be more quiet and serious than other pets, perhaps a lone wolf who prefers the company of its owner, rather than a sociable or mischievous type. This is another good sign for a working dog, such as a herder, as Capricorn animals enjoy this outlet for their energy.

Aquarius: The Independent Original

Aquarius owners tend to lead active, busy lives and need an animal who can either accompany them cheerfully or who won't make waves. Demanding or high-maintenance dogs are not for you. You might prefer unusual or oddball types of pets, such as dressed-up Chihuahuas who travel in your tote bag or scene-stealing, rather shocking hairless cats. Or you will acquire a group of animals who can play with one another when you are pursuing outside activities, as Oprah Winfrey does. You can relate to the independence of cats, who require relatively little care and maintenance.

Aquarius animals are not loners—they enjoy the companionship of humans or groups of other animals. They tend to be more independent and may require more training to follow the house rules. However, they can have unique personalities and endearing oddball behavior.

Pisces: The Soul Mate

This is the sign that can "talk to the animals." Pisces owners enjoy a deep communication with their pets, love having their animals accompany them, sleep with them, and show affection. Tenderhearted Pisces will often rescue an animal in distress or adopt an animal from a shelter.

Tropical fish are often recommended as a Pisces pet, and seem to have a natural tranquilizing effect on this sign. However, Pisces may require an animal that shows more affection than their fish friends.

Pisces animals are creative types, can be sensually seductive and mysterious, mischievous and theatrical. They make fine house pets, do not usually like to roam far from their owners, and have a winning personality, especially with the adults in the home. Naturally sensitive and seldom vicious, they should be treated gently and given much praise and encouragement.

CHAPTER 16

Your Gemini Personality and Potential: The Roles You Play in Life

The more you understand your Gemini personality and potential, the more you'll benefit from using your special solar power to help create the life you want. There's a life coach, personal trainer, career adviser, fashion expert, and matchmaker all built into your Gemini sun sign. Whether you want to make a radical change in your life or simply choose a new wardrobe or paint a room, your sun sign can help you discover new possibilities and make good decisions. You could tap into your Gemini power to deal with relationship issues, such as getting along with your boss or spicing up your love life. Maybe you'll be inspired by a celebrity sign mate who shares your special traits.

Let the following chapters help you move in harmony with your natural Gemini gifts. As the ancient oracle of Delphi advised, "Know thyself." To know yourself, as astrology helps you to do, is to gain confidence and strength.

You may wonder how astrologers determine what a Gemini personality is like. To begin with, we use a type of recipe, blending several ingredients. First there's your Gemini element: air. Air signs are distinguished by their mental orientation. Gemini functions like a mutable sign—constantly changing. Then there's your sign's polarity, which adds a positive, masculine, yang dimension. Let's not forget your planetary ruler: Mercury, the planet of communication, mental functioning. Add your sign's location in the zodiac: third, in the house of communication. Finally, stir in your symbol, the Twins, which indicate the dual nature of your sign.

This cosmic mix influences everything we say about Gemini. For example, you could easily deduce that an air sign with a Mercury ruling planet should have a quick mind and a facility with words. Is a Gemini likely to sit around the house? Only if there's a dual-line phone or a party going on. Gemini is the queen of multitasking, easily able to do two things at once. If you're a typical, social Gemini, a deserted island is unlikely to be your favorite vacation spot.

But all Geminis are not alike! Your individual astrological personality contains a blend of many other planets, colored by the signs they occupy, plus factors such as the sign coming over the horizon at the exact moment of your birth. However, the more Gemini planets there are in your horoscope, the more likely you'll recognize yourself in the descriptions that follow. On the other hand, if many planets are grouped together in a different sign, they will color your horoscope accordingly, sometimes making a communicative sign like yours appear more withdrawn. So if the Gemini traits mentioned here don't describe you, there could be other factors flavoring your cosmic stew. (Look up your other planets in the tables in this book to find out what they might be!)

The Gemini Man: Many Facets

The Gemini man is on a perpetual journey in search of the new. You seem to be forever in motion. Even when you're sitting still, your mind is racing. You are a lover of games on every level who can make a game of the most complicated situations. On the negative side, it is difficult for you to take anything or anyone too seriously. Weighty matters tend to drag you down, unless your mind is challenged by a crisis situation. You'd rather dabble in lots of different projects, then fly off when things get sticky.

In childhood, Gemini is the bright, funny little boy who gets bored in school and can devise some jolly pranks to amuse himself. You'll have many interests, which keep changing constantly. In your early years you should learn self-discipline as well as the satisfaction of setting goals and reaching them. Otherwise, you'll have a tendency to skim the surface of life, with much activity but few real accomplishments.

Young adulthood is an experimental time, and you're not about to deny yourself any adventures. Like the characters portrayed by Gemini idol Johnny Depp, you're the elusive and scintillating lover who dazzles, then disappears. A born flirt and charming chameleon who can't resist an exciting affair of the heart, you usually opt for several romantic experiences at once. This could result in your becoming a perennial playboy, even leading a double life, both hazards of the ever-curious and charming Gemini man.

In a Relationship

The woman who succeeds in tying Gemini down would be well advised to give him lots of rope and keep an open mind. This is likely to be a nontraditional marriage—exciting but not particularly stable. Though Gemini is not naturally inclined to be monogamous, he will stick with a woman who is bright, entertaining, sociable, interesting, and companionable. It would help if she is involved in his professional life, too, as well as having strong interests of her own. His hot-cold temperament and roving eye could cause his mate a great deal of insecurity, unless she is an independent person as well. This mercurial man makes the perfect husband for an intelligent woman who longs for a witty conversationalist, a flirtatious and inventive lover, and an ever-youthful companion throughout life. With Gemini, she'll never be bored.

The Gemini Woman: Talk Power

It's no surprise that the comedienne whose signature line is "Can we talk?" is a Gemini—Joan Rivers. Your verbal skills are legendary, giving you the ability to talk yourself into or out of any situation. Written and spoken words are your means of seduction, sales, and self-defense. You'll talk with your expressive hands (the Gemini part of the body), and use body language to add extra emphasis.

You're highly charged with nervous energy, seeming to be everywhere at once. And you have enough sides to your personality to dazzle even those close to you. One moment you are a capable executive, the next a little girl filled with wonder, the next an earthy sensualist, the next an expert in verbal karate, the next a comedienne. It's no wonder there are so many actresses under this sign. And, best of all, you do everything with a light, quicksilver touch, so the effort never shows.

While your brain is busily skipping about, juggling many people and projects at once, you manage to skip away from heavy emotional involvements. You're not one to be tied down in any way. However, though variety may be the spice of your life, it can also be hard to digest. You need a substantial anchor and truly caring relationships to get you through the tough times. If you learn to live with a few normal human flaws and foibles (you can't laugh everything off!) instead of constantly changing your mind, you'll find your twin sides working together more smoothly. Then you will have a much better idea of what you're really looking for.

The little Gemini girl is the bright, precocious one who learns to read and write ahead of everyone. She is very well-coordinated, moves quickly, and talks even more rapidly. She bores easily with her toys, and may even invent new games to play with them.

Gemini's problem is making up her mind. There is always something more interesting to do, a more exciting place to go, people who might be more fun. You must learn early to stick to one thing until you have mastered it—or you'll end up being the proverbial "jill-of-all-trades."

Propelled by a great reservoir of nervous energy, the young Gemini is likely to have more than one job, more than one boyfriend, and a full schedule of social activities. Juggling is second nature to you. The more balls in the air, the less likely you are to get bored. One challenge is to find situations that give you a chance to grow. Otherwise, you'll skip from job to job, love affair to love affair, at a great strain on your nerves.

When you find a man who stimulates you mentally as well

as emotionally and physically, you may be tempted to take a chance on love. It is important that you separate dream from reality here—and not confuse surface attraction with true communication. Otherwise, you may marry on impulse, quickly tire of the situation, and search for excitement elsewhere. Since you often retain your looks and youthful outlook, it is not unusual for you to finally settle with a much younger man.

In a Relationship

Keeping your foothold in the working world after marriage provides you with the outside stimulation you need and also the financial means to delegate the more boring routine tasks of housekeeping to someone else. If you apply your creativity to making the marriage special, you can keep the union lively, with no need to look for greener pastures. You're sure to promote a social life, entertain frequently, and decorate with flair and originality. Your relationship may also benefit if you take an active part in your husband's business. But too much togetherness can seem confining for your restless sign. If your husband is too possessive and demanding, you may be tempted to take flight. However, if you can negotiate enough room for personal freedom, you'll provide a life of sparkle and variety.

Gemini in the Family

The Gemini Parent

Geminis take a great interest in their child's different stages, watching the young personality unfold. You may find the early babyhood years most difficult, when the child is dependent and needs steady, routine care. After the child learns to communicate, you'll take on the role of teacher, introducing the child to the world of ideas and mental pursuits, helping with homework, and making difficult subjects easier to understand. One of your greatest assets as a parent is your own insatiable curiosity about the world, which you can communicate to the children by introducing them early to the world of ideas and books. You are also an excellent coach, teaching your child social abilities and the art of handling others at an early age. As your child matures, your youthful, ever fresh outlook makes you a wonderful friend and companion through the years.

The Gemini Stepparent

Your verbal skills and sense of humor will often come to the rescue in the initial stages of starting up a new family. You're a communicator who can quickly get shy youngsters to open up and difficult personalities to communicate. Your natural sociability and flair for entertainment encourages everyone to have fun, making family get-togethers seem like parties. Since you have many outside activities and interests, the children will be able to have as much time as they need alone with their parent. Soon your new family will find that you are a fun-loving addition to their lives, a wise adviser, and an excellent noncompetitive companion.

The Gemini Grandparent

You're an upbeat grandparent who still finds life an interesting adventure. You're always the life of the party, up on all the latest family gossip, as well as what's happening with the rest of the world. Visits with you are full of laughter and good stories! You'll take a special interest in your grandchildren's education and support them in whatever career path they choose. You may have a large extended family that reaches out to the children of your community. You'll give your own children plenty of space to rear the grandchildren as they please, never interfering with Mother's rules or taking over the grandchildren's upbringing.

"Never complain" was the motto of the Duchess of Windsor (a Gemini), and it could be yours, too. You accentuate the positive and keep a cheerful attitude. Your mentor should be the famous Gemini pastor Norman Vincent Peale, author of *The Power of Positive Thinking,* one of the most influential self-help books of all time. Dr. Peale lived a productive life well into his nineties, still writing and preaching. You, too, realize how the right mental attitude can influence any situation for the better, and you'll be sure to pass on your wisdom to your grandchildren.

CHAPTER 17

Gemini Fashion and Decor Tips: Elevate Your Mood with Gemini Style!

In this year of serious concerns, why not put joy and imagination into your life by creating a harmonious environment and expressing your sun sign's natural flair in everything you do and wear? There are colors, sound, fashion, and decor tips that fit Gemini like the proverbial glove and that could brighten every day. Even small changes in decor could make you feel "home at last." A simple change of color in your walls or curtains, your special music in the air, and a wardrobe makeover inspired by a Gemini designer or celebrity are natural mood elevators that boost your confidence and energy level. Even your vacations might be more fun if you tailor them to your natural Gemini inclinations. Try these tips to enhance your lifestyle and express the Gemini in you.

Gemini Fashion Secrets

Gemini always likes to do something interesting with your clothes and have fun with fashion, and never take your fashion image too seriously. Nicole Kidman dresses with great Gemini flair in clothes that get people talking. Annette Bening opts for simple, elegant clothes that set off her delicate beauty. Other Gemini beauties, like Liz Hurley, who once attended the Academy Awards in a gown held together with safety pins, and Mary Kate Olson enjoy looking downright outrageous, keeping their fans guessing! Some Geminis, like the late Marilyn Monroe, love to flaunt their sex appeal, making a game of it.

Since you have such a changeable personality, you'll probably experiment before you find the style that suits you. Double-duty clothes that change personality with a scene-stealing accessory or two are ideal for your gadabout life, when you're just too busy to fuss. A hairstyle that can be combed several different ways would satisfy your need for constant change. Add a witty, scene-stealing jewel or two, a dramatic scarf, or trendy shoes and handbag to quickly change your outfit's personality and you're ready to go!

Gemini often talks with the hands, so make your gestures count. Stay well-manicured and accent your expressive hands with hot-colored nail polish and fabulous rings.

Gemini Colors

The Gemini palette—soft silvery-gray, pale yellow, and airy Wallis Windsor blue—consists of great background colors, elegant ones you can live with over a period of time. They adapt to different seasons and climates, won't compete with your personality or distract from your total image. You can change the look of these colors at will, accenting them with bright touches or blending with other pastels. And they can tolerate a frequent change of accessories according to your mood of the moment.

Your Gemini Fashion Role Models

Some legendary fashion icons, like the late Duchess of Windsor, were born under your sign and you couldn't find better inspiration than this scandalous siren who made fashion history as well. We remember Wallis Simpson for her witty way with accessories, like those fabulous jewels she wore with casual

aplomb (some engraved with secret messages from the Duke).
Yet she never varied her signature swept-back hairdo or her
elegantly simple style of dressing.

The fashion duo Dolce & Gabbana, the with-it looks of
Anna Sui, or the newest androgynous menswear styles would
be fun for you to try on for size. Gemini models who express
your flair, like Naomi Campbell and Heidi Klum, have the
ability to change their image with their hair style, be a vamp
one moment, an innocent girl next door the next.

Gemini Home Makeover Tips

Your home should be multipurpose to accommodate your
many interests and ongoing projects, yet it should also be a
place where you can conduct your active social life, and finally,
a relaxing haven. Keep your atmosphere and colors light and
airy. Give heavy drapes, intense colors, and dark furniture a
pass.

Let the colors of your room be a background for all the
interesting things that will happen there. Pale neutrals and
pastels on the walls are versatile and easy to live with over
a period of time. (You might get quickly bored with more vibrant shades.) Then shift into color with bright slipcovers and
accessories to give your room a quick change of personality.

Since you may have several activities going on at once,
your decor strategy should help you avoid confusion and stay
on top of your schedule. Choose furniture that can be rear-
ranged in different combinations and settings. Clever cabinets
and storage containers allow you to sweep your projects out
of sight when friends drop in. Line a room with bookcases if
you're one of the Gemini readers who collect the latest magazines, books, and newspapers.

Set up your communications center carefully. (You're the
sign with a telephone on both sides of the bed and alongside
the bathtub.) Have a separate room or corner with a desk
where you can organize lists, equipment, and books so you
won't waste time looking for them. Many Geminis have houses
in more than one place (you're often bicoastal), so you can

186

switch environments. At each place, there should be a space to stash whatever you need to stay connected to your network. With a laptop computer, you can work wherever you go.

Geminis love to entertain casually and frequently, so your kitchen should be set up for impromptu parties, with plenty of glassware and buffet plates handy. Have multipurpose tables that can be set up anywhere and folding chairs for instant group seating. Then get ready to party!

Gemini Sounds

Gemini has sophisticated, eclectic musical tastes, and perhaps has accumulated a varied collection of sounds. You may enjoy instrumentals that require manual dexterity, such as piano concertos. In popular music, you pay attention to the words as well as the melody, so the witty lyrics of Cole Porter and the poetry of Bob Dylan appeal, as do the hottest rap artist and the latest experiment of Sir Paul McCartney. You like abstract classical music, but nothing too heavy or loud that might distract from conversation or bring on the blues. You're a natural disc jockey, so customize your own mix of musical moods on an iPod or CD recorder. Paula Abdul, Miles Davis, Alanis Morissette, rap music, Kylie Minogue, Cole Porter, Prince, Judy Garland, and continental tunes from Charles Aznavour would give you the full range of Gemini sounds.

Gemini Getaways

Sometimes you just have to get away from it all! But Gemini never likes to get too far away from civilization. Stay away from desert islands, unless you need some peace and quiet to write your novel. Stick to places where there's a lively social scene, some interesting scenery, local characters who provide good conversation, and an Internet café to keep up with your e-mail.

Improve your language skills by visiting a foreign country;

you'll have no trouble communicating in sign language, if necessary. Consider a language school in the south of France or in Switzerland, where you'll mix with fellow students of many nationalities while you perfect your accent. In the USA, visit some of the Gemini states: Wisconsin, Tennessee, Kentucky, Rhode Island, South Carolina, and Arkansas.

Lightness is the key to Gemini travel. Don't weigh yourself down with luggage. Dare to travel with an empty suitcase, then acquire clothes and supplies at your destination. Imagine how fast you'll speed through the airport! Invest in a fabulous carry-on that you can throw your life in and go.

Keep a separate tiny address book for each city, so the right numbers are always handy. Invest in beautifully designed travel cases and briefcases, since you're on the go so much. Spend some time looking for the perfect luggage, portable notebook computer, and a worldwide mobile phone to keep you in touch at all times.

CHAPTER 18

The Gemini Way to Stay Healthy and Age Well

This year we'll be focused on staying healthy to avoid the high costs of health care and to cope with stressful events. Some signs have an easier time than others committing to a health and diet regimen. Gemini usually dislikes routine and gets easily bored, unless there is variety and mental stimulation. It's important to design a unique program that incorporates health-building activities into your busy life. Astrology can clue you in to the specific Gemini tendencies that contribute to good or ill health. So follow these sun-sign tips to help yourself become the healthiest Gemini possible.

Diet Dos and Don'ts

Gemini is an on-the-go sign that does not usually have a weight problem, as long as you keep moving. If life circumstances force you to be sedentary, however, you may eat out of boredom and watch the pounds pile on. Your active social life can also sabotage your weight with sumptuous party buffets and restaurant meals where you enjoy sampling everything. Your challenge is to find a healthy eating system with enough variety so you won't get bored. Develop a strategy for eating out—at parties or restaurants—and fill up the buffet plates with salad or veggies before you taste all the desserts. Sociable Geminis on a diet can benefit from group support in a system like Weight Watchers. Or find a diet twin who'll support you and have fun losing weight together.

Calm Your Nerves

Gemini is associated with the nervous system, our body's lines of communication. If your nerves are on edge, you may be trying to do too many things at once, leaving no time for fun and laughter. When you've overloaded your circuits, it's time to get together with friends, go out to parties, do things in groups to release tension and bring perspective into your life. Investigate natural tension relievers such as yoga or meditation. Doing things with your hands—playing the piano, typing, craftwork—is also helpful.

Guard Your Lungs

Gemini is also associated with the lungs, which are especially sensitive. If you smoke, please consider quitting. Yoga, which incorporates deep breathing into physical exercise, brings oxygen into your lungs. Among its many benefits are the deep relaxation and tranquillity so needed by your sign. If you work in a closed environment, with inadequate ventilation, consider getting an air purifier to combat airborne flu viruses. If you are a frequent flyer, bolster your immune system with vitamins and antioxidants before you travel and plan your schedule ahead of time to make travel as stress-free as possible.

Exercise with Friends

Combine healthful activities with social get-togethers for fun and plenty of fringe benefits for everyone. Include friends in your exercise routines; join an exercise class or jogging club. Gemini excels at sports that require good timing and manual dexterity as well as communication with others, like tennis or golf. These are sports that usually take place in a clubby social atmosphere, which should motivate you to exercise frequently as you continue to improve your skills. Racquet sports are also good for travelers, who can easily find courts or clubs in other cities, enabling you to make new friends wherever you go.

Those who jog may want to add hand weights or upper-body exercises, which will strengthen the arms and hands. If you spend long hours at the computer, try an ergonomic keyboard for comfort and protection against carpal tunnel syndrome.

Stay Forever Young

Gemini thrives on social contact and mental stimulation and should remain active in the community. Expand your social network as much as possible to include young people with innovative ideas. Take courses at your local college, and challenge yourself by learning new skills. It is important for Gemini to protect nerve pathways, so be sure your chairs are ergonomic and watch for carpal tunnel syndrome if you use a computer. To protect your lungs, do everything you can to stop smoking, get regular flu shots, and improve the air quality in your home.

CHAPTER 19

Add Gemini Star Power to Your Career: What It Takes to Succeed in 2010

In today's tight job market, you'll need to pull out all the stops to land a great job. Gemini has a combination of talents and abilities that can make you a natural winner. Tops on the list is your ability to roll with the punches and come out on top. A quick study who can adapt to many situations and personalities, you're the zodiac's champion multitasker. If you develop and nurture these talents, you'll be more likely to find a career you truly enjoy, as well as one that rewards you financially. Here's to your success!

Where to Look for the Perfect Job

Follow your natural Gemini tendencies. Gemini has many winning cards to play in the career game. Your quick mind works best in a career where there is enough mental stimulation to keep you from getting bored. High-pressure situations that would be stressful to others are stimulating to you. Many things happening simultaneously—phones ringing off the hook, daily client meetings, constant changes—create a situation in which you thrive, getting to use all your communications skills.

Your ability to communicate with a variety of people works well in sales, journalism, public relations, politics, agent or broker work, personnel, or consulting—literally any job that requires verbal or writing skills. You who learn languages easily could be a language teacher or interpreter. Manual dexterity is another Gemini gift that can find craft, musical, or medical expression (especially surgery or chiropractic work).

What to avoid: a job that is too isolated, routine, detail-oriented, or confining. Stay away from companies that are hidebound, with rigid rules. Instead, look for a place that gives you strong backup as well as free rein. Gemini often succeeds in a freelance position, provided you have a solid support system to help with the details and routine chores.

Live Up to Your Leadership Potential

Gemini's natural analytical mind and way with words can be used to wheel and deal your way to the top. Master deal maker and real estate tycoon Donald Trump has written several books on his techniques that should make fascinating reading for ambitious Geminis. Be inspired and entertained by this colorful tycoon, who changed the skyline of New York and became a TV star, as well.

As a leader, Gemini is fun to work for—sociable, witty, and clever. Your office will be a beehive of activity, with telephone lines buzzing and clients coming and going. What is lacking in job security, you make up in opportunities for others to experiment, to develop flexibility and a sense of gamesmanship.

You operate best as a deal maker or an entrepreneur rather than a designer or producer. You often change your mind, so you should hire assistants who are adaptable enough to keep up with you, yet who can provide organization, follow-up, and structure. You rule multitasking, and sometimes have so many projects going on at once that others are dizzy, yet you are known for innovative ideas and cool analysis of problems. You are especially gifted in making a deal, coordinating the diverse aspects of a project.

How to Work with Others

You work beautifully on a team, where your light sense of humor, friendliness, and ability to express yourself clearly are appreciated. Your position should deal with the public in sales or communications. You are also skilled at office politics. It's all part of the game to you; you rarely get emotionally involved. Let someone else do the record keeping, financial management, or accounting. As a Gemini you can handle a position where you report to several different people or juggle several different assignments, though you may do less well if the job requires intense concentration, patience, and perseverance.

The Gemini Way to Get Ahead

As a Gemini, you bring some important assets to the table, such as your ability to think on your feet, to act quickly, and to get results. It's up to you to decide how to best utilize your talents and abilities to bring you the very highest return on the investment of your time and energy. Look for a job with plenty of variety and mental stimulation. Play up these attributes:

- Verbal and written communication skills
- Ability to handle several tasks at once
- Charm and sociability
- Manual dexterity
- Ability to learn quickly
- Analytical ability

CHAPTER 20

Learn from Gemini Celebrities

You know how much fun it is when you find a famous person who shares your sun sign—and even your birthday! Why not turn your brush with fame into an education in astrology? Celebrities who capture the media's attention reflect the current planetary influences, as well as the unique star quality of their sun sign. Who's in this year may be out next year. You can learn from the hottest stellar spotlight stealers what the public is responding to and what this says about our current values.

If one of your famous sign mates intrigues you, explore his personality further by looking up his other planets using the tables in this book. You may even find his horoscope posted on astrology-related Internet sites likd www.astrodatabank. com or www.stariq.com, which have charts of world events and headline makers. Then apply the effects of Venus, Mars, Saturn, and Jupiter to his sun-sign traits. It's a way to get up close and personal with your famous friend, and maybe learn some secrets not revealed to the public.

You're sure to have lots in common with your famous sign mates. Consider how Paul McCartney, Donald Trump, and Naomi Campbell have handled scandal and reinvented themselves. Do you have Gemini's way with words, like Bill Moyers, John F. Kennedy, and Joan Rivers? There are caring Geminis whose lives can inspire you to crusade for worthy causes, like Anderson Cooper and Angelina Jolie.

Get to know these famous Geminis better and learn what makes their stars shine brightly.

Gemini Celebrities

Raymond Burr (5/21/17)
Laurence Olivier (5/22/1907)
Naomi Campbell (5/22/70)
Douglas Fairbanks (5/23/1883)
Drew Carey (5/23/58)
Bob Dylan (5/24/41)
Priscilla Presley (5/24/45)
Roseanne Cash (5/24/50)
Kristin Scott-Thomas (5/24/60)
Dixie Carter (5/25/39)
Sir Ian McKellen (5/25/39)
Connie Sellecca (5/25/55)
Mike Myers (5/25/63)
Anne Heche (5/25/69)
Lauryn Hill (5/25/75)
John Wayne (5/26/1907)
Peggy Lee (5/26/20)
Miles Davis (5/26/26)
Stevie Nicks (5/26/48)
Lenny Kravitz (5/26/64)
Helena Bonham-Carter (5/26/66)
Vincent Price (5/27/11)
Henry Kissinger (5/27/23)
Tony Hillerman (5/27/25)
Louis Gossett, Jr. (5/27/36)
Siouxie Sioux (5/27/57)
Joseph Fiennes (5/27/70)
Paul Bethany (5/27/71)
Gladys Knight (5/28/44)
Rudolph Giuliani (5/28/44)
Kylie Minogue (5/28/68)
Bob Hope (5/29/1903)
John F. Kennedy (5/29/17)
Kevin Conway (5/29/42)
Anthony Geary (5/29/47)
Annette Bening (5/29/58)
Rupert Everett (5/29/59)
Benny Goodman (5/30/1909)

Prince Rainier (5/31/23)
Clint Eastwood (5/31/30)
Peter Yarrow (5/31/38)
Sharon Gless (5/31/43)
Tom Berenger (5/31/50)
Joe Namath (5/31/50)
Lea Thompson (5/31/61)
Brooke Shields (5/31/65)
Colin Farrell (5/31/76)
Andy Griffith (6/1/26)
Marilyn Monroe (6/1/26)
Edward Woodward (6/1/30)
Pat Boone (6/1/34)
Morgan Freeman (6/1/37)
Rene Auberjonois (6/1/40)
Jonathan Pryce (6/1/47)
Ron Wood (6/1/47)
Heidi Klum (6/1/73)
Alanis Morissette (6/1/74)
Hedda Hopper (6/2/1890)
Sally Kellerman (6/2/37)
Stacey Keach (6/2/41)
Marvin Hamlisch (6/2/44)
Tony Curtis (6/3/25)
Curtis Mayfield (6/3/42)
Deniece Williams (6/3/51)
Anderson Cooper (6/3/67)
Dr. Ruth Westheimer (6/4/28)
Bruce Dern (6/4/36)
Michelle Phillips (6/4/44)
Parker Stevenson (6/4/52)
Angelina Jolie (6/4/75)
Bar Rafaeli (6/4/85)
Bill Moyers (6/5/34)
Mark Wahlberg (6/5/71)
Sandra Bernhard (6/6/55)
Jessica Tandy (6/7/1909)
James Ivory (6/7/28)
Tom Jones (6/7/40)
Liam Neeson (6/7/52)

Prince (6/7/58)
Anna Kournikova (6/7/81)
Barbara Bush (6/8/25)
Joan Rivers (6/8/33)
Kathy Baker (6/8/50)
Juliana Margulies (6/8/66)
Kanye West (6/8/77)
Cole Porter (6/9/1892)
Helena Rubenstein (6/9/1892)
Charles Saatchi (6/9/43)
Michael J. Fox (6/9/61)
Johnny Depp (6/9/63)
Natalie Portman (6/9/81)
Prince Philip (6/10/21)
Lionel Jeffries (6/10/26)
Grace Mirabella (6/10/30)
Elizabeth Hurley (6/10/65)
Tara Lipinski (6/10/82)
Gene Wilder (6/11/35)
Chad Everett (6/11/37)
Adrienne Barbeau (6/11/45)
Shia LeBoeuf (6/11/86)
George Bush (6/12/24)
Timothy Busfield (6/12/57)
Basil Rathbone (6/13/1892)
Christo (6/13/35)
Tim Allen (6/13/53)
Ashley and Mary Kate Olsen (6/13/86)
Donald Trump (6/14/46)
Boy George (6/14/61)
Steffi Graf (6/14/69)
Mario Cuomo (6/15/32)
Waylon Jennings (6/15/37)
Helen Hunt (6/15/63)
Courteney Cox Arquette (6/15/64)
Corin Redgrave (6/16/39)
Sonia Braga (6/16/50)
Yasmine Bleeth (6/16/68)
Dean Martin (6/17/17)
Joe Piscopo (6/17/51)

Jason Patric (6/17/66)
E. G. Marshall (6/18/10)
Roger Ebert (6/18/42)
Paul McCartney (6/18/42)
Isabella Rossellini (6/18/52)
Gena Rowlands (6/19/34)
Phylicia Rashad (6/19/48)
Kathleen Turner (6/19/54)
Paula Abdul (6/19/63)
Danny Aiello (6/20/33)
Lionel Richie (6/20/40)
John Goodman (6/20/52)
Cyndi Lauper (6/20/53)
Nicole Kidman (6/20/67)

CHAPTER 21

Your Gemini Relationships with Every Other Sign: The Green Lights and Red Flags

Are you looking for insight into a relationship? Perhaps it's someone you've met online, a new business partner, a roommate, or the proverbial stranger across a crowded room. After an initial attraction, you may be wondering if you'll still get along down the line. Or why supposedly incompatible signs sometimes have magical attraction to each other. If things aren't working out, astrology could give you some clues as to why he or she is "not that into you."

Astrology has no magic formula for success in love, but it does offer a better understanding of the qualities each person brings to the relationship and how your partner is likely to react to your sun-sign characteristics. Knowing your potential partner's sign and how it relates to yours could give you some clues about what to expect down the line.

There is also the issue of the timing of a new relationship. From an astrological perspective, the people you meet at any given time provide the dynamic that you require at that moment. If you're a gadabout Gemini, you might benefit from the financial savvy and practical wisdom of a down-to-earth sign like Capricorn or Taurus at a certain time in your life.

The celebrity couples in this chapter can help you visualize each sun-sign combination. You'll note that some legendary lovers have stood the test of time, while others blazed, then broke up, and still others existed only in the fantasy world of film or television (but still captured our imagination). Traditional astrological wisdom holds that signs of the same element are naturally compatible. For Gemini, that would be fellow air signs Libra and Aquarius. Also favored are signs of complementary elements, such as air signs with fire signs (Aries, Leo, Sagittarius). In these relationships communication supposedly flows easily, and you'll feel most comfortable together.

As you read the following matches, remember that there are no hard-and-fast rules; each combination has perks as well as peeves. So when sparks fly and an irresistible magnetic pull draws you together, when disagreements and challenges fuel intrigue, mystery, passion, and sexy sparring matches, don't rule the relationship out. That person may provide the diversity, excitement, and challenge you need for an unforgettable romance, a stimulating friendship, or a successful business partnership!

Gemini/Aries

THE GREEN LIGHTS:

There is fast-paced action here. Gemini gets a charge of excitement. Aries gets constant changes to keep up with. Both are spontaneous, optimistic, and energetic. Differences of opinion only keep the atmosphere stimulating.

THE RED FLAGS:

Juggling life with you could have Aries seeing double. Aries is direct and to the point, but Gemini can't or won't be pinned down. This hyperactive combination could get on both your nerves unless you give each other plenty of space. Gemini, tone down the flirting. Aries must be number one!

SIGN MATES:

Gemini Annette Bening and Aries Warren Beatty

Gemini/Taurus

THE GREEN LIGHTS:

The sign next door can be your best friend as well as lover. In this case, you drag Taurus out of the house and into social life, adding laughter to love. Taurus has a soothing, stabilizing quality that supports your restlessness and allows you to be more creative than ever.

THE RED FLAGS:

Homebody Taurus usually wants one-on-one relations, while social Gemini loves to flirt with a crowd. You will have to curb roving eyes and bodies and plan to spend more time at home, which might cramp your style and leave you gasping for air. Infidelity can be serious business with Taurus, but taken lightly by Gemini. The line between freedom and license swings and sways here. You could feel Taurus is holding you back.

SIGN MATES:

Gemini Liam Neeson and Taurus Natasha Richardson
Gemini Steffi Graf and Taurus Andre Agassi
Gemini Anna Kournikova and Taurus Enrique Iglesias
Gemini Donald and Taurus Melania Trump

Gemini/Gemini

THE GREEN LIGHTS:

When Gemini twins find each other, you know you'll never be bored. There is enough multifaceted mental activity, games, and delightful social life to double your pleasure. Your partner will understand the complexities of your sign as only a fellow Gemini can.

THE RED FLAGS:

When the realities of life hit, you may go off in four directions at once. This combination lacks focus. It functions best in a light, creative atmosphere where there are no financial concerns. Serious practical problems could split your personalities and send you running elsewhere for protection and guidance.

SIGN MATES:

Twins Mary Kate and Ashley Olsen

Gemini/Cancer

THE GREEN LIGHTS:

This is a very public pair with charisma to spare. Your sparkling wit sets off Cancer poise with the perfect light touch. Cancer adds warmth and caring to Gemini. This sign's shrewd insight can make your ideas happen. You can go places together!

THE RED FLAGS:

It's not easy for Gemini to deliver the kind of devotion Cancer needs. There are too many other exciting options. Nor do you react well to the Cancer need to mother you or to Cancer pleas for sympathy. Their up-and-down moods get on your nerves. Why can't they learn to laugh away their troubles or to find new interests? When Cancer clings, Gemini does a vanishing act. You need to have strong mutual interests or projects to hold this combo together. But it has been done!

SIGN MATES:

Gemini Michael J. Fox and Cancer Tracy Pollan
Gemini Nicole Kidman and Cancer Tom Cruise

Gemini/Leo

THE GREEN LIGHTS:

Gemini good humor, ready wit, and social skills delight and complement Leo. Here is someone who can share the spotlight without trying to steal the show from the regal Lion. This is one of the most entertaining combinations. Steady Leo provides the focus Gemini often lacks, and directs the Twins toward achieving goals and status.

THE RED FLAGS:

Gemini loves to flirt and flit among many interests, romantic and otherwise. This is sure to irritate the Lion, who does one thing at a time and does it well. Gemini might be a bit bored with Leo self-promotion, and might poke fun at this sign's notorious vanity. The resulting feline roar will be no laughing matter!

SIGN MATES:

Gemini President J.F.K. and Leo Jacqueline Kennedy

Gemini/Virgo

THE GREEN LIGHTS:

You are both Mercury-ruled, and your deepest bond will be mental communication and appreciation of each other's intelligence. The Virgo Mercury is earthbound and analytical, while the Gemini Mercury is a jack-of-all-trades. Gemini shows Virgo the big picture; Virgo takes care of the details. Your combined talents make a stimulating partnership. Virgo becomes the administrator here, Gemini the idea person.

THE RED FLAGS:

Your different priorities can be irritating to each other. Virgo needs a sense of order. Gemini needs to experiment and is forever the gadabout. An older Gemini who has slowed down somewhat makes the best partner here.

SIGN MATES:

Gemini Courteney Cox and Virgo David Arquette

Gemini/Libra

THE GREEN LIGHTS:

Air signs Gemini and Libra have both mental and physical rapport. This is an outgoing combination, full of good talk. You'll never be bored. Libra's good looks and charm, as well as fine mind, could keep restless Gemini close to home.

THE RED FLAGS:

Both of you have a low tolerance for boredom and practical chores. The question of who will provide, do the dirty work, and clean up can be the subject of many a debate. There could be more talk than action here, leaving you turning elsewhere for substance.

SIGN MATES:

Tiger tamers Gemini Siegfried Fischbacher and Libra Roy Horn

Gemini/Scorpio

THE GREEN LIGHTS:

You're a fascinating mystery to each other. Gemini is immune from Scorpio paranoia, laughs away dark moods, and matches wits in power games. Scorpio intensity, focus, and sexual magnetism draw Gemini like a moth to a flame. You're intrigued by Scorpio secrets. Here's a puzzle that would be fun to solve!

And steamy Scorpio brings intensity and a new level of thrills to your sex life.

THE RED FLAGS:

Scorpio gets heavy, possessive, and jealous, which Gemini doesn't take seriously. To make this one last, Gemini needs to treat Scorpio like the one and only, while Scorpio must use a light touch, and learn not to take Gemini flirtations to heart.

SIGN MATES:

Gemini Prince Rainier and Scorpio Grace Kelly
Gemini Nicole Kidman and Scorpio Keith Urban

Gemini/Sagittarius

THE GREEN LIGHTS:

These polar opposites shake each other up happily. Sagittarius helps Gemini see higher truths, to look beyond the life of the party and the art of the deal. Gemini adds mental challenge and flexibility to Sagittarius.

THE RED FLAGS:

Gemini pokes holes in Sagittarius theories. Sagittarius can brand Gemini as a superficial party animal. Work toward developing nonthreatening, nonjudgmental communication. However, you can't talk away practical financial realities. You need a carefully thought-out program to make things happen.

SIGN MATES:

Gemini Marilyn Monroe and Sagittarius Joe DiMaggio
Gemini Angelina Jolie and Sagittarius Brad Pitt

Gemini/Capricorn

THE GREEN LIGHTS:

Capricorn benefits from the Gemini abstract point of view and lighthearted sense of fun. Gemini shows Capricorn how to enjoy the rewards of hard work. Support and structure are Capricorn gifts to Gemini. (Taking that literally, Capricorn Howard Hughes designed the famous bra that supported Gemini sexpot Jane Russell's physical assets!)

THE RED FLAGS:

Capricorn can be ultraconservative and tightfisted with money, which Gemini will not appreciate. The Gemini free-spirited, fun-loving attitude could grate against the Capricorn driving ambition. Gemini will have to learn to take responsibility and to produce solid results.

SIGN MATES:

Gemini Kylie Minogue and Capricorn Olivier Martinez

Gemini/Aquarius

THE GREEN LIGHTS:

In this open and spontaneous relationship, the pressure's off. You two air signs have room to breathe freely. At the same time, you can count on each other for friendship, understanding, and mental stimulation plus highly original romantic ideas. You'll keep each other entertained, and your love life will be fresh and stimulating.

THE RED FLAGS:

Be sure to leave time in your busy schedule for each other. If there is no commitment, you could both fly off. A sharing of causes, projects, or careers could hold you together.

Gemini Lisa Hartman and Aquarius Clint Black

Gemini/Pisces

THE GREEN LIGHTS:

You are both dual personalities in mutable, freedom-loving signs. You fascinate each other with ever-changing facets. You keep each other from straying by providing constant variety and new experiments to try together.

THE RED FLAGS:

At some point, you'll need a frame of reference for this relationship to hold together. Since neither likes structure, this could be a problem. Overstimulation is another monster that can rise to the surface. Pisces sensitive feelings and Gemini hyperactive nerves could send each other searching for more soothing, stabilizing alternatives.

SIGN MATES:

Gemini Donald Trump and Pisces Ivana Trump

CHAPTER 22

The Big Picture for Gemini in 2010

Welcome to 2010! You'll be working hard this year, but you will reap some terrific benefits as well. You'll need diplomacy to solve problems and meet challenges, particularly in the work arena. However, with your gift of gab and ability to engage anyone in a conversation, this shouldn't be a hurdle for you.

Your ruler, Mercury, begins the year in retrograde motion. Venus begins the year in Capricorn, in your eighth house. Granted, it's not the most auspicious of beginnings for a New Year, but on January 15 Mercury turns direct again, and it's suddenly easier to obtain a mortgage or loan. Your partner's income starts evening out as well. Check later in this overview section about other Mercury retrogrades this year and the areas of your chart they will impact.

Mars, the planet that symbolizes your sexuality and aggression, begins the year retrograde in Leo, your third house, and turns direct again on March 10. Until then, there may be disagreements and heated discussions with relatives as well as with neighbors. After March 10, you may be doing more traveling than usual, and you could get involved in some sort of community or neighborhood project. Mars will be in an excellent aspect to your sun, adding fuel and a certain flamboyance to your communication abilities. Mars makes it through six signs this year.

On January 13, Saturn turns retrograde in Libra, your fifth house, then moves back into Virgo and returns to Libra on July 21. While it's in Virgo, it urges you to meet your obligations concerning your home, parents, and family. You may be taking on additional responsibility at home, perhaps because of a family member who needs your help and support. While in Libra, where it will be for two and a half years, everything you do for fun and pleasure becomes a bit more structured. Instead of taking off on a whim for some exotic port, for example, you'll plan the trip. If you have children, you'll become more structured in your relationship with them; you will be setting up rules and restrictions. Even your creative work will change during the next two and a half years. You'll become more disciplined in your approach to your creative endeavors and set up a firm schedule for doing your work. Your network of friends and social acquaintances will be beneficial in terms of your creativity and in what you do for pleasure.

Pluto, the planet of profound transformation, continues its long journey through Capricorn, your eighth house, and keeps bringing about changes in resources that you share with others. Your partner or spouse could come into a windfall of money—or his or her finances may plunge. None of this will happen overnight, because Pluto will be in Capricorn until 2024. During the course of its long transit, your shared resources will undergo permanent transformation. Your interest in metaphysics will deepen too.

Pluto turns retrograde on April 6 and doesn't turn direct again until September 13. During this retrograde period, pay close attention to everything that happens concerning mortgages, loans, insurance, and taxes. Follow synchronicities; listen to your intuition.

Neptune—the planet that symbolizes our illusions, idealism, all forms of escapism, and our higher selves—continues its journey through Aquarius and your ninth house. Neptune has been in this position since 1998, so by now you're well aware of how it impacts professional matters. When it turns retrograde between May 31 and November 6, any dealings you have with education, publishing, or even foreign travel and foreigners may not be functioning quite as smoothly as usual. But you'll be injecting plenty of compassion and idealism into your career.

Uranus, the planet that symbolizes our individualism and sudden and unexpected change enters Aries on May 27 for a period of about seven years. Check your birth chart to find out exactly what area of your life will be affected by this transit. That area will experience sudden, unexpected change, new and exciting experiences, and insights. Uranus's job is to shake up the status quo and get us out of the comfortable ruts into which we often fall. The best way to navigate this seven-year transit is to embrace change. Try new things, go back to school, find a new career path, change jobs, and do whatever you feel will expand your universe and help you to evolve and achieve your potential. This transit should benefit you, because it will be forming a harmonious angle with your sun.

Uranus turns retrograde on July 5 and doesn't turn direct again until December 5. During this period, it retrogrades back into Pisces, your tenth house, and stirs up old issues with your career that you thought were resolved.

Jupiter, the planet of expansion and luck, enters Pisces and your tenth house on January 17, then speeds through it without any retrogrades and enters Aries on June 6. On July 23, it turns retrograde, slips back into Pisces in early September, and remains there throughout the rest of the year. It enters Aries again in late January 2011, where it remains until early June 2011. So look for expansion and good luck generally in your career, with friends, and in terms of your wishes and dreams for yourself. If you have a copy of your natal chart, by all means check to see where both Pisces and Aries fall in your chart. This will tell you a great deal about the specific area of your life where expansion is occurring.

Romance and Creativity

There are two notable time periods this year that favor romance and creative endeavors. Between April 25 and May 19, Venus will be in your sign. This transit increases your sex appeal, charisma, and general self-confidence. If you're uninvolved when the transit begins, you probably won't be when the transit ends. Venus in your sign accentuates all your normal traits and characteristics. If you get involved under this transit, your passions will be running the show! But because you're a Gemini who lives so much in your head, seduction for you always begins with the mind. You must be able to communicate with your partner.

The second great time period for romance falls between August 6 and September 8, when Venus is in fellow air sign Libra, transiting your fifth house of romance and creativity. This period should be very romantic if you're already involved and incredibly exciting if you're just getting involved. It's also a creative time, when your muse is so up close and personal that you feel you simply have to do something creative. So dust off those manuscripts and portfolios!

However, Venus will be retrograde between October 8 and November 18. A few bumps and bruises in relationship and creative endeavors could result.

Career

The best career dates this year occur when Venus transits your tenth house and Pisces—from February 11 to March 7. Also, great backup dates for making sales pitches, selling manuscripts, scheduling auditions, and just about any other professional endeavor fall between January 1 and May 27, while Uranus is making its final passage (except for retrogrades) through Pisces.

Another great time falls around the new moon in Gemini on June 12. This moon happens just once a year and sets the tone for the next year. Neptune forms a wide but harmonious angle to this moon, indicating that your ideals will play a major part in the year's events. This new moon should usher in many new opportunities in your personal life as well.

Best Times For

Buying or selling a home: July 10 to August 6, when Venus transits Virgo and your fourth house.

Family reunions: June 14 to August 6.

Financial matters: May 19 to June 14.

Signing contracts: When Mercury is moving direct!

Overseas travel, publishing, and higher-education endeavors: January 18 to February 11.

Mercury Retrogrades

Every year, Mercury—the planet of communication and travel—turns retrograde three times. During this period, it's wise not to sign contracts (unless you don't mind renegotiating when Mercury is moving direct), to check and recheck travel plans, and to communicate as succinctly as possible. Refrain from buying any big-ticket items or electronics during this time too. Often, computers and appliances go on the fritz, cars act up, data is lost—you get the idea. Be sure to back up all files before the dates below:

April 17–May 11: Mercury retrograde in Taurus. Old friends may surface, you may be dealing with issues from the past or from another life that you thought were resolved.

August 20–September 12: Mercury retrograde in Virgo, your fourth house of the home, family, parents. Communication snafus can be mitigated by communicating clearly and succinctly.

December 10–December 30: Mercury retrograde in Capricorn, your eighth house of shared resources.

Eclipses

Solar eclipses tend to trigger external events that bring about change according to the sign and the house in which they fall. Lunar eclipses trigger inner, emotional events according to the sign and house in which they fall. Any eclipse marks both beginnings and endings. The solar and lunar eclipse in a pair falls in opposite signs.

If you were born under or around the time of an eclipse, it's to your advantage to take a look at your birth chart to find out exactly where the eclipses will impact you.

Most years feature four eclipses—two solar and two lunar, with the set separate by about two weeks. In 2009, there was a lunar eclipse in Cancer on December 31, so the first eclipse in 2010 is a solar eclipse in the opposite sign, Capricorn. Below are the dates for this year's eclipses:

January 15: solar, Capricorn, your eighth house. Events concerning the affairs of this house—shared resources, metaphysics. Venus is also close to the eclipse degree, adding a protective quality.

June 26: lunar, Capricorn. Your eighth house is hit again. Emotions are stirred concerning the areas mentioned above.

July 11: solar, Cancer, your second house. External events concerning your finances and values.

December 21: lunar, Gemini, your first house. This one impacts your personal life.

Luckiest Day of the Year

There's at least one day a year when the sun and Jupiter link up in some way. This year, March 2 looks to be that day, with a nice backup on July 26.

Now let's find out what's in store for you, day by day.

CHAPTER 23

Eighteen Months of Day-by-Day Predictions: July 2009 to December 2010

Moon sign times are calculated for Eastern Standard Time and Eastern Daylight Time. Please adjust for your local time zone.

JULY 2009

Wednesday, July 1 (Moon in Libra to Scorpio 1:20 a.m.) Uranus goes retrograde in your tenth house today. You could display some erratic behavior. An offbeat approach to your career could result in confusion and delays. You tend to follow your own path, in spite of what others think.

Thursday, July 2 (Moon in Scorpio) The moon is in your sixth house today. Service to others is the theme of your day. You could be feeling somewhat emotionally repressed regarding your daily work. Don't let your fears hold you back. Help others where you can, but attend to your own concerns as well. Keep your resolutions about exercise.

Friday, July 3 (Moon in Scorpio to Sagittarius 11:12 a.m.) Mercury moves into your second house today. It's a good day for coming up with moneymaking ideas. You're focusing on your personal finances, and you're quick on your mental toes now. The focus is more material than intellectual. You get your ideas across.

Saturday, July 4 (Moon in Sagittarius)   The moon is in your seventh house today. You fit in well anywhere now. Cooperation is highlighted. Don't make waves; just go with the flow. Loved ones and partners are more important than usual. A contact could play a role.

Sunday, July 5 (Moon in Sagittarius to Capricorn 11:08 p.m.)   Venus moves into your first house. You're sensitive to the moods of others; you try to keep everyone in balance around you. You're good at developing friendships and making contact with old friends. You could also be looking or wishing for an expensive luxury item that will make your life easier.

Monday, July 6 (Moon in Capricorn)   The moon is in your eighth house today. If you are planning on making a major purchase, be sure that you and your partner are in agreement. Otherwise, you could encounter intense emotional resistance. Sex issues may play a role. Alternately, you explore mysteries of life, including past lives.

Tuesday, July 7 (Moon in Capricorn)   There's a lunar eclipse in your eighth house today. You have a strong emotional reaction related to a lover or partner, especially if it deals with shared belongings. Anything related to sex, death, rituals, and relationships may play a big role in your day.

Wednesday, July 8 (Moon in Capricorn to Aquarius 12:04 p.m.)   It's a number 2 day. A partnership plays an important role in your day. Family members are more important now. Be kind and understanding. There could be some soul-searching related to a relationship, but don't make waves. Just go with the flow.

Thursday, July 9 (Moon in Aquarius)   The moon is in your ninth house today. You could be launching a long trip or at least dreaming of one. You feel good about pursuing higher learning now. Ideas, philosophies, religion, and art interest you. A foreign country or a foreign-born person could play a role.

Friday, July 10 (Moon in Aquarius) It's a number 4 day. Control your impulses today. Take care of your obligations. Don't get sloppy. Emphasize quality. You're building a creative base for your future. Some hard work is required. Be methodical and thorough.

Saturday, July 11 (Moon in Aquarius to Pisces 12:44 a.m.) Mars moves into your first house today. Following up on yesterday's challenges, you are quite assertive now, letting others know exactly what you think and how you feel. You're more outgoing and aggressive. Others see you as ambitious. You see that your thoughts and feelings are aligned.

Sunday, July 12 (Moon in Pisces) The moon is in your tenth house today. Your career is about to take a new turn. You could gain a boost in your prestige now. You're well regarded by fellow workers; your warmth toward them is appreciated. Avoid any emotional displays in public.

Monday, July 13 (Moon in Pisces to Aries 11:40 a.m.) It's a number 7 day. Secrets, intrigue, and confidential information play a role. Investigate activities taking place behind closed doors. You work best on your own today. Keep your own counsel. Knowledge is essential to success. Gather information, but don't make any absolute decisions until tomorrow.

Tuesday, July 14 (Moon in Aries) The moon is in your eleventh house today. Friends play an important role in your day, especially a Libra and an Aquarius. You get together with a group of like-minded individuals and work toward a common goal. Focus on your wishes and dreams, and make sure that they are still a reflection of who you are.

Wednesday, July 15 (Moon in Aries to Taurus 6:30 p.m.) It's a number 9 day. Follow up on yesterday's energy and use the day for reflection, expansion, and concluding projects. Look beyond the immediate. Visualize the future, set your goals, and get to work. Consider ways to expand; get ready for a fresh start.

Thursday, July 16 (Moon in Taurus)   The moon is in your twelfth house today. You might feel a need to withdraw and work behind the scenes. A troubling matter from the past could rise up. It's a great day for a mystical or spiritual discipline. Your intuition is heightened.

Friday, July 17 (Moon in Taurus to Gemini 11:42 p.m.) Mercury moves into your third house today. There's a lot to communicate after a day of relative solitude. You get your ideas across as you go about your business, but it's more of an intellectual pursuit than an emotional one. You're witty, alert, and adaptable.

Saturday, July 18 (Moon in Gemini)   The moon is on your ascendant today. The way you see yourself is the way others see you. Your face is before the public. You're recharged for the month ahead; this makes you more appealing to the public. You're physically vital, and relations with the opposite sex go well.

Sunday, July 19 (Moon in Gemini)   It's a number 4 day. Stick to practical matters. You're seen as trustworthy and down to earth. Stick with this energy, and avoid trying to please everyone, and you can gain recognition, success, and fame for your hard work.

Monday, July 20 (Moon in Gemini to Cancer 12:52 a.m.) The moon is in your second house today. Money and material goods are important to you now and give you a sense of security. You may be dealing with payments and collecting what's owed to you. Look at your priorities in handling your income. Expect emotional experiences related to money.

Tuesday, July 21 (Moon in Cancer)   There's a solar eclipse in your second house today. External events allow you to see matters related to your finances more clearly now. You get a new perspective on something related to your values or possessions. You could decide to handle finances in a new manner.

Wednesday, July 22 (Moon in Cancer to Leo 12:28 a.m.)
The moon is in your third house today. Get in touch with others, especially relatives or neighbors. You'll have some things to talk about. Be careful while driving. Your thinking may be unduly influenced by the past.

Thursday, July 23 (Moon in Leo) It's a number 8 day. It's your power day. Now you can go far with your plans and achieve financial success. Expect a windfall. However, be aware that you're playing with power, so try not to hurt anyone.

Friday, July 24 (Moon in Leo to Virgo 12:24 a.m.) The moon is in your fourth house today. Stay at home or work at home, if possible. Your intuition is highlighted. Spend time with your family and loved ones. But also find time to focus inward in quiet meditation.

Saturday, July 25 (Moon in Virgo) It's another good day to stick close to home. Tidy the house, tie up loose ends, and attend to details. Take time to write in a journal. You can write from a deep place now with lots of details and colorful descriptions. Pay attention to any health concerns.

Sunday, July 26 (Moon in Virgo to Libra 2:26 a.m.) It's a number 2 day. It's all about working together. Partnerships are highlighted. Cooperation is stressed. Don't make waves now. Go with the flow.

Monday, July 27 (Moon in Libra) The moon is in your fifth house. Be yourself. Follow your heart related to a relationship. It's also an especially good day for pursuing a creative project or for spending time with children.

Tuesday, July 28 (Moon in Libra to Scorpio 7:57 a.m.) It's a number 4 day. Tear down the old in order to rebuild. Be methodical and thorough. Revise and rewrite. You're in the right place at the right time. Missing papers or a lost object is recovered.

Wednesday, July 29 (Moon in Scorpio) The moon is in your sixth house today. It's a service day. Help others who are relying on you. Do a good deed. Take care of any health issues. Make any medical appointments that you've been putting off.

Thursday, July 30 (Moon in Scorpio to Sagittarius 5:10 p.m.) It's a number 6 day. Yesterday's energy related to service continues into your Thursday. Diplomacy wins the way. Be sympathetic, kind, and tolerant. Avoid confrontations. Try to make other people happy.

Friday, July 31 (Moon in Sagittarius) Venus moves into your second house today. Bolster your finances. You can make money through the arts now. Watch your spending. You could be feeling somewhat extravagant in your desires to purchase a luxury item.

AUGUST 2009

Saturday, August 1 (Moon in Sagittarius) The moon is in your seventh house. Loved ones and partners are more important than usual. You're dealing with partnerships, personal and business. Be careful that others don't manipulate your feelings. A legal matter comes to your attention.

Sunday, August 2 (Moon in Sagittarius to Capricorn 5:09 a.m.) Mercury moves into your fourth house today. You're doing your homework related to an intellectual pursuit. You study hard to prepare yourself for a test of some sort. Alternately, you could be exploring the details of a real-estate matter.

Monday, August 3 (Moon in Capricorn) The moon is in your eighth house. Your experiences could be more intense, especially related to your belongings as well as things that you share. It's a good day for dealing with mortgages, insurance, and investments. An interest in metaphysics could also play a role in your day, especially an exploration of life-after-death questions.

Tuesday, August 4 (Moon in Capricorn to Aquarius 6:08 p.m.)   It's a number 8 day. Business dealings go well. You could pull off a financial coup. You're being watched by people in power. Be courageous and honest. Also, be aware that fear of failure can attract tangible experiences that reinforce the feeling.

Wednesday, August 5 (Moon in Aquarius)   There's a lunar eclipse in your ninth house today. You could experience an emotional reaction to a matter dealing with either long-distance travel or higher education. Friends or a group association could play a role. Make sure your wishes and dreams are compatible with the plans.

Thursday, August 6 (Moon in Aquarius)   The moon is in your ninth house. Yesterday's energy flows into your Thursday. Your mind is active, and you seek new experiences. You can create positive change through your ideas. Any publishing projects go well. A foreign-born person or a foreign country could play a role in your day.

Friday, August 7 (Moon in Aquarius to Pisces 6:35 a.m.)   It's a number 2 day. Cooperation is highlighted. Partnerships are key to your day. You get along well with others. Don't make waves. Don't rush or show resentment. Let things develop.

Saturday, August 8 (Moon in Pisces)   The moon is in your tenth house. Even though it's a weekend, your mind is on your career or professional matters. You get along well with co-workers, possibly during an off-duty activity. Be careful about mixing your personal life with professional matters.

Sunday, August 9 (Moon in Pisces to Aries 5:24 p.m.)   It's a number 4 day. Get organized. Be methodical and thorough.

You're in the right place at the right time. Keep in mind that you're building a creative base for your future.

Monday, August 10 (Moon in Aries)   The moon is in your eleventh house today. Your sense of security is tied to your relationships and to your friends. Focus on your wishes and dreams. Examine your overall goals. Those goals should be an expression of who you are. Social consciousness plays a role. Your interests are so diverse that others might think you lack depth.

Tuesday, August 11 (Moon in Aries)   The moon is in your eleventh house today. You have deeper contact with friends now, especially with a Libra and an Aquarius. You join a group of like-minded individuals to raise social awareness regarding an issue. Follow your wishes and dreams.

Wednesday, August 12 (Moon in Aries to Taurus 1:51 a.m.) It's a number 7 day. You work best on your own. Secrets, intrigue, and confidential information play a role. Knowledge is essential to success. Express your desires, but avoid self-deception. Maintain your emotional balance.

Thursday, August 13 (Moon in Taurus)   The moon is in your twelfth house. Like yesterday, it's a good day to stay out of sight. Work behind the scenes. Avoid public appearances. A matter from the past, possibly from your childhood, could be haunting you. Confide in a close friend you can trust.

Friday, August 14 (Moon in Taurus to Gemini 7:27 a.m.) It's a number 9 day. Complete a project. Clear up odds and ends. Don't start anything new today. Take an inventory on where things are going in your life. Strive for universal appeal.

Saturday, August 15 (Moon in Gemini)   The moon is on your ascendant today. You're feeling physically vital and recharged for the rest of the year. You're assertive and outgoing. Your appearance and personality shine. You get along well with the opposite sex.

Sunday, August 16 (Moon in Gemini to Cancer 10:14 a.m.)   It's a number 2 day. Use your intuition to focus on a relationship issue. Process everything that happened yesterday. Cooperation is highlighted. Be supportive. Don't make waves.

Monday, August 17 (Moon in Cancer)   The moon is in your second house today. It's a good day for finances and money matters. Consider your priorities in spending your income. Put off any big purchases for another few days. Your values play an important role in your day.

Tuesday, August 18 (Moon in Cancer to Leo 10:57 a.m.) It's a number 4 day. Persevere to get things done today. Stay focused. Don't get sloppy. Missing papers or objects are found. You're in the right place at the right time. Like yesterday, be practical with your money.

Wednesday, August 19 (Moon in Leo)   The moon is in your third house today. The focus of your activities is more mental than physical. You communicate your thoughts and ideas well. But make sure you control your emotions. Avoid arguments, especially with relatives. You could receive an invitation to a social event. Neighbors play a role in your day.

Thursday, August 20 (Moon in Leo to Virgo 11:01 a.m.) There's a new moon in your third house today. That means there's some opportunity that's offered to you. It's a doorway to something new. It could relate to a neighbor or relative. You communicate your thoughts well.

Friday, August 21 (Moon in Virgo)   The moon is in your fourth house. You're dealing with the foundations of who you are and who you are becoming. Retreat to a private place for meditation. It's a good day for dream recall. It's best to work on your own and stay focused. It's time to eliminate a bad habit.

Saturday, August 22 (Moon in Virgo to Libra 12:12 p.m.) It's a number 8 day, your power and money day. Unexpected money arrives. It's a good day to play the lottery. Think big; take a risk.

Sunday, August 23 (Moon in Libra)   The moon is in your fifth house today. Take time now to consider your options related to a creative project. There's greater depth now in a romantic relationship. Be emotionally honest. You can go deep inside now for inspiration. Children play a role in your day.

Monday, August 24 (Moon in Libra to Scorpio 4:17 p.m.) It's a number 1 day. You're at the top of your cycle again. You can take the lead on a new project. You get a new beginning. Don't be afraid to turn in a new direction now.

Tuesday, August 25 (Moon in Scorpio)   With Mars moving into your second house today, pursue a tough business matter. You're extremely competitive now. Use your mental abilities to focus on a relationship issue. You sound very convincing, especially related to a creative idea or project.

Wednesday, August 26 (Moon in Scorpio)   Venus moves into your third house. You find harmony, especially when combining the mental and the artistic. You get along well with others in your daily life.

Thursday, August 27 (Moon in Scorpio to Sagittarius 12:16 a.m.)   The moon is in your seventh house. Partners, business and personal, play an important role in your day. You get along well with others. You can fit in just about anywhere. But you are feeling somewhat restless and might be analyzing and reanalyzing a relationship.

Friday, August 28 (Moon in Sagittarius)   You see the big picture, not just the details. Make good use of your sense of humor. Like yesterday, you're feeling restless and impulsive. Spiritual values arise. Worldviews are emphasized. Think abundance.

Saturday, August 29 (Moon in Sagittarius to Capricorn 11:45 a.m.)   It's a number 6 day. It's another service day.

Diplomacy is stressed. Be kind and understanding. Do a good deed for someone. You offer advice and support.

Sunday, August 30 (Moon in Capricorn)   The moon is in your eighth house. You could be dealing with an inheritance or a legacy. Matters related to shared property are on the table. You're sensitive and intuitive; you could take an interest in a metaphysical or spiritual topic, such as life after death.

Monday, August 31 (Moon in Capricorn)   It's a number 8 day. Focus on a power play. Business dealings go well, especially if you open your mind to a new approach. Unexpected money arrives. Remember that you're playing with power, so be careful not to hurt others.

SEPTEMBER 2009

Tuesday, September 1 (Moon in Capricorn to Aquarius 12:43 a.m.)   The moon is in your ninth house. Escape from the usual routine. You're a dreamer and a thinker, but now you're ready for a new experience, and you have the energy to follow through.

Wednesday, September 2 (Moon in Aquarius)   Groups and social events are highlighted today. Your individuality is stressed. Your visionary abilities are heightened. Play your hunches. Look beyond the immediate.

Thursday, September 3 (Moon in Aquarius to Pisces 12:59 p.m.)   It's a number 8 day. Go for it! It's your power day. Take a chance. You attract financial success, especially if you open your mind to a new approach. You pull off a financial coup. A gamble pays off.

Friday, September 4 (Moon in Pisces)   The full moon is in your tenth house. You gain a big boost in prestige related to your profession. You harvest what you've sown. Business dealings go well. Your life is more public than usual. You're more emotional and warm toward coworkers.

Saturday, September 5 (Moon in Pisces to Aries 11:15 p.m.)   It's a number 1 day. You're at the top of your cycle today. Be independent and creative; refuse to be discouraged by naysayers. You're determined and courageous.

Sunday, September 6 (Moon in Aries)   Mercury goes retrograde in your fifth house. That means there could be some miscommunication or misunderstanding with loved ones. A creative project could be stalled. Leave extra time when traveling. Children could be more difficult than usual over the next three weeks. Things will get better!

Monday, September 7 (Moon in Aries)   The moon is in your eleventh house. You work well with others, especially in a group. Friends play an important role. You work for the common good, but don't forget about your own wishes and dreams.

Tuesday, September 8 (Moon in Aries to Taurus 7:19 a.m.) It's a number 4 day. Make good use of your organizational skills. Persevere to get things done. Be methodical and thorough; emphasize quality. Take care of your obligations. Be practical with your money.

Wednesday, September 9 (Moon in Taurus)   The moon is in your twelfth house. You communicate your deepest feelings to a trustworthy friend, but otherwise you keep your thoughts and feelings to yourself. You feel best working behind the scenes. Take time to reflect and meditate.

Thursday, September 10 (Moon in Taurus to Gemini 1:18 p.m.)   It's a number 6 day and another service day. Be generous, tolerant, and diplomatic with those who complain and want more from you. Focus on making people happy. Offer your advice and support, but don't spread yourself too thin.

Friday, September 11 (Moon in Gemini)   Pluto goes direct in your eighth house. You're often analytical, but logic trumps emotions. However, you tend to be obsessive about achieving your goals. If you've been in financial trouble, the picture should start improving. If it's already good, expect even more positive news related to finances.

Saturday, September 12 (Moon in Gemini to Cancer 5:20 p.m.) It's a number 8 day. Yesterday's energy flows into your Saturday. It's your power day, and a good day to open your mind to a new approach. Expect a windfall. You can go far with your plans and achieve financial success. But keep in mind you're playing with power, so be careful not to hurt others.

Sunday, September 13 (Moon in Cancer) The moon is in your second house. The energy of the past two days continues with an emphasis on finances. The overall financial picture takes a turn for the better.

Monday, September 14 (Moon in Cancer to Leo 7:40 p.m.) It's a number 1 day. You're at the top of your cycle again. Get out and meet people and have new experiences. Stress originality. In romance, if you're interested, something is developing.

Tuesday, September 15 (Moon in Leo) The moon is in your third house today. No doubt you're taking care of your everyday needs. Be especially careful when driving. You make your point and get your ideas across. However, control your emotions, especially when talking with relatives or neighbors.

Wednesday, September 16 (Moon in Leo to Virgo 8:56 p.m.) It's a number 3 day. Your charm and wit are appreciated today. Your imagination is keen now. You're curious and inventive. You communicate well, and you're warm and receptive to what others say.

Thursday, September 17 (Moon in Virgo) The moon is in your fourth house. Spend time with your family and loved ones. A parent may play a role. Take time to settle into a quiet place to meditate. You're dealing with the foundations of who you are and who you are becoming.

227

Friday, September 18 (Moon in Virgo to Libra 10:26 p.m.)
There's a new moon in your fourth house. An opportunity
arises related to your home or home life. If you're interested
in moving, you could get an offer on your house. Alternately,
you might find the land or house you've been looking for, or
you find something just right to beautify your home.

Saturday, September 19 (Moon in Libra)   The moon is in
your fifth house. Your emotions tend to overpower your intellect. You're emotionally in touch with your creative side. You
feel strongly attached to loved ones, particularly children. But
eventually you need to let go. Animals play a role.

Sunday, September 20 (Moon in Libra)   Venus moves
into your fourth house. It's a good day for your love life. Stay
home and cuddle with your lover. It's also a good day for the
arts, especially for something that you work on at home.

*Monday, September 21 (Moon in Libra to Scorpio 1:52
a.m.)*   It's a number 8 day. It's your power day. You pull off
a financial coup. Expect a windfall. You're being watched by
people in power. Be courageous. Remember that you're playing with power, so be careful not to hurt others.

Tuesday, September 22 (Moon in Scorpio)   The moon is
in your sixth house. Help others, but don't ignore your own
needs. You're compassionate and sensitive. You tend to think
a lot about whatever you're involved in. Keep your resolutions about exercise; watch your diet.

*Wednesday, September 23 (Moon in Scorpio to Sagittarius
8:44 a.m.)*   It's a number 1 day. You're at the top of your
cycle. Take the lead on a project and don't be afraid to turn in
a new direction. Stress originality. Get out and meet people
and have new experiences. In romance, make room for a new
love, if that's what you want.

Thursday, September 24 (Moon in Sagittarius)   The moon
is in your seventh house. You get along well with others. Cooperation and partnership are emphasized. Go with the flow. Let

things develop on their own. Think of yourself as part of the process. Through a partnership, you become whole. The other half helps you realize your full potential.

Friday, September 25 (Moon in Sagittarius to Capricorn 7:19 p.m.)   It's a number 3 day. You're curious and inventive. Take time to relax. Spread your good news to friends, and listen to their stories. Enjoy the harmony, beauty, and pleasures of life. Expect an invitation.

Saturday, September 26 (Moon in Capricorn)   The moon is in your eighth house. Your experiences are more intense than usual; they could relate to control issues about shared possessions. Best to focus on your sense of stability. You could be dealing with an inheritance, taxes, insurance, or investments. Metaphysical concepts, such as life after death, could play a role.

Sunday, September 27 (Moon in Capricorn)   Your responsibilities increase as a result of events yesterday. You may feel overworked. Self-discipline and structure are key. Other air signs—Libra and Aquarius—play prominent roles. Maintain emotional balance.

Monday, September 28 (Moon in Capricorn to Aquarius 8:07 a.m.)   It's a number 6 day. Focus on making people happy. Be generous and tolerant. Do a good deed. Go to the aid of someone who needs help. A domestic adjustment works out for the best. Diplomacy wins the day, especially with someone who argues or complains.

Tuesday, September 29 (Moon in Aquarius)   Mercury goes direct in your fourth house. That means any confusion and miscommunication that you've been experiencing, especially related to your home life, recede into the past. You get your ideas across. Everything works better, including computers and other electronic equipment.

Wednesday, September 30 (Moon in Aquarius to Pisces 8:27 p.m.)   It's a number 8 day. Focus on a power play. Open your mind to a new approach that could bring in big bucks. Business discussions go well.

OCTOBER 2009

Thursday, October 1 (Moon in Pisces) The moon is in your tenth house today. Your life is more public. It's a good day for sales and dealing with the public. Business is highlighted. You're feeling warm and emotional toward fellow workers. You're more responsive now to their needs.

Friday, October 2 (Moon in Pisces) Imagination is highlighted. Watch for psychic events. Keep track of your dreams, including your daydreams. Ideas are ripe. You're compassionate, sensitive, and inspired. Make good use of your imagination.

Saturday, October 3 (Moon in Pisces to Aries 6:21 a.m.) It's a number 9 day. Finish whatever you've been working on, but don't start anything new today. Clear your desk for a new cycle. Set your goals and get to work. Strive for universal appeal. You're up to the challenge.

Sunday, October 4 (Moon in Aries) There's a full moon in your eleventh house. It's a great time for initiating projects, launching new ideas, and brainstorming, especially with a group of like-minded individuals. Friends play an important role, but emotions could be volatile. You're passionate, but impatient.

Monday, October 5 (Moon in Aries to Taurus 1:34 p.m.) It's a number 2 day. Use your intuition to get a sense of your day. Be kind and understanding. The spotlight is on cooperation. Marriage plays a key role. Show your appreciation to others.

Tuesday, October 6 (Moon in Taurus) The moon is in your twelfth house. You prefer working on your own and keeping your own counsel. You could be holding in anger that you need to deal with openly. Your thinking is influenced by the past and your subconscious mind. It's a great day for a mystical or spiritual discipline. Your intuition is heightened.

Wednesday, October 7 (Moon in Taurus to Gemini 6:47 p.m.) It's a number 4 day. Emphasize quality with whatever you're doing. Be methodical and thorough. Tear down in order to rebuild. Be practical with your money. You may feel inhibited in showing affection.

Thursday, October 8 (Moon in Gemini) The moon is on your ascendant. The way you see yourself is the way others see you. You're recharged for the month ahead; this makes you more appealing to the public. You're physically vital, and relations with the opposite sex go well.

Friday, October 9 (Moon in Gemini to Cancer 10:48 p.m.) It's a number 6 day. It's a service day. Help others where you can, but take care of any health issues. Make a medical appointment that you've been putting off.

Saturday, October 10 (Moon in Cancer) The moon is in your second house. Expect emotional experiences related to money. You identify with your possessions or whatever you value. You feel best when surrounded by familiar objects, especially in your home environment. It's not the objects themselves that are important, but the feelings and memories you associate with them. Put off making any major purchases.

Sunday, October 11 (Moon in Cancer) Yesterday's energy flows into your Sunday. Beautify your home. Take care of home repairs. Snuggle with your loved one. You're somewhat moody and sensitive to other people's moods. It's a good day to spend time near a body of water.

Monday, October 12 (Moon in Cancer to Leo 2:03 a.m.) Jupiter goes direct in your ninth house. You're undergoing an expansion related to higher education or long-distance travel. You're a dreamer and a thinker with big ideas. You're also interested in breaking away from the usual routine.

Tuesday, October 13 (Moon in Leo)   The moon is in your third house. Get your ideas across as you go about your everyday activities. You may be in the car a lot. Stay in conscious control of your emotions. Matters from the past could arise.

Wednesday, October 14 (Moon in Leo to Virgo 4:46 a.m.)   Venus moves into your fifth house today. You feel a strong attraction to the opposite sex. You get along well with children and young people. Any creative talent in the arts is highlighted.

Thursday, October 15 (Moon in Virgo)   The moon is in your fourth house. Don't ignore domestic matters. If possible, stay home or work at home. Find some quiet time for yourself to consider everything that has taken place recently. Family and loved ones play a major role.

Friday, October 16 (Moon in Virgo to Libra 7:30 a.m.)
Mars moves into your third house. You're resourceful as usual. But you might show a sharp edge, an unexpected aggressiveness. Think before you speak, especially around family members. Try to avoid jumping to conclusions before you have all the information.

Saturday, October 17 (Moon in Libra)   The moon is in your fifth house. You're emotionally in touch with your creative side. But you tend to suppress the intellect in favor of emotion. There's greater depth in a relationship, but you could be somewhat possessive of a lover.

Sunday, October 18 (Moon in Libra to Scorpio 11:23 a.m.)
There's a new moon in your fifth house. Yesterday's energy continues with the added possibility of a new creative project coming your way. You feel strongly attached to loved ones, particularly children. Animals play a role.

Monday, October 19 (Moon in Scorpio)   The moon is in your sixth house. It's a service day. You improve, edit, and refine the work of others. Help others, but don't deny your own needs. Keep your resolutions about exercise; watch your diet. Attend to details related to your health.

Tuesday, October 20 (Moon in Scorpio to Sagittarius 5:50 p.m.)   It's a number 8 day. It's a powerful day for finances and making money, especially an unexpected windfall. You have a chance today to gain recognition and fame.

Wednesday, October 21 (Moon in Sagittarius)   The moon is in your seventh house. Personal relations are key to your day. Loved ones and partners are more important than usual. Women, in particular, play a prominent role. It's difficult to remain detached and objective. Be careful that others don't manipulate your feelings.

Thursday, October 22 (Moon in Sagittarius)   You see the big picture. Don't limit yourself. A partner could play a role. There's passion in a relationship, but you feel a sense of wanderlust. Look for ways to grow and expand your base. However, watch your diet, or your waist could also expand!

Friday, October 23 (Moon in Sagittarius to Capricorn 3:40 a.m.)   It's a number 2 day. The energy of the past two days continues. The focus remains on partnerships and cooperation. Use your intuition to get a sense of your day. Be supportive, patient, kind, and understanding.

Saturday, October 24 (Moon in Capricorn)   The moon is in your eighth house. Things tend to get more emotionally intense than usual, especially if you're dealing with shared resources or belongings. You could attract the attention of powerful people. Look into any issues related to taxes, insurance, or investments.

Sunday, October 25 (Moon in Capricorn to Aquarius 3:08 p.m.)   It's a number 4 day. Get everything in order. You can overcome any bureaucratic red tape. You're in the right place at the right time. Emphasize quality. Revise and rewrite. You're building a creative base for your future.

Monday, October 26 (Moon in Aquarius)   The moon is in your ninth house. You're thinking and talking a lot about your philosophy of life, about your ideas on how things should work, about why certain things are happening. You analyze and scrutinize. While you lay it all out for friends or a group, you don't feel much emotional commitment to correcting the situation.

Tuesday, October 27 (Moon in Aquarius)   Like yesterday, friends or a group plays a role in your day. Stress your individuality. Play your hunches. Look beyond the immediate. Find new ways of doing something important. New ideas and options are the rule. Help others, but dance to your own tune.

Wednesday, October 28 (Moon in Aquarius to Pisces 3:46 a.m.)   Mercury moves into your sixth house. You're methodical and thorough in dealing with any mental activities. You like everything in order. You communicate well and get your ideas across, especially when you're helping others. Don't forget to speak out about health issues.

Thursday, October 29 (Moon in Pisces)   Any kind of creative effort takes on greater meaning. You're very serious. You could be struggling through a writer's block, but you know you're doing something important. In romance, you could take an interest in an older person.

Friday, October 30 (Moon in Pisces to Aries 1:57 p.m.)   It's a number 9 day. Complete a project. Clear up odds and ends; make room for something new. Get ready for a new cycle. Accept what comes your way, but don't start anything new.

Saturday, October 31 (Moon in Aries)   The moon is in your eleventh house. You might feel a need to withdraw today and work behind the scenes as you initiate something new. A troubling matter from the past could rise up. It's a great day for a mystical or spiritual discipline. Your intuition is heightened. Stress your originality, but avoid naysayers.

Sunday, November 1—Daylight Saving Time Ends (Moon in Aries to Taurus 7:45 p.m.)   It's a number 8 day. Focus on a power play. Business dealings go well, especially if you remain flexible and keep your mind open to an unusual approach. Unexpected money arrives. Keep in mind that you're playing with power, so be careful not to hurt others.

Monday, November 2 (Moon in Taurus)   The full moon is in your twelfth house, which tends to illuminate some hidden issue that you can see clearly. You could be dealing with an issue that relates to a matter from a past life. It's a good day for remembering your dreams.

Tuesday, November 3 (Moon in Taurus to Gemini 11:53 p.m.)   It's a number 1 day. You're at the top of your cycle. You make connections that others overlook. You're determined and courageous. Stress originality. In romance, something new is developing. Refuse to deal with people who have closed minds.

Wednesday, November 4 (Moon in Gemini)   Neptune goes direct in your ninth house. You're highly intuitive; you could take an interest in out-of-the-ordinary beliefs and philosophies. A pursuit of the higher mind or an advanced study of the arts attracts your attention.

Thursday, November 5 (Moon in Gemini)   With the moon on your ascendant, you get recharged for the month ahead, and that makes you more appealing to the public, particularly the opposite sex. You focus on your emotional self. Your thoughts and feelings are aligned.

Friday, November 6 (Moon in Gemini to Cancer 2:43 a.m.) It's a number 4 day. Your organizational skills are emphasized. Tear down in order to rebuild. Hard work is called for. Revise and rewrite. Be practical with your money.

Saturday, November 7 (Moon in Cancer)   Venus moves into your sixth house. You spread your love when you help others now. You feel emotionally attached to the workplace and the people there. Alternately, you could get involved romantically with someone you know from the workplace.

Sunday, November 8 (Moon in Cancer to Leo 5:23 a.m.) It's a number 6 day. A domestic adjustment works out for the best. Be understanding and avoid confrontations. Be aware that you could face emotional outbursts or someone making unfair demands. Diplomacy wins the way.

Monday, November 9 (Moon in Leo) The moon is in your third house. Your communications with others are subjective. Take what you know and share it with others, but control your emotions. That's especially true when dealing with siblings or neighbors. Your thinking could be unduly influenced by the past.

Tuesday, November 10 (Moon in Leo to Virgo 8:31 a.m.) It's a number 8 day again. It's your power day. You attract financial success. Business discussions go well. Be courageous. You have a chance to gain recognition and fame.

Wednesday, November 11 (Moon in Virgo) The moon is in your fourth house. Stay close to home. Work at home, if possible. Spend time with your family and loved ones. Get out and enjoy the fall, or beautify your home.

Thursday, November 12 (Moon in Virgo to Libra 12:23 p.m.) It's a number 1 day. You get a new beginning. Be independent and creative; refuse to be discouraged by naysayers. Stress originality. In romance, a flirtation turns more serious.

Friday, November 13 (Moon in Libra) The moon is in your fifth house. You're emotionally in touch with your creative side. You love what you're doing. You're more protective and nurturing toward children. Animals play a role. Your emotions tend to overpower your intellect.

Saturday, November 14 (Moon in Libra to Scorpio 5:25 p.m.) It's a number 3 day. Your popularity is on the rise.

Your imagination is keen. You're curious and inventive. You communicate well. You're warm and receptive to what others say. Remain flexible.

Sunday, November 15 (Moon in Scorpio)   As Mercury moves into your seventh house, the energy from your Saturday expands. You tend to spend time with creative, witty, and well-spoken people. You get along well with others and can resolve any disagreements.

Monday, November 16 (Moon in Scorpio)   There's a new moon in your sixth house. An opportunity arises, especially one related to service work. You get a fresh start. Make sure you take care of any health needs. Proper diet and exercise are key.

Tuesday, November 17 (Moon in Scorpio to Sagittarius 12:23 a.m.)   It's a number 6 day. Yesterday's energy flows into your Tuesday as your service to others is highlighted. Do a good deed for someone. Focus on making people happy! Be sympathetic, kind, and compassionate. Your advice and assistance will be appreciated.

Wednesday, November 18 (Moon in Sagittarius)   The moon is in your seventh house. Partnerships, both personal and business, are highlighted. You get along well with others. You can fit in just about anywhere. A legal matter comes to your attention.

Thursday, November 19 (Moon in Sagittarius to Capricorn 10:01 a.m.)   It's a number 8 day. Focus on a power play. Money matters go well. Expect a windfall. You attract financial success, especially if you open your mind to a new approach.

Friday, November 20 (Moon in Capricorn)   The moon is in your eighth house. Your experiences are more emotionally intense than usual. You could be dealing with a matter concerning shared resources or possessions. Security is an important issue with you. Alternately, an interest in metaphysics plays a role in your day. You could be dealing with a mystery.

Saturday, November 21 (Moon in Capricorn to Aquarius 10:11 p.m.) It's a number 1 day. You're at the top of your cycle. You get a fresh start. Don't be afraid to turn in a new direction. Trust your hunches. Intuition is highlighted. You're inventive. You're determined and courageous. Stress originality.

Sunday, November 22 (Moon in Aquarius) The moon is in your ninth house. You may feel a need to get away. You yearn for a new experience.

Monday, November 23 (Moon in Aquarius) Your individuality is stressed. Your visionary abilities are heightened. Play your hunches. Look beyond the immediate. You get a new perspective on life.

Tuesday, November 24 (Moon in Aquarius to Pisces 11:08 a.m.) It's a number 4 day. Control your impulses to wander off course. Stay focused. Persevere to get things done. Fulfill your obligations. You're building foundations for an outlet for your creativity.

Wednesday, November 25 (Moon in Pisces) The moon is in your tenth house. Professional concerns are the focus. You could get a promotion. You're emotional and warm toward coworkers. Your life is more public.

Thursday, November 26 (Moon in Pisces to Aries 10:11 p.m.) It's a number 6 day. It's another service day. Diplomacy is called for in dealing with others, especially someone who might make unfair demands on your time. An adjustment in your domestic life may be necessary.

Friday, November 27 (Moon in Aries) The moon is in your eleventh house. You find strength in numbers and meaning through friends and groups. Work for the common good, but keep an eye on your own wishes and dreams. A Libra and an Aquarius play a role in your day.

Saturday, November 28 (Moon in Aries) It's a great time for initiating projects, launching new ideas, and brainstorming. Emotions can be volatile. You're passionate, but impatient. Imprint your style. Wear bright colors. Avoid reckless behavior.

Sunday, November 29 (Moon in Aries to Taurus 5:35 a.m.) It's a number 9 day. Complete a project. Clear up odds and ends. Take an inventory on where things are going in your life. It's a good day to make a donation to a worthy cause. Use the day for reflection, expansion, and concluding projects, but don't start anything new.

Monday, November 30 (Moon in Taurus) The moon is in your twelfth house. Work behind the scenes. Start something new, but keep it to yourself for now. You're sensitive.

DECEMBER 2009

Tuesday, December 1 (Moon in Taurus to Gemini 9:24 a.m.) With Uranus moving into your tenth house, you're entering a period where you'll feel best working on your own. Start a new business, especially if you can work with a partner, preferably someone you love. That's because Venus is now in your seventh house of partnerships.

Wednesday, December 2 (Moon in Gemini) The full moon is in your first house. You reap what you've sown related to your self-image. The way you see yourself is the way others see you. You feel recharged for the month ahead; this makes you more appealing to the public. Relations with the opposite sex go well.

Thursday, December 3 (Moon in Gemini to Cancer 11:01 a.m.) It's a number 2 day. Use your intuition to get a sense of your day. Be kind and understanding. Your intuition focuses on relationships.

Friday, December 4 (Moon in Cancer) The moon is in your second house of money and finances. Money and material goods are important to you and give you a sense of security.

You identify emotionally with your possessions or whatever you value. Watch your spending.

Saturday, December 5 (Moon in Cancer to Leo 12:08 p.m.) Mercury moves into your eighth house. You're asking a lot of questions as you try to get to the bottom of a problem or mystery. It could involve shared possessions or resources, or it could relate to a deeper mystery of the unknown, such as life after death.

Sunday, December 6 (Moon in Leo) The moon is in your third house. You get your ideas across, especially in dealings with neighbors and siblings. You could be taking one or more short trips today. Drive carefully and take time to check up on your mother.

Monday, December 7 (Moon in Leo to Virgo 2:07 p.m.) It's a number 6 day. Focus on making people happy. It's a service day. Do a good deed. Visit someone who is ill or someone in need of help. Diplomacy wins the way. Be helpful, but dance to your own tune.

Tuesday, December 8 (Moon in Virgo) The moon is in your fourth house. Stick close to home. Retreat to a private place. Take time to meditate and consider everything that has been taking place recently. Spend time with your family and work on a home-repair project.

Wednesday, December 9 (Moon in Virgo to Libra 5:48 p.m.) It's a number 8 day, your power day. Be courageous. A financial coup could come your way. Business discussions go well. Open your mind to a new approach that could bring in new income.

Thursday, December 10 (Moon in Libra) The moon is in your fifth house. Your creative assets are emphasized. You bring more emotional depth to any creative project that you're working on. Any involvement with children and animals goes well. A relationship can reach new levels, but you might be feeling somewhat possessive.

Friday, December 11 (Moon in Libra to Scorpio 11:32 p.m.)　　It's a number 1 day. Get out and meet people and have new experiences. Express your opinions dynamically. In romance, a flirtation could turn serious. Make sure that it's what you want.

Saturday, December 12 (Moon in Scorpio)　　The moon is in your sixth house. Keep your resolutions about exercise and diet. Help others where you can. Don't fret about any health issues. Don't let your fears hold you back, especially in your daily work. Confront and overcome them.

Sunday, December 13 (Moon in Scorpio)　　You're passionate. Your sexuality is heightened. Any conflicts, however, could be more intense than usual. Dig deep for information. Be aware of things happening in secret and of possible deception.

Monday, December 14 (Moon in Scorpio to Sagittarius 7:25 a.m.)　　It's a number 5 day. Change and variety are highlighted. Think outside the box. Take risks; experiment. Get a new point of view. You're especially versatile and changeable.

Tuesday, December 15 (Moon in Sagittarius)　　The moon is in your seventh house. The emphasis turns to partnerships. Loved ones and partners play a role. It's all about working together. Stay emotionally balanced. You could also be dealing with a legal matter or contract.

Wednesday, December 16 (Moon in Sagittarius to Capricorn 5:32 p.m.)　　There's a new moon in your seventh house. You get an opportunity and could be negotiating or signing a contract. You're taking the initiative with your partner, and emotions could get volatile. It's difficult to maintain an objective and detached point of view. Be careful not to let others manipulate your feelings.

Thursday, December 17 (Moon in Capricorn)　　The moon is in your eighth house. Yesterday's energy flows into your Thursday. Your experiences are intense. The issue at hand could be a joint project or possessions that you share. Try not

241

to manipulate or control the matter. Your actions, for better or worse, could be attracting the attention of powerful people.

Friday, December 18 (Moon in Capricorn) Your ambition and drive to succeed are highlighted. You're feeling financially flush. However, don't speculate or take any unnecessary risks. Your responsibilities increase. You may feel stressed.

Saturday, December 19 (Moon in Capricorn to Aquarius 5:39 a.m.) It's a number 9 day. Finish what you've started. Complete a project. Look beyond the present. Strive for universal appeal. Spiritual values surface. Clear up odds and ends. Take an inventory on where things are going in your life.

Sunday, December 20 (Moon in Aquarius) Mars goes retrograde in your third house. You could be feeling aggressive related to your communication with neighbors or relatives. But you tend to internalize the anger and hold back. Eventually, you need to allow it to come to the surface and confront whatever you're feeling.

Monday, December 21 (Moon in Aquarius to Pisces 6:42 p.m.) It's a number 2 day. Don't make waves. Don't rush or show resentment. Let things develop. The spotlight is on cooperation. Your emotions and sensitivity are highlighted. Show your appreciation to others.

Tuesday, December 22 (Moon in Pisces) The moon is in your tenth house. You gain an elevation in prestige related to your profession and career. Business is highlighted. Material success and financial security play roles in your day. You make a strong emotional commitment to your profession.

Wednesday, December 23 (Moon in Pisces) Your imagination is highlighted. Watch for psychic events. Universal knowledge, eternal truths, and deep spirituality are emphasized. Don't fall into a trap of self-deception.

Thursday, December 24 (Moon in Pisces to Aries 6:40 a.m.) It's a number 5 day. Promote new ideas; follow your curiosity. You're versatile. Be careful not to spread out and diversify too much.

Friday, December 25 (Moon in Aries)   Venus moves into your eighth house. You could have a relationship with some-one you've known in a past life. You could decide to attend a metaphysical class and explore mysteries of life and death. You could inherit money. Whatever happens, it'll be a positive experience. Merry Christmas!

Saturday, December 26 (Moon in Aries to Taurus 3:27 a.m.) Mercury goes retrograde in your eighth house. That means you can expect some delays and glitches in communication over the next three weeks, especially related to your shared possessions, taxes, mortgages, or insurance issues. Relax and control your emotional reactions to situations. If you're look-ing into a metaphysical subject, expect some misunderstand-ing or miscommunication.

Sunday, December 27 (Moon in Taurus)   The moon is in your twelfth house. Stay out of public view. Difficult issues from your past might surface. Confide your thoughts and feel-ings to a close friend. Relations with women can be difficult.

Monday, December 28 (Moon in Taurus to Gemini 8:15 p.m.)   It's a number 9 day. Finish a project and get ready for something new. Take time to relax and reflect on every-thing that's been taking place; look for ways to expand and move beyond any perceived limitations.

Tuesday, December 29 (Moon in Gemini)   The moon is in your first house. You're sensitive to other people's feelings. You may feel moody, withdrawn one moment, happy the next, then sad. It's all about your emotional self. Your feelings and thoughts are aligned. You're dealing with the person you are becoming.

Wednesday, December 30 (Moon in Gemini to Cancer 9:46 p.m.)   It's a number 2 day. Use your intuition to get a sense of the day. Focus on your direction. Where are you going and

243

why? The spotlight is on cooperation. Help comes through friends and loved ones, especially a partner.

Thursday, December 31 (Moon in Cancer)   There's a lunar eclipse in your second house. You experience an emotional reaction related to money issues or your values. Look at your priorities in handling your income. Put off making any major purchases. It's time to come to terms with what it is that you really value.

HAPPY NEW YEAR!

JANUARY 2010

Friday, January 1 (Moon in Cancer to Leo 10:42 p.m.) Your New Year begins with Mercury retrograde—a major pain for you, since this planet rules your sign. That said, the moon is in compatible fire sign Leo, so you're in rare form among neighbors and relatives. It's a good day to kick back, relax, and enjoy your free time.

Saturday, January 2 (Moon in Leo)   You and a relative are involved in lively discussions today. The conversation should be positive, but resist the temptation to talk over the other person. Cultivate the art of listening. If you're going back to work on Monday, be sure to have your schedule firmed up so you don't lose valuable time figuring things out.

Sunday, January 3 (Moon in Leo to Virgo 10:53 p.m.)   Tend to details at home. Your kids, partner, and perhaps even your parents may need additional emotional support now. Or, just as likely, a home-improvement project that was pushed to the back burner over the holidays now needs to move forward to restore order at home!

Monday, January 4 (Moon in Virgo)   The beginning of the workweek features Mercury still in retrograde motion, so be sure to communicate clearly and succinctly to avoid misunderstandings. Mars is also retrograde, in Leo, your third house, which may add to your frustration when it comes to communication. Be sure that you're following an exercise routine so you can burn off some of your energy. It'll help deal with these retrograde planets.

Tuesday, January 5 (Moon in Virgo)   If you've procrastinated with preventive health stuff, today is the day to make those appointments. And you may want to consider signing up for a yoga or Pilates class to maintain your flexibility. It's never too early in the year to nurture yourself.

Wednesday, January 6 (Moon in Virgo to Libra 12:59 a.m.) Romance and creative endeavors are on your mind today. You may consider taking some time to dive into your multiple creative projects and sort through them. A friend is helpful in this regard. Chose the project that really calls out to you, and get to work!

Thursday, January 7 (Moon in Libra)   You have a complex network of friends and acquaintances. You may want to put together a newsletter for your client list or start a blog to keep the conversation going with friends and relatives. Be sure you have the time to commit to any long-range creative project before you leap in.

Friday, January 8 (Moon in Libra to Scorpio 6:01 a.m.) Research and investigation are the day's hallmarks. Whether the research is related to work or to something else, you're on top of things. Don't hesitate to delegate if you need to. Trusted employees or coworkers can be helpful when you're up against a deadline.

Saturday, January 9 (Moon in Scorpio)   In six days, there will be a solar eclipse in Capricorn, and you may be feeling the effects already. This eclipse will impact your eighth house of shared resources, so if it's suddenly easier to obtain a mortgage or loan, thanks to the upcoming eclipse. You and a coworker or employee may spend some time discussing work issues. Lighten up on yourself. Get out and have some fun!

Sunday, January 10 (Moon in Scorpio to Sagittarius 2:10 p.m.) The moon enters your opposite sign, and suddenly you're on fire with ideas. Whatever issue you've been mulling over is now much clearer to you. It seems that you have a grasp of the larger implications. If you don't like what you see, then change your thoughts and intentions.

Monday, January 11 (Moon in Sagittarius) You're the life of the party, and even if there isn't a party, you create one through your magnetic presence. Your usual gift of gab is accelerated, if that's possible, but you'll have to be careful about blurting what's on your mind, particularly if you're dealing with someone who is very sensitive.

Tuesday, January 12 (Moon in Sagittarius) Watch your sarcasm today. It may put off the wrong people, and afterward, you'll wish you could take back what you said. The Sagittarius moon has wit in excess, and occasionally, that wit sharpens into unintended bluntness and barbs. Your mood is upbeat, and that's always a good place from which to launch a manifestation. What kinds of experiences would you like to have in your life?

Wednesday, January 13 (Moon in Sagittarius to Capricorn 12:54 a.m.) Saturn turns retrograde in Libra, your fifth house, and remains that way until May 30. Over the course of the next several months, you'll be seriously evaluating what you want in a romantic relationship, in your creative endeavors, and for pure fun and pleasure.

Thursday, January 14 (Moon in Capricorn) Unless you have a natal Capricorn moon or Capricorn rising, this moon probably isn't your favorite. But it enables you to focus on what you want and to lay down a strategy for attaining it. You have to adjust your mental attitude concerning resources you share with others. But your flexibility is one of your survival mechanisms. You come through the test with flying colors.

Friday, January 15 (Moon in Capricorn to Aquarius 1:17 p.m.) Two events today: a solar eclipse in Capricorn and

Mercury turns direct in Capricorn. Venus is close to the degree of this moon, so the eclipse should be quite positive generally. Expect new opportunities to surface related to resources you share with others. Mercury turning direct is always great news for you. Pack your bags; send out your e-mails.

Saturday, January 16 (Moon in Aquarius)   You've got terrific ideas today; don't hesitate to fine-tune them so that you can present them to the people who call the shots. If you're the one who calls the shots, you're fine-tuning everything in order to make the ideas comprehensible to other people.

Sunday, January 17 (Moon in Aquarius)   Jupiter enters Pisces and your tenth house today. During the next several months, your career opportunities should expand enormously. You're in the right place at the right time for major career leaps, for networking with the right people, and for being recognized by peers and other professionals.

Monday, January 18 (Moon in Aquarius to Pisces 2:18 a.m.)   Venus enters Aquarius, your ninth house, where it will be until February 11. This transit facilitates the quickness of your intellect and makes it likely that romance sparks with a foreigner or with someone whose worldview is different from yours. Since Venus also represents the arts and money, it's possible that you'll be making money from an artistic project.

Tuesday, January 19 (Moon in Pisces)   The moon joins Jupiter in Pisces, in your tenth house. The combination expands your intuition and allows you to intuitively pick up on information you need concerning your career and professional relationship. There could be some travel for professional matters over the next few days.

Wednesday, January 20 (Moon in Pisces to Aries 2:37 p.m.) You meet with a group that supports your passions and ideals. The group could be anything—from a bunch of writers to theater buffs to people whose political ideals match yours. Take what you learn today, and figure out a way to integrate it into your daily life.

Thursday, January 21 (Moon in Aries)   Social invitations are coming your way. You may have to juggle your schedule around, but don't deny yourself fun if you're in the mood! The Aries moon fires up your passions and urges you to follow your bliss.

Friday, January 22 (Moon in Aries)   Today, a number of planets are lined up in compatible signs, which serves you in a positive way. So rather than thinking in terms of your weekend plans, take a deeper look at where you are in your life—and where you would like to be. Then bring your energy into alignment with the desire by seeing yourself in that new place. Back it with emotion.

Saturday, January 23 (Moon in Aries to Taurus 12:41 a.m.) The moon enters Taurus and your twelfth house. This is usually a good day for housecleaning of the metaphorical variety. In other words, dig into yourself and get rid of beliefs that no longer serve your best interests. You could engage in a symbolic gesture by cleaning your closets, garage, or attic.

Sunday, January 24 (Moon in Taurus)   If you're more stubborn today, there's a good reason. The Taurus moon is one of the most stubborn in the zodiac. It's probably exactly what is called for today too. Someone may be trying to convert you to his or her way of thinking. But you want none of it.

Monday, January 25 (Moon in Taurus to Gemini 7:12 a.m.) The moon enters your sign, a high point in every month. Gone is the angst you sometimes feel when you can't make up your mind. Your head and heart are in complete agreement. So tackle something you've postponed dealing with, or get out and shore up your contacts.

Tuesday, January 26 (Moon in Gemini)   With Mercury now moving in direct motion and the moon in your sign, you should consider sending out a newsletter or some other type of communication to your e-mail contacts. Whether it's business or pleasure, the time is ripe. If you find that a newsletter or regular e-mail is too time-consuming, then consider starting up a blog.

Wednesday, January 27 (Moon in Gemini to Cancer 10:02 a.m.)   Your emotional focus shifts to finances. Perhaps those holiday bills are coming due, or you're eyeing some big-ticket item. Just be sure that if you go the credit card route, you'll have the money soon to pay it off. Better yet, if you can't afford the item, put off the purchase until you can.

Thursday, January 28 (Moon in Cancer)   Home and family are on your mind today. One or both of your parents figure into the day's events, and if you have kids, so do they. An issue that surfaces in some way, shape, or form today is nurturing.

Friday, January 29 (Moon in Cancer to Leo 10:10 a.m.) You may be sticking close to home over the weekend. Your neighborhood or community is the feature for today and to-morrow. However, there's a good chance that you'll be out in front of the public more than you usually are. So look your best!

Saturday, January 30 (Moon in Leo)   The full moon in Leo receives a powerful beam from Mars, so there's sure to be plenty of activity and action. Also, Saturn forms a wide but beneficial angle to this moon, suggesting that the news you hear today is serious and beneficial. If, for instance, you're a writer in search of an editor, then Saturn's angle indicates that the offer is solid.

Sunday, January 31 (Moon in Leo to Virgo 9:23 a.m.) Something at home or with your family needs attention. It's detail stuff, but if you tend to it today, it ceases to be annoying. If you postpone or procrastinate, then the challenge shows up again next month.

FEBRUARY 2010

Monday, February 1 (Moon in Virgo)   If you live where it's cold now, then February is probably not your best month. However, you can mitigate any blueness you might feel due to weather by maintaining a cheerful, upbeat mood as best you can. Strive to cheer up the people around you, and do something for someone else.

Tuesday, February 2 (Moon in Virgo to Libra 9:42 a.m.) Romance and pleasure are highlighted today, as are relationships generally. The Libra moon seeks emotional balance, but that could be the most difficult thing to achieve today unless you work at it. But you're flexible. It's one of your greatest strengths.

Wednesday, February 3 (Moon in Libra)   The moon hooks up with Saturn again. This combination can make you somewhat somber, so resist taking anything too personally. This combination will occur for the next two and a half years, and you'll have to learn that not everything someone says about you is a criticism.

Thursday, February 4 (Moon in Libra to Scorpio 12:56 p.m.) Your daily work and health routines are highlighted. If you don't have a regular exercise routine already, then today is the perfect time to start one. Be sure it's something you know you can stick to. You also may be experimenting with various diets or nutritional programs.

Friday, February 5 (Moon in Scorpio)   Someone's got your number today and knows which buttons to push. Take a few deep breaths when you're around this individual and keep your opinions to yourself. You'll have a chance later this month to express your feelings. But today is the day to back off.

Saturday, February 6 (Moon in Scorpio to Sagittarius 8:04 p.m.)   The moon enters your opposite sign and forms a beneficial angle with Venus. As a result, love and romance are highlighted, but thanks to the position of the moon, there could be some issues that need to be brought out into the open. Once they are, things improve immeasurably.

Sunday, February 7 (Moon in Sagittarius)   Tell the truth. If you exaggerate, or even tell a little white lie, it will come back to haunt you down the line. This doesn't mean that you have to blurt out what you feel about someone else, especially if it will hurt that person's feelings.

Monday, February 8 (Moon in Sagittarius)   Your business or romantic partner is highlighted today. If you're self-employed and have a partner, then you may be negotiating or renegotiating terms in your contract. Or you may be hashing out the details. Don't shortchange yourself just to be agreeable.

Tuesday, February 9 (Moon in Sagittarius to Capricorn 6:45 a.m.)   The moon joins Pluto in Capricorn, your eighth house. This powerful combination can put you in the driver's seat where loans and mortgages, taxes and insurance are concerned. There's another aspect to the eighth house worth noting—it symbolizes things that go bump in the night. So don't be surprised if you have some sort of psychic experience during the next few days.

Wednesday, February 10 (Moon in Capricorn)   Mercury enters Aquarius and your ninth house, where it remains until March 1. This transit certainly helps if you're a writer or work in the publishing or travel business, education or law. Your communication skills are sharper; you enjoy greater ease in whatever you present, sell, or do. There may be more frequent communication with people who live overseas.

Thursday, February 11 (Moon in Capricorn to Aquarius 7:25 p.m.)   Venus enters Pisces and your tenth house, where it remains until March 7. During this period, your career benefits in very nice ways, with recognition by peers and bosses, a bonus, a raise, or perhaps even a promotion. If you have ideas you want to pitch or projects you hope to get off the ground, this transit allows you to do so with style.

Friday, February 12 (Moon in Aquarius)   The new moon in Aquarius should usher in opportunities for foreign travel and any kind of dealings with foreign countries. New educational opportunities are also part of this package. If you're a writer looking for a publisher, this moon may bring exactly the right editor. If you're published already, this new moon could increase your sales to foreign countries.

Saturday, February 13 (Moon in Aquarius)   You're just itching to get moving—on a trip, a new project, a new relationship, or perhaps even a quest of some kind. Thanks to Neptune's proximity to yesterday's new moon, your idealism is heightened. You hunger to integrate that idealism more readily into your daily life.

Sunday, February 14 (Moon in Aquarius to Pisces 8:24 a.m.)   Happy Valentine's Day! Celebrate with quality time together with your partner. If you're not involved right now, the dates between April 25 and May 19 should correct that situation!

Monday, February 15 (Moon in Pisces)   A boss or someone with whom you work may be on your case about something. The issue belongs to the other person, not to you, so just keep your own counsel, and don't allow the situation to veer out of control. It's not worth the hassle. Your intuition is especially strong today. Use it.

Tuesday, February 16 (Moon in Pisces to Aries 8:31 p.m.) You're pursuing a line of inquiry or investigation that falls outside the box. Don't be intimidated by naysayers who may tell you it won't work. You're the best judge of what will work or not work.

Wednesday, February 17 (Moon in Aries)   Friends or any groups to which you belong may be helpful today. Now that you've got your vision of what is possible, you'll need people who can help out. Tap your friends. Tap your virtual friends. Start a blog that puts forth your ideas.

Thursday, February 18 (Moon in Aries)   You're taking giant steps today toward ... well, you aren't sure. It's a mysterious adventure into the unknown. One thing's for sure. The new moon in Aquarius six days ago is having unexpected repercussions for your personal philosophy. New ideas that come to you now are expanding your belief system.

Friday, February 19 (Moon in Aries to Taurus 6:56 a.m.) If you're in need of solitude today, indulge yourself. You're in a good place for some internal housecleaning, and you are preparing yourself for the moon entering your sign on Sunday. So tie up obligations; clear your desk. These things are signs that you're ready for whatever the moon in your sign will bring.

Saturday, February 20 (Moon in Taurus)   You're feeling relentless emotionally about an issue, a relationship, or a desire that you have. If what you're feeling bothers you, get to the root of it. What is making you uncomfortable? On the other hand, if you don't mind feeling relentless, then use the energy in a positive way, to enhance an area of your life.

Sunday, February 21 (Moon in Taurus to Gemini 2:47 p.m.) The moon enters your sign. Finally, your heart and your head are in complete agreement. The duality for which Gemini is famous could be more pronounced today, but it certainly doesn't trouble you. Onward!

Monday, February 22 (Moon in Gemini)   Networking and touching base with friends and professional contacts are important today. You sometimes act as a connector among people, and it's impossible to know how or when these connections will benefit you or someone within your circle. On other fronts, your gift of gab is at a monthly high.

Tuesday, February 23 (Moon in Gemini to Cancer 7:29 p.m.) Your emotional focus may shift to finances. This is fine, as long as you don't obsess about what you *don't* have. It's always best to be appreciative for what you do have so that you manifest more of the same in your life.

Wednesday, February 24 (Moon in Cancer)   You may be seeking ways to fully integrate your values into what you do creatively, how you make your living, or both. Or you may just be looking for a way to integrate these values more fully into your daily life. Today is ideal for figuring out the logistics.

Thursday, February 25 (Moon in Cancer to Leo 9:09 p.m.) Your community or neighborhood is your focus today. Perhaps a relative or a neighbor seeks to enlist your help for a project. You know you'll enjoy the socializing and networking, but before you commit, be sure you have time to do the work.

Friday, February 26 (Moon in Leo)   This transit is excellent for any kind of writing and communication. You may be doing some traveling today, but it's mostly short-distance stuff. Whether you're running errands or running the show, look your best. Tomorrow, you'll be glad that you did.

Saturday, February 27 (Moon in Leo to Virgo 8:53 p.m.) Things at home could feel a tad unsettled today. It's as if you know you're forgetting something, but can't recall what that something is. It'll come to you. In the meantime, take care of details with your family, partner, and kids.

Sunday, February 28 (Moon in Virgo)   Today's full moon in Virgo brings news about your home and family. Powerful Pluto forms a beneficial angle to this moon, so the news should put you in charge. However, there could be some conflict between responsibilities and home and professional responsibilities.

MARCH 2010

Monday, March 1 (Moon in Virgo to Libra 8:32 p.m.) Mercury enters Pisces and your tenth house, where it will be until March 17. During this period, your career and professional relationships are highlighted. You may be traveling for business and can certainly use this time frame for pitching ideas, pushing your own agenda forward, and expanding your network of contacts.

Tuesday, March 2 (Moon in Libra)   This moon is usually quite pleasant for you. It deepens your artistic sense, ramps up your social needs so that you spend more time with other people, and generally makes life smoother. You're more flirtatious, so if you're not involved in a relationship now, you may be before the end of the month. Spend some time today with your muse. He or she is ready and waiting.

Wednesday, March 3 (Moon in Libra to Scorpio 10:12 p.m.)
Your daily work routine takes some surprising turns today. You may be tapped for some sort of research project. You're excited about it but could feel some doubt about whether you're up to the task. Of course you're up to it. Change is your middle name.

Thursday, March 4 (Moon in Scorpio)   It's a bottom-line sort of day. Whatever it is you're after, you're able to find it by following your hunches. Even if your hunches lead you in some odd directions, don't worry about it. A dose of serendipity will keep things interesting.

Friday, March 5 (Moon in Scorpio)   There are reasons for everything, even if you can't discern them when events are happening. You can connect the dots on an intuitive level if you can shut off your inner chatter for a few minutes. Sit quietly, calm your mind, and pose your question.

Saturday, March 6 (Moon in Scorpio to Sagittarius 3:37 a.m.)   The moon enters your opposite sign, and suddenly your business or romantic partner (or both) may be demanding more of your time. Go with the flow. You actually have the big picture today—or are close to grasping it—and that's exactly what is needed in this situation. Wait until the moon is in your own sign before making any major decisions.

Sunday, March 7 (Moon in Sagittarius)   Venus enters Aries, where it will be until March 31. During this period, your social life picks up, and romance with a friend or some-one you meet through friends is possible. This transit also favors any kind of publicity and promotion you do for your company, your product, or any creative endeavors. Your passions are running high during this period—jealousy, love, envy.

Monday, March 8 (Moon in Sagittarius to Capricorn 1:15 p.m.)   Today it becomes easier to obtain a mortgage, a rate reduction in insurance, or a loan. You may be exploring things that go bump in the night: ghosts, legends, witchcraft, life after death, or communication with the dead.

Tuesday, March 9 (Moon in Capricorn)   You're able to make long-range plans in a way that eludes you at other times. It's as if you can see the light at the end of the tunnel regardless of how long the tunnel is. The only challenging thing about this moon is that you may have to make emotional adjustments throughout the day to maintain your equilibrium. Think of it as fine-tuning.

Wednesday, March 10 (Moon in Capricorn)   Mars turns direct in Leo, your third house. This movement should ramp up your communication abilities and trigger a lot of activity with relatives, as well as with neighbors and other members of your community. Your energy should increase and so will your drive to look and feel your best.

Thursday, March 11 (Moon in Capricorn to Aquarius 1:44 a.m.)   Finally, a moon that feels good to you. The air- and fire-sign moons are the most comfortable, but the Aquarius moon holds a broad appeal for that part of you interested in divination systems, oracles, and the order beneath the chaos. This moon allows you to access the deep parts of your intuition.

Friday, March 12 (Moon in Aquarius)   If you think you've got the answers to a pressing issue, then you probably do. The challenge is to implement what you've learned in a measured, efficient way. But you're always innovative, and you'll figure it all out. One of your most valuable survival skills is the ability to adapt.

Saturday, March 13 (Moon in Aquarius to Pisces 2:44 p.m.) Even though it's Saturday, you may have a new idea that you anticipate using next week at work. You'll work on it today, and you may test it out on friends and family. Whatever this is, you're on the cutting edge, and your bosses and peers will sit up and take notice.

Sunday, March 14—Daylight Saving Time Begins (Moon in Pisces) Your intuition is running the show today. Regardless of what you're doing, experience nudges you to try something new or to travel in a different direction. Even your conscious mind is able to intuitively grasp people, situations, and events, sizing things up in a matter of seconds.

Monday, March 15 (Moon in Pisces) Today's new moon in Pisces ushers in a whole new chapter in your career. New opportunities, new people, and new situations surface. You may change career paths or choose to work out of your home. Both Uranus and Mercury are within a degree of this new moon, indicating that the opportunities that arise do so suddenly and unexpectedly, and there's a lot of discussion about things generally.

Tuesday, March 16 (Moon in Pisces to Aries 2:32 a.m.) Your social life takes a definite upswing. But you're restless and impatient and may be somewhat short-tempered, so think before you speak and keep your sarcasm to a minimum! Friends are helpful now, and if you join a group, be sure it's one whose interests match your own.

Wednesday, March 17 (Moon in Aries) Mercury enters Aries, your eleventh house, where it will be until April 2. During this transit, expect lots of involvement and discussions with friends and groups about your wishes and dreams. It's an excellent time for publicity and promotion for your company's products or services or for your own creative endeavors. This transit forms a beneficial angle to your sun, so your usually excellent communication skills are enhanced.

Thursday, March 18 (Moon in Aries to Taurus 1:30 p.m.)   Whenever the moon enters Taurus and your twelfth house, you may feel a need to withdraw, to get off by yourself. You're essentially cleaning out the hidden stuff you haven't dealt with and making room for the new that will arrive when the moon enters your sign on Saturday. Since the universe loves symbolic gestures, clean out your closet today!

Friday, March 19 (Moon in Taurus)   There are certain times when solitude suits you. Today, you're deeply enmeshed in a project that requires solitude and time to think, brainstorm, and imagine. You may choose to spend the day with a trusted family member or close friend who understands and supports what you're doing.

Saturday, March 20 (Moon in Taurus to Gemini 9:29 p.m.) The moon enters your sign, and life suddenly becomes much easier! Gone is the conflict between head and heart. You're in the Gemini groove, and that means saying what you think when you think it, and networking with people far and wide.

Sunday, March 21 (Moon in Gemini)   Your gift of gab serves you well today. It attracts a new romantic interest or someone who can help you professionally. Through your vast network of contacts, other people connect through you, and everyone benefits. With Venus in Aries right now, it's possible that you meet someone new through friends. Or a friend becomes something more!

Monday, March 22 (Moon in Gemini)   The best things come in twos today; two calls, two e-mails, two letters, or even two opportunities. Play your game straight and honestly, but keep to yourself what is no one else's business. Don't gossip or play favorites.

Tuesday, March 23 (Moon in Gemini to Cancer 3:16 a.m.) Your focus shifts to finances and what you value. How much money do you need in the bank to feel secure? And if it's not money that makes you feel secure, what does: a home, tangible assets, or your family? These questions are some that will haunt you at some level today.

Wednesday, March 24 (Moon in Cancer)   Your parents figure into the day's events. One or both of them may need your time, energy, and nurturing. Or perhaps you're the one who is nurtured by them. One thing is for certain: Home and family are your priority.

Thursday, March 25 (Moon in Cancer to Leo 6:40 a.m.) There are times when you're in the mood to strut your stuff. So go for it. Whether you're showing off your writing, photography, acting, some other creative endeavor, or just yourself, do it with style. You'll need recognition from others today.

Friday, March 26 (Moon in Leo)   If you have siblings, then today you have more contact than usual with them. Your neighbors may also be involved in the day's activities. You may get tapped for a neighborhood or community project. Other people like your easygoing nature and your ability to talk to anyone.

Saturday, March 27 (Moon in Leo to Virgo 7:58 a.m.) The Virgo moon can be picky and critical. You may attract criticism from someone in your family, or you may be criticizing someone close to you. If the first scenario happens, ignore it. If you're the one doing the criticizing, back off and apologize. Nothing is gained by being critical of yourself or of others.

Sunday, March 28 (Moon in Virgo)   You may be sticking pretty close to home today. Your roots are calling to you, and you may want to figure out why. What is it about the past that sticks with you? What's the source of your nostalgia?

Monday, March 29 (Moon in Virgo to Libra 8:22 a.m.) Today's full moon in Libra should be quite pleasant for you. It occurs in your fifth house of romance, in a fellow air sign. So

259

expect news about a romantic relationship or a creative project. Saturn is within nine degrees of this moon, so whatever the day brings, it's serious stuff. You'll have to meet your responsibilities and obligations.

Tuesday, March 30 (Moon in Libra)   Get out and have some fun today. Life should never be all work, work, work. When it is, you tend to lose your perspective on what's really important. So do what you enjoy. Indulge yourself. Tomorrow, you'll be glad that you did.

Wednesday, March 31 (Moon in Libra to Scorpio 9:42 a.m.) Venus enters Taurus, where it will be until April 25. Any relationship that begins under this transit is likely to be private, perhaps even secretive. If you're involved already, then this transit should bring some quality time to the relationship. You and your partner spend a lot of time together.

APRIL 2010

Thursday, April 1 (Moon in Scorpio)   Coworkers or employees may get on your nerves today. It's not anything blatant, but an accretion of small things that bug you. Best course? Keep your own counsel, put some distance between yourself and these other people, and don't create a confrontation.

Friday, April 2 (Moon in Scorpio to Sagittarius 1:54 p.m.) Mercury enters Taurus and your twelfth house, where it will remain until June 10. During part of this time—April 17 to May 11—Mercury will be retrograde. This transit gives you the opportunity to work in seclusion. There will be a lot going on behind the scenes, and you'll be mentally stubborn, definitely a good thing during this period.

Saturday, April 3 (Moon in Sagittarius)   The moon enters your opposite sign, shifting your focus to partnerships, both romantic and professional. There may be some lively discussions with business partners, but your communication skills are so sharp that you can talk circles around just about anyone. You make your point and hear arguments from no one.

Sunday, April 4 (Moon in Sagittarius to Capricorn 10:08 p.m.) The moon enters Capricorn, so your emotional focus shifts to long-range plans and strategies and how to implement them. You may be concerned about filing your tax return or paying an insurance bill. It might be to your benefit to hire an accountant for the taxes and enlist the help of a trusted friend for the long-range plans.

Monday, April 5 (Moon in Capricorn) Nostalgia may be setting in. You may be fiddling with your digital photos and searching for just the right ones to print, and feelings about the past sweep through you. Or perhaps you run into someone you haven't seen for a while and catch up on old times. You get the idea. The past has its hold over all of us. But your point of power lies in the present.

Tuesday, April 6 (Moon in Capricorn) Pluto turns retrograde in Capricorn and doesn't turn direct again until September 13. The effects are subtle, because Pluto moves so slowly. Over the next few months, you'll be examining your beliefs about resources you share with others—a spouse, parent, child, or business partner. By the time Pluto turns direct again, you'll have a clearer idea about this particular area of your life.

Wednesday, April 7 (Moon in Capricorn to Aquarius 9:51 a.m.) The moon enters fellow air sign Aquarius, always a welcome reprieve after the heavy-handed Capricorn moon. Today your emotions take you into foreign lands. Your services or product may expand to overseas markets, or you may hear from friends who live in other countries.

Thursday, April 8 (Moon in Aquarius) Aren't you the visionary! Everyone around you says so, and even if you don't feel much like a visionary, you've got your finger on the pulse of the public right now. You can come up with the newest trend before it hits a tipping point. Get busy.

Friday, April 9 (Moon in Aquarius to Pisces 10:48 p.m.) Clear your desk; meet your obligations. Professional matters are vitally important today. There's a certain way for things to be done, especially on a Friday, and if you do them in this way, you get to take off from work early. Your intuition is running hot and furiously all weekend. Heed it.

Saturday, April 10 (Moon in Pisces)   If it's spring where you live, get out and about this weekend. The need to do so will nearly overwhelm you. Wrap up family or professional obligations early, and hit the road for the rest of the weekend. You may want to bring your laptop with you, and stay at some spot that has wireless Internet. Geminis can't stray too far from the connected world!

Sunday, April 11 (Moon in Pisces)   You delve into your intuitive abilities quite by accident today. The repercussions surprise you, and you may begin to investigate this curious area more deeply. Sign up for a course or a seminar on enhancing and using your intuition. Tax day is Thursday. Are you ready to send off your return?

Monday, April 12 (Moon in Pisces to Aries 10:31 a.m.) The fire-sign moon always brings a change of emotional pace. Today's focus shifts to friends and your own wishes and dreams. If you feel you aren't close enough yet to what you want, then lay out a new plan and get to work. The results will astonish you.

Tuesday, April 13 (Moon in Aries)   Concentrate on your own path today. It's the kind of thing you do well when you're focused. Set your sights, and go after what you want—a job, a relationship, a home, a romantic interest, whatever. You're writing the script of your life. Make it a fantastic script!

Wednesday, April 14 (Moon in Aries to Taurus 7:55 p.m.) Today's new moon in Aries attracts new opportunities for following your own bliss and for new friendships and group associations. Neptune forms a beneficial angle to this moon, so your ideals and compassion also come into play.

Thursday, April 15 (Moon in Taurus)   You're withdrawing somewhat today, getting into a solitary frame of mind so that you can complete something you've been working on. Your taxes, perhaps? A creative project? A home-improvement project? Whatever it is, finish it by Saturday, when the moon enters your sign, signaling a high point in the month.

Friday, April 16 (Moon in Taurus)   You're releasing old stuff to make way for the new. So tie up loose ends and make symbolic gestures like cleaning your closets, your garage, or your attic. The universe loves symbolism. Then create a list of what you would like to do or accomplish in the next few days, when the moon is in your sign. Back up computer files! Mercury turns retrograde tomorrow.

Saturday, April 17 (Moon in Taurus to Gemini 3:09 a.m.) Mercury turns retrograde in Taurus until May 11. You should know the drill by now. But in case you don't remember, reread the big-picture section about how this retrograde may impact you. People you haven't seen in a while may surface during this retrograde. Also, issues you've buried could pop up again. Deal with them.

Sunday, April 18 (Moon in Gemini)   Network and communicate. Those are your priorities today. However, with your ruler now retrograde for several weeks, the communication angle requires a bit more tact and skill. If you have to communicate with people you don't particularly like, then do so through e-mail. In fact, do all of it through e-mail. There's less chance of miscommunication.

Monday, April 19 (Moon in Gemini to Cancer 8:40 a.m.) It's time to review your finances, not your favorite task. So let technology and software make it easier for you. Enter your accounts and balances in one place, buy an external hard drive so you can back up your records, and set up your banking options online. It may take you some time to get it all set up, but once you do, you'll wonder what took you so long.

Tuesday, April 20 (Moon in Cancer)   You stick close to home today, if not physically, then mentally and emotionally. Your parents may figure into the day's events and nostalgia of all kinds certainly will. Scrapbooks are outdated; get your digital photos in one place where they won't be lost if your computer crashes. External hard drives and memory sticks are both good options.

Wednesday, April 21 (Moon in Cancer to Leo 12:43 p.m.) If you're a writer, in the travel business, in sales, or in education, this moon should bring out the best in you. You're in the groove called showmanship, and other people are drawn to what you're doing or proposing. Today, you could sell anyone virtually anything.

Thursday, April 22 (Moon in Leo) Mars is also in Leo now, and the combination of the two planets ramps up your impatience and restlessness. You may be feeling the need to travel, but if possible hold off until Mercury turns direct on May 11. Virtual travel all you want, but make your plans after Mercury turns direct again.

Friday, April 23 (Moon in Leo to Virgo 3:25 p.m.) Home and family. Parents. Kids. Your roots. Genealogy. All of those areas come up today. So take your time, sift through the events and emotions you experience, and tend to things at home. By Sunday, when Venus enters your sign, you'll be back on top of the world.

Saturday, April 24 (Moon in Virgo) Tend to details. It will enable you to connect the dots in a situation or in a relationship. Even if you don't have the full picture yet, you soon will. This is the first step to getting there. If it's spring where you live, be sure to take time to get out and enjoy the change in seasons.

Sunday, April 25 (Moon in Virgo to Libra 5:18 p.m.) Venus enters your sign, where it will be until May 19. This period will be one of the most romantic and creative that you experience all year. So get yourself into the right frame of mind, embrace all possibilities, and let your self-confidence shine.

Monday, April 26 (Moon in Libra) In addition to Venus's transit through your sign, the moon is in Libra today, your fifth house of romance. Talk about a terrific recipe for love and romance and for all creative ventures. Even if you're involved right now, you and your partner benefit from this combination of planets.

Tuesday, April 27 (Moon in Libra to Scorpio 7:30 p.m.) Your focus shifts to research, investigation, and your daily work. If you've been looking for a job or hoping to find a new job, today is great for sending out résumés, touching base with people you've contacted earlier, and for generally consolidating your physical energy. Use e-mail and the phone when possible.

Wednesday, April 28 (Moon in Scorpio) Today's full moon in Scorpio brings news and insights related to your daily work. It could be that new job! Pluto forms a beneficial angle to this moon, which puts you in the driver's seat. Mercury is opposed to the moon, so you're very forceful in your communications.

Thursday, April 29 (Moon in Scorpio to Sagittarius 11:36 p.m.) The moon enters your opposite sign, which shifts your emotional focus to business and romantic relationships. Given Venus's position in your sign right now, it's likely that you're in a very nice place for love and romance. Your muse is at your beck and call as well.

Friday, April 30 (Moon in Sagittarius) In another twelve days, Mercury turns direct again. Keep that in mind as your nomadic tendencies take root today, urging you to pack it in and get out of town. For now, stick close to home.

MAY 2010

Saturday, May 1 (Moon in Sagittarius) Your focus shifts to partnerships, both romantic and business. You may be in search of the big picture today. Don't bother gathering facts. Go with your gut, your first impressions; let your intuition guide you. Tomorrow, you'll be glad you did.

Sunday, May 2 (Moon in Sagittarius to Capricorn 7:00 a.m.)
When the moon and Pluto hook up, power issues surface. Unless you have your natal moon or rising in Capricorn, the combination is challenging. You have to adjust your attitude to fully understand the situation, which could involve taxes, insurance, or even a psychic experience.

Monday, May 3 (Moon in Capricorn) You're making long-range plans of some kind today. Whether it involves your personal or your professional life, make the plans realistic, then back them up with the full power of your emotions and intentions. When you set your sights on something, mountains can move. So get busy!

Tuesday, May 4 (Moon in Capricorn to Aquarius 5:52 p.m.) The Aquarius moon suits you, and so do the day's activities and events. You may be considering a return to college—or may be heading off for the first time this fall. If not college, then perhaps graduate school. Regardless of which it is, learning and curiosity are in the air, and you are certainly in your element.

Wednesday, May 5 (Moon in Aquarius) Planning a trip overseas? Then be sure you don't buy a ticket or make your reservations until after Mercury turns direct on May 11. If you absolutely have to travel, then be aware that sudden changes in your itinerary and schedule are likely. Be as flexible as possible, and consider carrying your luggage onto the plane with you rather than checking it.

Thursday, May 6 (Moon in Aquarius) With Venus still in your sign and the moon in fellow air sign Aquarius, you're in rare form today. Other people look to you for answers or insights and are receptive to your ideas.

Friday, May 7 (Moon in Aquarius to Pisces 6:34 a.m.) Your emotions are erratic and unpredictable today. But you have such unusual insights into professional situations and relationships that you barely notice your emotional roller coaster. A boss or peer has information that you may need before making a decision.

Saturday, May 8 (Moon in Pisces)   Intuition and imagination are your hallmarks today. Well, you have plenty of both as it is, but today, these two characteristics carry you to exactly where you need to go. Whether it's contacting a client or finding a particular piece of information, you take a nontraditional route.

Sunday, May 9 (Moon in Pisces to Aries 6:30 p.m.)   Friends and social connections figure into the day's events. You may decide to have a small party at your place, or you and a group of friends head out for a hiking trip, to the beach, or to some nearby town. It's a day to celebrate spring and express gratitude for all that you have.

Monday, May 10 (Moon in Aries)   Tomorrow, Mercury turns direct. So hold on for just another couple of days before making those travel reservations or signing a contract. For today, make a list of what you would like to do or tackle the day after Mercury turns direct.

Tuesday, May 11 (Moon in Aries)   Mercury turns direct in Taurus, your twelfth house. What you've learned about your own motives and unconscious during the past several weeks can now be integrated into your daily life. As Mercury begins its forward movement, start getting your thoughts and priorities in order. On June 10, Mercury will enter your sign, where it will be until June 25. That's the time to prepare for right now.

Wednesday, May 12 (Moon in Aries to Taurus 3:49 a.m.) The moon hooks up with Mercury in your twelfth house. This combination allows you to tap in to your inner resources. People from the past may reappear in your life, and issues from the past you thought were resolved may crop up once again. But you have the resilience to deal with this stuff.

Thursday, May 13 (Moon in Taurus)   Today's new moon in Taurus ushers in opportunities to work behind the scenes at something you enjoy doing. Both Jupiter and Uranus form beneficial angles to this moon, suggesting a suddenness to events that somehow expand your world in a positive way.

Friday, May 14 (Moon in Taurus to Gemini 10:19 a.m.) Your artistic sense is boosted today. Whether it's gourmet food that you're after or perhaps some kind of painting or other artistic work, the search is on. What begins as a quest for a particular thing turns into something much larger that helps illuminate who you are. Engage other people. They're helpful.

Saturday, May 15 (Moon in Gemini) Finally, with the moon in your sign, you're on top of the world again. Even if you're now sure there are two of you (that's why they call you the twin!), you're in the perfect spot to engage those various parts of yourself and put them to work doing . . . well, whatever. You change your mind every five minutes. Isn't that part of the fun?

Sunday, May 16 (Moon in Gemini to Cancer 2:47 p.m.) As the moon enters nurturing Cancer, you may pull at the bit as your emotions shift and eddy, seeming to follow the moods of the people around you. Changeable Gemini! Let this water-sign moon soothe you. Let its intuitive knowledge seep into you.

Monday, May 17 (Moon in Cancer) You may be fretting about finances. But the more you worry, the likelier it is that you draw more of the same. So redirect your thoughts. Reach for something more positive and uplifting. And then watch your reality shift!

Tuesday, May 18 (Moon in Cancer to Leo 6:07 p.m.) Early this evening, the moon enters Leo, a fire sign that's compatible with your sun. This moon can make things seem larger and more important than they really are, so avoid drama, especially with relatives and neighbors. Better to express Leo's drama through clothing, writing, or some other creative endeavor.

Wednesday, May 19 (Moon in Leo)   Venus enters Cancer and will be there until June 14. This transit should be very good for your finances generally. Someone who owes you money may repay it, a check you've been expecting finally arrives, or perhaps you land a contract of some kind. This transit also spells a rather nice period with your home life and in your relationship with your parents..

Thursday, May 20 (Moon in Leo to Virgo 8:59 p.m.)   Pay attention to details today, particularly in your home life and in your career. It's one of those days when your job is to connect the dots—in a relationship, with an idea, or in a project. With Mercury now moving in direct motion, that process should be much easier.

Friday, May 21 (Moon in Virgo)   Venus is now moving in a harmonious angle with the moon, so today should be quite romantic and creative. If you're not involved with anyone right now, you're having so much fun at whatever you're doing that it doesn't matter. In fact, your mantra has become: If it doesn't feel good, don't do it.

Saturday, May 22 (Moon in Virgo to Libra 11:50 p.m.)
The moon enters fellow air sign Libra and stirs up your creative urges. Your muse is up close and personal, so if you've got a creative project in the works, indulge yourself today and for the next three days. After all, timing really is everything.

Sunday, May 23 (Moon in Libra)   Balance is the key today. And if you're balancing a number of different obligations and responsibilities, you may have to delegate some of them to free up time for yourself. Be sure that whomever you delegate to is someone you trust and who will get the job done.

Monday, May 24 (Moon in Libra)   There are days where teamwork and cooperation are called for. So gather your supporters, and find out what's on their minds. Cultivate the art of really listening. What are you hearing? Just as important, what are you *not* hearing?

Tuesday, May 25 (Moon in Libra to Scorpio 3:18 a.m.)
You may try a new type of exercise today, something you consider doing routinely. Whether it's a specific workout at the gym, or a yoga or Pilates class, commit yourself to it for a specified period of time—a month, six months, or whatever feels right. You may increase your intake of vitamins, and try a new nutritional program too.

Wednesday, May 26 (Moon in Scorpio) A bottom-line sort of day. You may feel mired early in the day—in a project, an issue, or a particular thought process—but by early afternoon, you've hit your stride. Research and investigation are highlighted. You may have to adjust your attitude in some way to reap the benefits of your research.

Thursday, May 27 (Moon in Scorpio to Sagittarius 8:16 a.m.)
Today is major. First, the full moon in Sagittarius, your opposite sign, brings insights and news about a partnership—either romantic or business. Uranus, which enters Aries today, forms a wide but beneficial angle to this moon, adding an element of excitement and unpredictability to events. For information on Uranus's seven-year transit through Aries, read about it in the overview section. But know this for sure: This transit should be positive for you.

Friday, May 28 (Moon in Sagittarius) As the days are winding down toward summer, your eyes are on a vacation or a trip overseas. If it's in the planning stage, Mercury moves retrograde between December 10 and December 30, so you've got plenty of time before then. Your trip may be more immediate, in fact, like this weekend. Get away with your partner. You've earned some time together!

Saturday, May 29 (Moon in Sagittarius to Capricorn 3:44 p.m.) Unless you have a natal moon or rising in Capricorn, this moon probably isn't your favorite. That said, use the energy to ground an idea or project. Use it to make long-range plans or goals. One possible use for this moon? Draw up a will.

Sunday, May 30 (Moon in Capricorn)   Saturn turns direct in Libra, a very nice bonus for your love life, your creativity, and whatever you do for sheer enjoyment. Now you can easily integrate what you've learned about cooperation and teamwork into your daily life.

Monday, May 31 (Moon in Capricorn)   Neptune turns retrograde in Aquarius and remains that way until November 6. The effects are subtle, because Neptune moves so slowly, but over the next several months, you'll be learning about your capacity for compassion and clarifying your ideals.

JUNE 2010

Tuesday, June 1 (Moon in Capricorn to Aquarius 2:08 a.m.) The moon joins Neptune retrograde in Aquarius, your ninth house. The combination urges you to take a deeper look at your ideals. Are they your ideals or ideals you have adopted from family and friends? Once you determine this, you can weed out what really isn't you and define your own ideals.

Wednesday, June 2 (Moon in Aquarius)   You're on the cutting edge of something today—an idea, an emotion, or a trend. How can you use this professionally? Or personally? You're usually the one who spreads the word, so get busy. Whatever this cutting edge is, you'll want others to know about it.

Thursday, June 3 (Moon in Aquarius to Pisces 2:34 p.m.) As the moon enters the career sector of your chart, your emotions shift in that direction. Whether you're dealing with a peer relationship or a relationship with a boss or coworker, allow your intuition to guide you. Forget preparation for whatever is going on today. Go with your hunches.

Friday, June 4 (Moon in Pisces)   Imagination is your biggest asset today. Well, that and your gift of gab. Combine the two for a winning ticket in whatever you tackle. On the home front, an issue may require your attention, but you don't allow it to detract from what you're doing professionally.

Saturday, June 5 (Moon in Pisces) The year's almost half over. Are you satisfied with the direction you're headed? If not, make new plans and get to work. The results will astonish you.

Sunday, June 6 (Moon in Pisces to Aries 2:51 a.m.) Another major transit begins today as Jupiter enters Aries, joining Uranus in your eleventh house. Read about this transit in the big-picture section. There will be more frequent events in your life that occur suddenly and without warning, but which in some way expand and broaden who you are. With both Jupiter and Uranus forming harmonious angles to your sun, your opportunities are going to expand tremendously.

Monday, June 7 (Moon in Aries) Mars enters Virgo and your fourth house, where it will be until July 29. This transit certainly energizes your home life and could cause some friction with family members. But if you handle things with an even, upbeat disposition, from a base of good feelings rather than hostility, things will work out in everyone's favor. Mars in Virgo can be quite fussy and picky, so be sure not to turn those characteristics on the ones you love.

Tuesday, June 8 (Moon in Aries to Taurus 12:42 p.m.) The moon enters stubborn and resilient Taurus, your twelfth house. Time to do some housecleaning—either metaphorically or literally. Symbolic gestures—cleaning out your closets, attic, or garage—are great because the universe responds to them. As soon as you make space for the new, it arrives!

Wednesday, June 9 (Moon in Taurus) You may be working hard to meet a deadline on a project. You'll make the deadline, so don't worry about that. But perhaps next time, it would be better not to wait until the eleventh hour to complete something. In other words, plan ahead!

Thursday, June 10 (Moon in Taurus to Gemini 7:12 p.m.) Mercury enters your sign. Between now and June 25, you're on a roll, able to pitch ideas, sell ideas, and talk up a storm with just about anyone. Use this energy to your advantage. If you want to sign up for a course or workshop, do so. If you feel like traveling, get out and do that. As the old song says, "Feed your head!"

Friday, June 11 (Moon in Gemini)   Today, you may feel as if there are four of you. Or perhaps six. After all, both the moon and your ruler, Mercury, are in your sign. So the many facets of your personality are all working seamlessly together. And tomorrow the picture gets even prettier: There's a new moon in your sign! Prepare for it now by listing the experiences, people, and situations you would like to attract into your life.

Saturday, June 12 (Moon in Gemini to Cancer 10:51 p.m.)
The new moon in Gemini happens just once a year and sets the tone for the next year. This moon forms a harmonious angle to Neptune and a challenging angle to Saturn. That said, any new moon is what *you* make of it, so focus on the opportunities that you'll be attracting into your life during the next year. These opportunities can appear in any area of your life, but you'll have to be alert for them and act quickly, decisively. Even if you don't have the full picture, your intuition is sharp, so let it lead the way.

Sunday, June 13 (Moon in Cancer)   How do you nurture yourself and others? Well, if you're like many Geminis, then you probably nurture best through the mind and intellect. You help to foster curiosity in others. You give people books, turn them on to certain Web sites and ideas, and are a virtual repository of trivia and information. Your brand of nurturing expands the conscious thought process.

Monday, June 14 (Moon in Cancer)   Venus enters Leo and your third house, where it will be until July 10. During this period, your communication skills are remarkable. If you're a writer, you may want to focus solely on your writing for the next few weeks. This transit also is beneficial for travel and for relationships with relatives and neighbors. In terms of romance, if you're not involved, then watch out! Your new romantic interest may live in your neighborhood.

Tuesday, June 15 (Moon in Cancer to Leo 12:55 a.m.)   Today you talk circles around the competition. Your weapon and your gift, as always, are words, your command of language. But be gentle with people who just don't get what you're trying to communicate. Sometimes the best defense is to simply remain quiet. Yes, that's tough!

Wednesday, June 16 (Moon in Leo)   You and a relative may get together or talk at length today, perhaps about summer vacation plans. A family gathering could be in the offing. Everyone is looking to you for answers and ideas. Shine on!

Thursday, June 17 (Moon in Leo to Virgo 2:41 a.m.)   Details haunt you today. The faster you deal with them, the quicker things are resolved. You may want to catch up on things like dentist and doctor appointments if you've been procrastinating. Or perhaps seek out alternative healers. A new nutritional program may be on your day's list as well.

Friday, June 18 (Moon in Virgo)   It's a perfect day for catching up on e-mails, phone calls, and even letters. You're in a perfectionist frame of mind, which helps you to dot the Is and cross the Ts, things that the Virgo moon requires. With Mercury still in your sign, look over contracts and negotiate some more or sign them.

Saturday, June 19 (Moon in Virgo to Libra 5:13 a.m.)   Romance is in the air. Even if you're not involved with anyone just now, your thoughts are on romance and love. But rather than operate from a basis of lack, imagine what you would like in a romantic relationship. Visualize yourself with this person. Back the visualization with intense emotion. Then get out of the way so the universe can go to work on bringing that special person into your life.

Sunday, June 20 (Moon in Libra) With Venus forming a nice angle to the moon in Libra, spend time with your partner today. Plan a special dinner, take in a movie or a museum exhibit, or spend the evening in a café. In other words, do something you both enjoy, and be honest and open in your communications with each other.

Monday, June 21 (Moon in Libra to Scorpio 9:14 a.m.) Unless you have a natal moon or rising in Scorpio, this probably isn't your favorite moon. It requires that you adjust your attitude or thinking in some way so that you can adapt to a rapidly changing situation. There are few signs more adaptable than you are. But if someone issues a bottom-line ultimatum, just walk away.

Tuesday, June 22 (Moon in Scorpio) Research and investigation are the hallmarks of the moon in Scorpio. But it takes place on an inner, intuitive level within your complicated emotions. You're trying to understand a relationship with a partner, coworker, peer, or friend, and the insights you need come from a stranger.

Wednesday, June 23 (Moon in Scorpio to Sagittarius 3:11 p.m.) As the moon enters your opposite sign, your partner—business or romantic—may have a request. The request will help you to grasp the big picture of this relationship. What you do with this information or insight depends on whether you're pleased or distressed about it.

Thursday, June 24 (Moon in Sagittarius) Tomorrow, Mercury leaves your sign and enters Cancer. So do some real Gemini things today, to honor Mercury. Network. Browse through a bookstore. Read. Socialize. Dig for information. Sell something. Pitch an idea. Engage in a long discussion.

Friday, June 25 (Moon in Sagittarius to Capricorn 11:22 p.m.) Mercury enters Cancer and transits there until July 9. This shifts your daily mental focus toward money. You may be concerned that you're not earning enough or that you're spending too much. Rather than focusing on what you *don't* have, be grateful for what you *do* have. Once you can appreciate that, half your battle is won.

Saturday, June 26 (Moon in Capricorn) The lunar eclipse in Capricorn will be an emotional wakeup call. Saturn forms a wide but challenging angle to this moon, indicating that you will have to meet obligations and live within the rules. Let's say you're applying for a mortgage and have great credit. You're not worried about getting a mortgage. But you discover that your credit is drying up, and it's not going to be as easy as you had hoped. Now what? Focus on what you want—not on what you don't have.

Sunday, June 27 (Moon in Capricorn)   You may be preparing for some presentation during the week, so today you gather your material. Preparation may require several phone calls or an e-mail exchange with a boss or peer. But you're on top of things, and once you begin to organize the material and bring your considerable communication skills to bear against it, you step into the winner's court.

Monday, June 28 (Moon in Capricorn to Aquarius 9:53 a.m.)   Feeling restless and nomadic? Then it's time to schedule a trip to some far-flung corner of the globe that satisfies not only your itch to travel but becomes creative fodder too. With Mars now forming a beneficial angle to Venus, you may want to include the kids and one of their friends.

Tuesday, June 29 (Moon in Aquarius)   You're the visionary who recognizes patterns and trends before they reach a tipping point. Other people figure you've got the answers. Even if you don't, you know where to go to find the answers. Your worldview is undergoing subtle shifts, particularly in terms of spirituality.

Wednesday, June 30 (Moon in Aquarius to Pisces 10:11 p.m.)   If you're interviewing for a new job today or doing anything professionally that is outside of your normal routine, allow your imagination and intuition to lead the way. You may be connecting with someone you have known in a past life. The recognition, on some level, will be mutual.

Thursday, July 1 (Moon in Pisces)   More career stuff is on the table today. If you're considering a job or career change, then today is ideal for sending out résumés and touching base, by phone or e-mail, with prospective employers. Set up your interviews.

Friday, July 2 (Moon in Pisces)   Plan something fun for yourself this weekend. You've worked hard this week and earned a break. Perhaps a trip out of town will satisfy your nomadic tendencies. Invite your partner or a friend or even your parents. Follow your instincts and urges, regardless of how outlandish they may seem.

Saturday, July 3 (Moon in Pisces to Aries 10:45 a.m.)   The moon in Aries is certainly a friendly one for you. Ideas rush through you so quickly it's difficult to seize them. Keep a pad of paper with you so you can scribble down an idea when it occurs to you. A computer file is also handy, but be sure to keep a hard copy!

Sunday, July 4 (Moon in Aries)   Whether you've stuck close to home this weekend or gone out of town, it's an ideal day for gatherings with friends and family. You're filled with ideas for making the weekend memorable for everyone. If you're on deadline for a project, you may have to sneak off for a few hours by yourself today to work on it.

Monday, July 5 (Moon in Aries to Taurus 9:30 p.m.)   Uranus turns retrograde in Aries, your eleventh house, and begins its movement back into Pisces. This movement may have you reexamining certain friendships and revamping your wishes and dreams. Read more about it in the big-picture section. With the moon entering Taurus today, you're finishing up a work project and dealing with the remnants of the holiday weekend.

Tuesday, July 6 (Moon in Taurus)   Old friends may begin to surface in your life. These reconnections can occur in person, through phone, or by e-mail. You and a coworker or employee may find common ground for a joint project or may join forces to pitch an idea.

Wednesday, July 7 (Moon in Taurus) If you don't have a regular exercise routine already, start one today. Make sure it's something that you'll be able to follow through on. In other words, don't take up marathon running if you've never jogged before. Start gently. Maybe a yoga class?

Thursday, July 8 (Moon in Taurus to Gemini 4:51 a.m.) A high point in the month. Your inner and outer selves are in agreement on the most fundamental issues. If you have any outstanding financial issues to tackle, tend to them today. Tomorrow, Mercury enters Leo, your third house, and you may be hitting the road for business or pleasure or both.

Friday, July 9 (Moon in Gemini) Mercury enters Leo, where it will be until July 27. This transit should trigger a lot of activity and discussions with neighbors and relatives. Your grasp of language and your communications, both written and verbal, will have a flair, a kind of pizzazz that dazzles others. So use Mercury's energy to pitch an idea, to boost your sales quota, or to finish that book you started!

Saturday, July 10 (Moon in Gemini to Cancer 8:38 a.m.) Venus enters Virgo, your fourth house. Whether you're involved, married, or single, this transit makes for smooth sailing at home, with parents and kids, and it lasts until August 6. It's square to your sun sign, which may make you somewhat picky about romantic interests. In terms of creative projects, you're urged to pay close attention to details.

Sunday, July 11 (Moon in Cancer) Today's total eclipse in Cancer occurs in your second house of finances. This can be both good or not so good. Solar eclipses are like double new moons, so you can expect financial opportunities, but some other financial avenue may end. Mars forms an exact and beneficial angle to the eclipse degree, indicating a lot of activity surrounding this eclipse.

Monday, July 12 (Moon in Cancer to Leo 9:54 a.m.)   The Leo moon stimulates your showmanship. Your relatives play a part in the day's events. You may be hosting or directing some sort of project in your neighborhood or community that puts you more out in front of the public.

Tuesday, July 13 (Moon in Leo)   The moon joins Mercury in your third house, a terrific combination for any kind of communication. Your conscious mind and your intuition work well together, and anything that you communicate today comes off with pizzazz. Your relatives may figure into the day's activities.

Wednesday, July 14 (Moon in Leo to Virgo 10:15 a.m.)   The moon joins Venus in your fourth house. Intuitively, you know exactly what's going on in a romantic relationship. But on a conscious level, you may have misgivings about the relationship or feel that it needs some fine-tuning. Don't push too hard for change. Go with the flow.

Thursday, July 15 (Moon in Virgo)   If you're feeling self-critical today, turn your thoughts away from that toward something more uplifting and positive. This moon can cause you to scrutinize every emotion, to tear apart every conversation and break it down into its components. That's fine, but not for a steady diet.

Friday, July 16 (Moon in Virgo to Libra 11:25 a.m.)   The moon enters fellow air sign Libra, your fifth house. This transit shifts your emotional focus to love, romance, creativity, and children, if you have any. You're called upon to be more cooperative, to engage in teamwork. The cooperation factor comes into play in a romantic relationship, and the teamwork may be connected to a creative project.

Saturday, July 17 (Moon in Libra)   The moon joins Saturn in your fifth house. Yes, this will be happening for at least two days a month for the next two and a half years. Until you get used to the combination's energy, you may experience an exaggerated sense of responsibility toward a relationship or a creative project. But that's fine. From this conjunction, you learn—among other things—how to make the best use of your free time.

Sunday, July 18 (Moon in Libra to Scorpio 2:43 p.m.) Some sort of attitude adjustment is in store for you today. Nothing serious. But it could involve your agenda for tomorrow with work-related projects and responsibilities. You may be searching for something special, and if you follow your intuitive leads, you probably find it before the moon changes signs on Tuesday.

Monday, July 19 (Moon in Scorpio)　　Today's moon forms a harmonious angle with Jupiter, which has slid back into Pisces, so in terms of career matters, there's a strong, even flow to the day. You're reaping the benefits once again of Jupiter's expansiveness in terms of your career. New professional opportunities may be surfacing. Be on your toes!

Tuesday, July 20 (Moon in Scorpio to Sagittarius 8:49 p.m.) Your emotional focus shifts to the big picture of whatever it is that you're involved in today. Rather than trying to connect the dots or examining the details, go for the bigger vision. A romantic or business partner proves helpful. An Aries and a Leo individual help you to find your stride.

Wednesday, July 21 (Moon in Sagittarius)　　Saturn turns direct in Libra—a definite bonus for your love life and your creative projects. You're now able to integrate what you've learned about obligation and responsibility more fully into your daily life. Saturn is forming a harmonious angle with your sun for the next two and a half years, and it's helping you build the right structures and foundations in your life.

Thursday, July 22 (Moon in Sagittarius)　　In a week, Mars will link up with Saturn in Libra. You may be feeling the impact of this combination already. You may be approached, in fact, to head up a creative project. Mars gives you the energy to do it, and Saturn provides the proper structure. The only

280

question that remains is whether you have the time to commit to this.

Friday, July 23 (Moon in Sagittarius to Capricorn 5:40 a.m.)   Unless you have a natal moon or rising in Capricorn, this moon probably isn't your favorite. However, it serves a purpose in that it prompts you to examine or implement long-range goals and to take an honest look at your financial situation. Depending on your age, you may be saving for a house, a vacation, or your retirement!

Saturday, July 24 (Moon in Capricorn)   You're puttering around your place today, and you can't relax. It seems that you must make your time count for something, so you begin to rearrange furniture, paintings, or pictures. Then you tackle your joint financial picture. You could decide to apply for a home-equity loan to make some additions to your home.

Sunday, July 25 (Moon in Capricorn to Aquarius 4:39 p.m.)   Today's full moon in Aquarius forms a beautiful and exact angle to Jupiter and to Uranus. So any news that arrives around this time will be sudden and unexpected and should be upbeat and in some way expand your options.

Monday, July 26 (Moon in Aquarius)   It you've got the urge to hit the road, then by all means indulge the desire. Mercury is moving direct right now, but will be retrograde between August 20 and September 12, so plan your trip around those dates. If you're the type who doesn't need to plan ahead, then hop in your car and leave.

Tuesday, July 27 (Moon in Aquarius)   Mercury enters Virgo, your fourth house, and will be there until October 3, because it will be retrograde part of that time. This transit favors all kinds of communication and travel with family members. It's also good for catching up on doctor and dentist appointments and for completing home-improvement projects.

Wednesday, July 28 (Moon in Aquarius to Pisces 5:00 a.m.)
Mercury and Mars travel together for another day, galvaniz-

ing things on the home front. There could be some minor tensions with family members or with peers and coworkers, but patience and listening both go a long way. In fact, open up a discussion so that everyone can air his or her opinions.

Thursday, July 29 (Moon in Pisces)   Mars enters Libra, joining Saturn in your fifth house. This transit lasts until September 14 and is sure to make you much more cooperative and more aware of just how far this cooperation and team spirit can take you. What you learn can be applied to any area of your life, of course, but will be most important in your romantic relationships, in your creative projects, and with your kids.

Friday, July 30 (Moon in Pisces to Aries 5:42 p.m.)   The moon hooks up with Jupiter in Aries, enhancing that part of you that thinks outside the box. If your ideas seem grandiose, don't worry about it. Jupiter shows you what is possible. Start implementing the ideas when the moon is in your sign.

Saturday, July 31 (Moon in Aries)   Another day to brainstorm and enjoy the company of friends and family who fully support your ideas. You may have some ideas about stuff to do around your home. Before you run out and spend a lot of money, be sure that the checks have cleared!

AUGUST 2010

Sunday, August 1 (Moon in Aries)   Today you're off the beaten path, which is exactly where you should be with this moon. A couple of friends may be along for the ride, but you're definitely the leader! Don't hesitate to think outside the box. Discuss your ideas with your companions. Brainstorm. And then get out and have some fun. That's one thing the Aries moon encourages.

Monday, August 2 (Moon in Aries to Taurus 5:13 a.m.)   The moon enters your twelfth house, and by now you know what that means. Tie up loose ends, tackle something that requires completion by Wednesday, and have your mind on what you would like to do when the moon enters your sign the day after tomorrow. You're making way for new experiences, people, situations, and opportunities.

Tuesday, August 3 (Moon in Taurus)   Resoluteness is your middle name today. You're so intent on whatever you're doing that you don't even pause to answer the phone or e-mail. Now *that* is really a rarity for you. But you are primed and prepared for the moon entering your sign tomorrow, a high point every month.

Wednesday, August 4 (Moon in Taurus to Gemini 1:54 p.m.) If the day starts on a sour note, don't despair. By this afternoon, you're at the peak of your game. Use your power wisely. Resist the temptation during these peak days to throw your weight around, or you'll regret it later.

Thursday, August 5 (Moon in Gemini)   Books, information, networking. With both Mars and Saturn in fellow air sign Libra, you're in a very social mood and taking this networking stuff quite seriously. Good thing. The contacts you make from now to the end of the month will be quite beneficial for you. Tomorrow, Venus joins Mars and Saturn in Libra, sweetening the romantic pot considerably!

Friday, August 6 (Moon in Gemini to Cancer 6:50 p.m.) Venus enters Libra, teaming up with both Mars and Saturn. This trio of planets makes for an intriguing mix of serious romancing and creative drive. If you're involved already, then things begin to really take off. You and your partner see eye to eye on most things and, before the transit ends on September 8, may take the relationship to a whole new level.

Saturday, August 7 (Moon in Cancer)   With the moon in intuitive Cancer and Venus teaming up with Mars and Saturn in Libra, you have a unique opportunity to create something that will make you a lot of money. So dust off that old manuscript and get busy!

Sunday, August 8 (Moon in Cancer to Leo 8:23 p.m.)   This could be a touch-and-go sort of day. You fret about money, then feel somewhat directionless. This evening your mood lifts. The Leo moon usually lifts your spirits, so allow this feeling to follow you into tomorrow. And don't overlook the fact that some of the best things in life are right under your nose!

Monday, August 9 (Moon in Leo)   Today's new moon in Leo should be exciting and unpredictable. New opportunities to write, publicize, and promote yourself and your own creative work or your company's product or services come your way. New opportunities for travel may come your way as well. These opportunities probably will surface quickly and unexpectedly.

Tuesday, August 10 (Moon in Leo to Virgo, 8:02 p.m.)   Your home and family take priority today. Even if these responsibilities conflict with your professional obligations, tend to things at home before you tackle anything else. It's all in the details.

Wednesday, August 11 (Moon in Virgo)   Sometimes, life's best treasures are uncovered where we least expect to find them. So today, remain focused on exploring these treasures as they appear, and notice how the discovery and exploration make you feel. Carry this feeling with you throughout the day and into tomorrow.

Thursday, August 12 (Moon in Virgo to Libra 7:44 p.m.)   This evening, you come into your own. It's as if a massive weight has fallen off your shoulders, and now you're free to do what you enjoy with the people you enjoy. Your creativity plays a major role in the day's activities, particularly this evening. Be sure to carve some time for conversing with your muse.

Friday, August 13 (Moon in Libra)   With Saturn, Venus, and Mars also in Libra, you're compelled to delve into your creative projects and have fun! If travel is what you enjoy doing, then today's adventures on the road could include romantic interludes. Whenever Venus and Mars travel together in a romantic sign like Libra, the chemistry is just about perfect.

Saturday, August 14 (Moon in Libra to Scorpio 9:27 p.m.) Your passions run deeply and furiously. Play your hand quitly, revealing little or nothing about your agenda and intentions. You'll have a much clearer picture of what's really going on when the moon enters Sagittarius on Tuesday. Allow your intuition to guide you through the next few days.

Sunday, August 15 (Moon in Scorpio) In a few days, Mercury turns retrograde in Virgo, your fourth house. Start preparing by scheduling travel plans on either side of August 20 and September 12. Be sure to make backups of computer files at home and work on August 19. If you've been considering the purchase of a big-ticket item, buy it on either side of these Mercury retrograde dates.

Monday, August 16 (Moon in Scorpio) You're living with such intensity today that it's easy to forget that life is continuing around you. Slow down and take time to eat, to make small talk with coworkers and employees, and to find your own center. Ground yourself in the real world; then proceed at a more measured pace.

Tuesday, August 17 (Moon in Scorpio to Sagittarius 2:35 a.m.) You begin to gain a larger perspective on some pressing issues, situations, and relationships. Your business or romantic partner, in fact, gets the ball rolling, perhaps through something he or she says. You may have to pull back emotionally from the situation before you gain clarity.

Wednesday, August 18 (Moon in Sagittarius) This moon forms favorable angles to both Jupiter and Uranus, so batten down the hatches. It's going to be a wild day. But at the end of the day, your life will be expanding in some way. Perhaps you find a new business partner. Perhaps your friends rally to your support just when you need them most.

Thursday, August 19 (Moon in Sagittarius to Capricorn 1:18 a.m.) Back up computer files today, and wrap up preparations for your travel plans. Mercury turns retrograde tomorrow. For today, finish up loan or mortgage applications,

complete what you can at work, and clear your desk for to
morrow. You'll be reviewing, revising, and revamping unt
September 12.

Friday, August 20 (Moon in Capricorn)   Mercury turn
retrograde in Virgo, your fourth house. For a deeper look a
how this will affect you, reread the section on Mercury re
rogrades in the big-picture overview. Issues involving home
health, and family that you thought were resolved could su
face again. People you haven't seen in a long time may com
back into your life.

**Saturday, August 21 (Moon in Capricorn to Aquarius 10:3
p.m.)**   This evening you feel a hundred percent more up
beat than you did earlier in the day. The Aquarius moon stir
up your ideas and gets your adrenaline pumping. If you're
writer, this moon could bring contact with your editor or pub
lisher. It's possible that your books or your company's produc
will be expanding to an overseas market.

Sunday, August 22 (Moon in Aquarius)   With a predom
nance of planets in air signs now, you're in a social, upbea
mood and eager to do some networking, make new contact
and solidify the contacts you have. So you either attend a so
cial function or throw one yourself. Your ideas and the wa
you present them win support from unexpected sources.

Monday, August 23 (Moon in Aquarius)   You may b
feeling the impact already of tomorrow's full moon in Pisce
You'll be hearing career news and could hear it as early a
today. Full moons usually operate for a few days on eithe
side of the exact date. Mars is still in Libra, along with Venu
so conditions are perfect for romance! There could be new
about a creative project as well.

**Tuesday, August 24 (Moon in Aquarius to Pisces 11:1
a.m.)**   The full moon in Pisces forms a strong and benef
cial angle to Pluto in your eighth house, indicating that yo
benefit from other people's energy, time, and resources. Whe

hey are applied to your career, a major break might land in our lap. Be alert to seize the opportunity when it arrives.

Wednesday, August 25 (Moon in Pisces)   Intuition and imagination are the keys to success today. Whether you're dealing with career issues or a situation in some other area of your life, you probably have a good idea already what's going on. Use your imagination and intuition to solve the issue. Then back it up with facts and action.

Thursday, August 26 (Moon in Pisces to Aries 11:49 p.m.) The moon joins Jupiter and Uranus in Aries. This powerful trio makes harmonious angles to your sun, energizing you physically, mentally, emotionally, and spiritually. Whatever you attract into your experience today expands your life in some way. And whatever it is manifests itself suddenly and without warning.

Friday, August 27 (Moon in Aries)   Trailblazer, entrepreneur, pioneer—in some way, shape, or form, you represent the hyperbole today. In a sense, you're out there pounding the metaphorical brush in search of a trend or an idea that no one has tapped into yet. Your information and social network stands behind you.

Saturday, August 28 (Moon in Aries)   As the summer winds down, you're on fire with plans that will carry you through to the end of the year. You may want to refine and polish your plan for the rest of the year. Remember to keep the plans reasonable, but don't be afraid to dream big.

Sunday, August 29 (Moon in Aries to Taurus 11:36 a.m.) The moon enters your twelfth house. You may be spending the day with yourself, working on something behind the scenes. You could be on deadline for something or may just need some time alone to relax.

Monday, August 30 (Moon in Taurus)   Spiff up your environment in some way. The Taurus moon is fond of beauty,

so you may want to consider adding some artwork or pho-
tographs to your office or home. If you have kids and one of
them is artistic, have him or her create a drawing or painting
for you. Cut flowers are always an added plus!

Tuesday, August 31 (Moon in Taurus to Gemini 9:20 p.m.)
What better way to end the month and start the next one?
With the moon in your sign, you're in a very good place to
make your dreams come true. All you have to do is figure out
a strategy for making it happen.

SEPTEMBER 2010

Wednesday, September 1 (Moon in Gemini)   Flexibility
and the ability to adapt to any situation are your greatest assets today. You'll have to think on your feet and make snap
decisions concerning a situation or event at home or work.
But at the end of the day, you're pleased with the results.

Thursday, September 2 (Moon in Gemini)   With Mars, Venus, and Saturn forming favorable angles to the moon, your
life is in very good shape. It's possible that a creative project
takes center stage. If so, you find the correct structure for the
project and pull it off without a hitch.

Friday, September 3 (Moon in Gemini to Cancer 3:51 a.m.)
Your emotional focus shifts to your values—what you value
most, why you value it, and how you can integrate these values
more fully into your daily life. The nurturing qualities of the
moon are turned on your own concerns. In others words, you
nurture *you*.

Saturday, September 4 (Moon in Cancer)   As you move
into the long Labor Day weekend, you may be sticking close
to home, continuing some improvement projects. If you're
having guests over, you'll be busy with them. But if Labor Day
is just a time for you to chill and get on track for the fall, then
be sure to nurture yourself.

Sunday, September 5 (Moon in Cancer to Leo 5:46 a.m.)
In another week, Mercury will turn direct again and communication snafus will be history. But for now, mind your Ps and Qs when communicating with others. Virtual travel all you want, but don't make reservations until after September 12. With the moon in dramatic Leo today, strut your stuff and don't hesitate to toot your own horn!

Monday, September 6 (Moon in Leo)   If you're involved in a relationship, you may be hoping for more recognition from your partner—you know, like a surprise gift or a bouquet of flowers. But rather than fretting about it, acknowledge your partner in some way. Plan a special dinner. Make a gesture. Sometimes, the best gestures are the simplest.

Tuesday, September 7 (Moon in Leo to Virgo 5:54 a.m.)
Prepare today for tomorrow's new moon in Virgo. Make a list of what you want to manifest into your experience. Be as wild and imaginative as you want. With the moon entering Virgo today, you'll be dealing with the most fundamental parts of your life.

Wednesday, September 8 (Moon in Virgo)   Today's new moon in Virgo could bring an opportunity to sell your home, if your place is on the market, or an opportunity to buy a home. Saturn forms a wide conjunction to the degree of this moon, suggesting that there will be a lot of discussion and perhaps some travel around this date. Venus also enters Scorpio, where it will be through the end of the year. Until October 8, it will be moving in direct motion and should bring a certain smoothness to your daily work life.

Thursday, September 9 (Moon in Virgo to Libra 5:02 a.m.)
The moon joins forces with Saturn in your fifth house. Sometimes, this combination can put a damper on what you do for fun and pleasure. Or it seems that you need structure to your activities. However this manifests for you today, focus on your own pleasure and creative endeavors.

Friday, September 10 (Moon in Libra)   Balance, cooperation, and teamwork are the hallmarks of the day. You hit your stride creatively and use recent experiences as fodder for expressing a particular emotion or theme. You find the correct structure or venue for creative expression. In love and romance, someone older than you may grab your attention.

Saturday, September 11 (Moon in Libra to Scorpio 5:2. a.m.) Tomorrow Mercury turns direct, so just hold off another day before you sign a contract or firm up travel plan For today, focus on your health routine—everything from exercise to nutrition to any bad habits you want to break. The exercise routine you had this summer may not be suitable to the fall, so make adjustments.

Sunday, September 12 (Moon in Scorpio) Mercury turn direct! It's safe to pack your bags, sign contracts, update your Web site, or contact people on your e-mail loop. Since Mercury rules your sign, it's likely that you feel the transition from retrograde to direct motion more strongly. If you've had a big ticket item on your buy list, then go looking tomorrow. Give Mercury a day to settle in.

Monday, September 13 (Moon in Scorpio to Sagittarius 8:5. a.m.) Pluto turns direct in your eighth house. The effects of this movement will be subtle, but over the next several month some things will come more easily to you—mortgages, insurance, loans, and the use of other people's resources. You will also be more aware of sharing what you have with others.

Tuesday, September 14 (Moon in Sagittarius) Mars enters Scorpio, your sixth house, where it will be until October 28. This transit brings a bottom-line kind of attitude to your daily work life. Since Venus is also in this sign, an office flirtation could become something much more. You're after transformational experiences now.

Wednesday, September 15 (Moon in Sagittarius to Capricorn 4:30 p.m.) The moon joins Pluto in Capricorn. If Capricorn is prominent in your birth chart in some way, then you'll want to keep track of these lunar transits in Capricorn, especially

cially while Pluto is also in this sign. With practice, you'll be able to anticipate what kinds of experiences may surface.

Thursday, September 16 (Moon in Capricorn)   Synchronicities that occur today may be especially meaningful. Pay close attention to the circumstances, the people involved, and the theme or pattern. Does the synchronicity involve numbers? Names? Places? What's the message?

Friday, September 17 (Moon in Capricorn)   You usually aren't the best long-range planner on the block. However, today you do it with such ease that you may astonish the people around you. What others don't realize is that when you're focused on something, your planning skills are exceptional.

Saturday, September 18 (Moon in Capricorn to Aquarius 3:35 a.m.)   You've got a lot on your plate today. But you're an excellent multitasker and shouldn't hesitate to delegate some responsibilities if you need to. With Mercury now direct, you can move forward with travel plans, educational plans, and communications of all sorts.

Sunday, September 19 (Moon in Aquarius)   If you're not involved in a committed relationship right now, then you may be before Venus completes its transit of Scorpio at the end of the year. Emotions and passions are intense with Venus in Scorpio, and with Mars in the same sign, that intensity may be evident in a romantic relationship. It could also find expression in a creative venture.

Monday, September 20 (Moon in Aquarius to Pisces, 4:15 p.m.)   With the moon entering the career sector of your chart, you may be fretting about the direction your professional life is headed. You're probably doing just fine, but if you have any insecurities in the career area, this moon may exacerbate them. Advice? Go with the flow.

Tuesday, September 21 (Moon in Pisces)   Use your imagination to bring about something new in the way you approach your career and professional matters. If you can imagine it, then you can manifest it! It could be something as simple as an attitude adjustment or something as complex as putting together a résumé and looking for another job or even a different career path.

Wednesday, September 22 (Moon in Pisces)   Now that Uranus has retrograded back into Pisces, the moon links up with it once again, bringing an eccentricity to your emotional responses. Your responses are unusual. Your emotions feel strange to you. Yet your insights are brilliant and cutting-edge. Try to bring both to bear on career matters. In some weird way, the eccentricity and the insights will work together.

Thursday, September 23 (Moon in Pisces to Aries 5:47 a.m.) Today's full moon in Aries should be exciting, unpredictable, and perhaps even downright strange. But you'll hear news concerning a friendship or a group to which you belong and concerning a dream or wish you have for yourself.

Friday, September 24 (Moon in Aries)   Don't hesitate to think outside the box today. In fact, it's what the day's events and situations require! With Mars in Scorpio and the moon in fire sign Aries, you are inclined to act on your hunches and to blaze your path.

Saturday, September 25 (Moon in Aries to Taurus 5:17 p.m.) Both Mars and Venus are opposed to this moon, which can create some emotional discomfort. Your feelings, for instance, may get hurt more easily than usual. What is intended as a casual remark by someone in your environment is blown out of proportion, and suddenly you're on the defensive.

Sunday, September 26 (Moon in Taurus)   As you go through your day, be aware of what changes you would like to bring about in your life and envision how those changes might occur. In other words, if you want to earn more money, should you be pounding the pavement with your résumés, or should you change your beliefs about money? Is action called for, or should you work on your beliefs?

Monday, September 27 (Moon in Taurus)   Your artistic sense is heightened. You want to beautify your environment in some way. Some feng shui may be in order. Find the area of your house that represents the area of your life you want to beautify and get busy. Prosperity, for instance, lies in the southeast corner. Its color is purple. Fame lies to the south; its color is red. You get the idea.

Tuesday, September 28 (Moon in Taurus to Gemini 3:12 a.m.)   What a nice way to wind down the month of September. The moon enters your sign, and now you're in your element. Pick an activity that interests you and dive in. You won't fail. In fact, you'll succeed beyond your wildest dreams.

Wednesday, September 29 (Moon in Gemini)   With Saturn in air sign Libra, and the moon in your own sign, you're able to find a structure or venue that is perfect for what you're doing and involved in. Whether it's a relationship, a creative project, or simply something that fires you up, trust your instincts.

Thursday, September 30 (Moon in Gemini to Cancer 10:47 a.m.)   Your mother or another nurturing female in your life may have advice or insights you should hear. You, in turn, have advice or insights for someone in your life for whom *you* are the nurturer. What goes around comes around.

OCTOBER 2010

Friday, October 1 (Moon in Cancer)   With Mercury now in direct motion, that big-ticket item you've had your eye on now has your name on it! Whether you pay cash or charge it, be sure you've got the money in your account. This moon forms a beneficial angle to both Venus and Mars, so it's possible you and your romantic partner may be considering a change in your relationship. Moving in together, perhaps. Or even setting a date for marriage.

Saturday, October 2 (Moon in Cancer to Leo 3:22 p.m.) Your day may feel like a marathon, running here and there, trying to do too much at once. It's best if you slow down and tackle one thing at a time. Even though you're a multitasker, today's energies ask that you shine and perfect one task before you move on to another. Take note of your internal dialogues. Are they primarily positive or negative? Uplifting or critical?

Sunday, October 3 (Moon in Leo)   Mercury enters Libra, joining Saturn in your fifth house. This transits lasts until October 20, and during this period, your conscious thoughts may seem overconcerned with responsibilities and obligations. With all creative endeavors, you'll have the perfect structure in place for success.

Monday, October 4 (Moon in Leo to Virgo 5:00 p.m.)   Fundamentals are at the heart of it all today. Whatever your political and spiritual beliefs, these things are on your mind today. You may be working for a group or organization that represents your interests, passions, and beliefs. If you're a volunteer, you'll have to watch your time commitment. If you're paid, you throw yourself wholeheartedly into the job.

Tuesday, October 5 (Moon in Virgo)   Time to clean house. Not your physical home, but your mental, emotional, and spiritual home. You'll be sweeping away cobwebs, chasing dust bunnies, and generally cleaning out the beliefs that no longer work for you. This is something you probably should have done before now, but Geminis tend to stay on the move so constantly that it's difficult to find the time. From now on, do your cleaning while you're at the gym, in the car, or out walking.

Wednesday, October 6 (Moon in Virgo to Libra 4:52 p.m.) The moon joins Saturn in Libra once again. Today, you're in charge of your creative flow. Your muse is up close and personal, whispering urgently, offering guidance and direction. Listen and then integrate this guidance into your creative endeavors.

Thursday, October 7 (Moon in Libra)   Today's new moon in Libra should usher in new creative opportunities, a new romantic relationship (if you're uninvolved), and will bring opportunities for all the kinds of things you enjoy doing. Both Saturn and Mercury form wide but beneficial conjunctions to this moon, indicating a lot of activity and discussion around the time of this moon.

Friday, October 8 (Moon in Libra to Scorpio 4:52 p.m.) Venus turns retrograde today in Scorpio and turns direct again on November 18. This can create some bumps and bruises in your romantic and work relationships. There could be some physical discomforts at work.

Saturday, October 9 (Moon in Scorpio) The moon hooks up with Venus retrograde. In your creative ventures, you may be revisiting issues that you thought were resolved or may be tempted to trash what you're working on and start over. Definitely don't do that! Carefully go through your project, and look for the weaknesses and strengths.

Sunday, October 10 (Moon in Scorpio to Sagittarius 7:09 p.m.) With the moon in your opposite sign, there could be some tension today with a business or romantic partner. Or you may be feeling insecure in one of these relationships. In truth, there's probably not much wrong in the relationship arena. Things will look much better when the moon enters Aquarius.

Monday, October 11 (Moon in Sagittarius) You're reaching for the bigger picture, the broader canvas, rather than trying to connect the dots. Let your nature take you far and wide today—through the Internet and e-mail—culling and disseminating information.

Tuesday, October 12 (Moon in Sagittarius) You easily forget how popular you are when your phone doesn't ring, right? Or when the only mail in your in-box is ads. Perhaps it's time to put up your own blog and invite everyone you know to drop by for coffee and conversation. Then you won't feel so isolated.

Wednesday, October 13 (Moon in Sagittarius to Capricorn 1:17 a.m.) The moon and Pluto are holding hands together in your eighth house. This can be excellent for obtaining mortgages and loans. However, with Venus retrograde in Scorpio, you may want to wait until after November 18 to buy something like a car.

Thursday, October 14 (Moon in Capricorn) Think back to your most pleasant and delightful memory. How old were you? How did you feel when this event occurred? Now try to conjure those same emotions, and apply them to a situation in your life now that you hope will improve. Sometimes, improvement happens simply through adjusting your emotions.

Friday, October 15 (Moon in Capricorn to Aquarius 11:24 a.m.) With the moon entering fellow air sign Aquarius, your thoughts are turning toward travel, education, or perhaps even a publishing venture of some kind. Maybe it's time to get out that manuscript you stuck away in your closet and go to work on it! Mercury and Saturn form harmonious angles to this moon, so there should be structured discussions (as opposed to sitting around and talking) today.

Saturday, October 16 (Moon in Aquarius) Fasten your seat belt. It's going to be a wild, hectic day, but it's the sort of rush you enjoy and usually handle well. You're working up to the full moon in Aries on Friday, which may bring a lot of social invitations. Your phone will be ringing frequently; the mail in your in-box stacks up. Enjoy the ride!

Sunday, October 17 (Moon in Aquarius to Pisces 11:52 p.m.) Think for yourself. If a boss or peer instructs you to do something you know is questionable or even flat-out wrong, don't do it. Refuse. It's time to stand up for what you believe. Intuitively, you already know what to do about this.

Monday, October 18 (Moon in Pisces) You take a professional risk and just hope that it pays off. You actually don't need to worry about it. You have excellent instincts and, as long as you follow them, should do just fine. Right now Mars forms a harmonious angle to this moon, increasing the likelihood that your stamina remains strong, even intense.

Tuesday, October 19 (Moon in Pisces)   Pisces is the only other sign besides Gemini represented by two of something. So when the moon is in Pisces, there can be conflicts between your head and your heart. Your head says to do one thing; your heart is screaming to do another. The best way to reconcile this is to wait until the moon is in Aries.

Wednesday, October 20 (Moon in Pisces to Aries 12:24 p.m.) Mercury enters Scorpio, your sixth house, where it remains until November 8. This transit should bring about a lot of discussion with coworkers. Research and investigation will be part and parcel of your work routine for the next few weeks. You may feel things more intensely, and your conscious mind will be receptive to other people's thoughts and feelings.

Thursday, October 21 (Moon in Aries)   Friends and groups are highlighted. You and several other people may be hot on the trail of a new trend or idea. Don't worry about how you'll market the idea. Just nurture its emergence into the world—and into your experience—and the rest will take care of itself.

Friday, October 22 (Moon in Aries to Taurus 11:31 p.m.) Today's full moon in Aries should bring news concerning a friendship or a wish or dream that you have. Neptune forms a wide but beneficial angle to this moon, indicating an element of compassion to events. Later tonight, as the moon enters Taurus, you'll feel like kicking back and taking it easy. In fact, the next couple of days will have you turning down social invites. You're in the mood for some alone time.

Saturday, October 23 (Moon in Taurus)   The moon is opposite Mars in Scorpio, so there could be some friction between you and a partner or coworker or employee. You may dig in your heels about a particular issue, refusing to change your mind or budge from your position. The other person is

297

equally stubborn. Wait until the moon is in your sign to make any decisions about the conflict.

Sunday, October 24 (Moon in Taurus) If it's fall where you live, you may want to get out and about today and refresh your spirit through some sort of physical exercise. A hike. A run. Even a long walk might feed your soul. Whatever you encounter today—externally or internally—becomes creative fodder. You're good at connecting those kinds of dots today.

Monday, October 25 (Moon in Taurus to Gemini 8:48 a.m.) Things are really getting good. The moon enters your sign, and you begin to do what you're best at: networking, culling and disseminating information, writing and communicating. Today you may organize your energy around a particular project, relationship, or concern. If you're passionate about something, that passion is communicated to others.

Tuesday, October 26 (Moon in Gemini) If your thoughts seem to be humming along in a gloom-and-doom direction today, stop. The more you find to appreciate, the likelier it is that you attract even more of the same.

Wednesday, October 27 (Moon in Gemini to Cancer 4:15 p.m.) Tomorrow, Mars enters your opposite sign. As it prepares to make that shift, you could be experiencing tension with a business or romantic partner. Or you may suddenly grasp the big picture of this relationship and not like what you see. What you experience under this transit will depend to a large degree on your state of mind.

Thursday, October 28 (Moon in Cancer) Mars enters Sagittarius, where it will be until December 7. This transit energizes the partnership sector of your chart. You could find a new business partner, be attracted to someone romantically, experience tension. The bottom line, though, is that Gemini and Sagittarius, despite the fact that they are opposite signs, often get along beautifully. So if you meet someone during this transit, there may be a chemical attraction.

Friday, October 29 (Moon in Cancer to Leo 9:39 p.m.) The dramatic Leo moon can exaggerate events and emotions so that things either seem really fantastic or really awful. However, since Leo is compatible with your sun sign, your feelings today probably fall under fantastic. Try not to make any decisions based on emotions today. Wait a few days. Then decide.

Saturday, October 30 (Moon in Leo) You may be asked to get involved in a neighborhood or community project. You really want to be a part of this, but could be feeling time constraints. Balance your need with reality and then decide if you can commit. Don't commit just to please.

Sunday, October 31 (Moon in Leo) With the moon entering Virgo tonight, you're on your toes, paying close attention to everything that happens, to everything you feel. Try not to be overanalytical, but take what you learn and apply it in a positive way to a project you're involved in.

NOVEMBER 2010

Monday, November 1 (Moon in Leo to Virgo 12:51 a.m.) The structures in your life are now strengthening. Thank Saturn in Libra for that. If you're in a relationship that hasn't changed much in a while, then Saturn will either take things to a deeper level of commitment or you could decide to end it. In terms of your creative ventures, you're either encountering restrictions in that area or building stronger structures.

Tuesday, November 2 (Moon in Virgo) Someone in your family requires your focus and concentration. It may be time to gather everyone together for a family reunion and work in a discussion about any pressing issues. Best to do this while everyone is relaxed rather than calling some huge family pow-wow.

Wednesday, November 3 (Moon in Virgo to Libra 2:19 a.m.) The moon joins Saturn in Libra, your fifth house. A lightbulb goes on inside your head, and insights pour in about a creative project you're working on. You may have to revise your project or, at the very least, tweak and fine-tune it. But the end result will be a vastly improved product.

Thursday, November 4 (Moon in Libra) Balance and fairness are at the core of events today. As a sign represented by two of something (the twins), you're probably well aware of what genuine balance is. You can usually see the other side of the issue just as clearly as you can your own side. But that doesn't make it any easier to use the knowledge.

Friday, November 5 (Moon in Libra to Scorpio 3:16 a.m.) It's another one of those bottom-line sort of days. There could be a pressing issue or concern at work that requires investigation to get to the core of what's really going on. You're up to the task, but it may take a couple of days to gather the information you require.

Saturday, November 6 (Moon in Scorpio) Today's new moon in Scorpio ushers in work opportunities and opportunities in the maintenance of your health. You may start a new nutritional or exercise program, find a new job, hire a new trainer, or sign up for a new exercise class. There could be a lot of discussion concerning these new opportunities. At least one of them will prove to broaden and expand your career. Neptune also turns direct today, in Aquarius, enabling you to more fully integrate your compassion and ideals into your worldview.

Sunday, November 7—Daylight Saving Time Ends (Moon in Scorpio to Sagittarius 4:28 a.m.) The moon enters your opposite sign, joining Mars in your seventh house. This combination should fire you up emotionally and intuitively. You'll be able to grasp the broader implications of a situation or relationship. If you're involved right now, then your sex life should heat up!

Monday, November 8 (Moon in Sagittarius) Mercury enters Sagittarius, joining Mars and the moon in your seventh house. With three planets now in the partnership sector of your chart, you and a business or romantic partner may be having a lot of discussions concerning your respective needs and expectations. It clears the air and allows you both some breathing room.

Tuesday, November 9 (Moon in Sagittarius to Capricorn 9:37 a.m.) The moon enters Capricorn, joining Pluto in your eighth house. Once again, you're in the power seat. But you may have to adjust your attitude slightly to reap the benefits of this conjunction. They say that everything is about timing, and that certainly applies to the events today. Act when you feel the time is right.

Wednesday, November 10 (Moon in Capricorn) If you've got the time, give some thought to your long-range plans. Whether you're tackling issues like retirement, insurance, financing college, or applying for a mortgage, strive to think beyond the immediate future.

Thursday, November 11 (Moon in Capricorn to Aquarius 5:33 p.m.) In another week, Venus turns direct again, and then you can make your travel plans for the holidays. You may also want to revisit your daily work plans. There could be something there that needs fine-tuning or adjustment. Employee or coworker issues, perhaps.

Friday, November 12 (Moon in Aquarius) Whenever the moon links up with Neptune, there's a visionary quality to whatever you do. It's possible that today you volunteer for a charitable organization or even just volunteer to help out a neighbor, friend, or family member. If more of us could cultivate the art of giving, the world at large would benefit too.

Saturday, November 13 (Moon in Aquarius) Indulge your nomadic feelings. Get on the Internet and virtual travel. Pick a spot, and learn about it. This is the kind of thing you're good at—gathering information. Then figure out the expenses for your trip to this place. If you feel you can afford it, make your reservation after Venus turns direct on November 18.

Sunday, November 14 (Moon in Aquarius to Pisces 6:25 a.m.)   The moon links up with Uranus in your career sector. This won't happen many more times before Uranus enters Aries again. So wrap up outstanding issues and projects in your career, and clear up space for new opportunities and situations.

Monday, November 15 (Moon in Pisces)   If you feel torn between two opposing desires or needs today, blame the moon in Pisces. It, like Gemini, is represented by two of something—two fish, headed in opposite directions. So if you feel like there are four of you, each with different needs and desires, that's why. Best way to navigate this? Indulge one, then the other. If nothing else, it will make for an exciting and unpredictable day.

Tuesday, November 16 (Moon in Pisces to Aries 7:00 p.m.)   The Aries moon is much more comfortable for you, than a Pisces moon. In fact, after several days of feeling uncertain and doubtful about everything, today you get together with friends. If you're part of a group—a book group, a theater group, a writing group, whatever—you may meet with members of that group too.

Wednesday, November 17 (Moon in Aries)   Off you go pursuing something that no one else sees. You're the trailblazer today, the entrepreneur, the pioneer.

Thursday, November 18 (Moon in Aries)   Venus turns direct, so your love life should improve immeasurably. This movement also brings creative projects up front and center. In addition, Jupiter turns direct, back in Pisces once again. This movement should expand your career opportunities through the end of the year.

Friday, November 19 (Moon in Aries to Taurus 6:05 a.m.)   With the moon in earth sign Taurus, your focus is on practicality, efficiency, and doing things correctly, even if it takes longer. The reward for your diligence comes when the moon enters your sign on Sunday.

Saturday, November 20 (Moon in Taurus) This transit may bring up emotional issues from the past—deep memories that have been hidden for years—and may find you visiting someone in a hospital or nursing home. You're emotionally strong, and if the day involves others, your strength becomes theirs.

Sunday, November 21 (Moon in Taurus to Gemini 2:46 p.m.) The full moon in Taurus occurs in a late degrees, so those of you born between May 18 and May 20 will feel it the most. You can expect sudden, unexpected good news that somehow expands your opportunities and insights. Venus forms a challenging angle to this moon, but it isn't all that serious. If anything, watch your spending.

Monday, November 22 (Moon in Gemini) Breathe. Does it sound like a sigh of relief? The moon is in your sign again, a high point of every month. You're running around, trying to get ready for the Thanksgiving holiday. Whether you're staying in town or leaving, you feel pressure to get things lined up. But admit it. This is the sort of pressure you enjoy.

Tuesday, November 23 (Moon in Gemini to Cancer 9:14 p.m.) With every planet now moving in direct motion, the deck is certainly stacked in your favor and the field is wide-open. This trend continues until December 10, when Mercury turns retrograde for the last time this year. So take advantage of all this forward motion and apply your energy in the area of your life where you feel you need it most.

Wednesday, November 24 (Moon in Cancer) If you celebrate Thanksgiving, then chances are you are caught up in travel plans or meal preparations or both. If guests are coming in from out of town, be sure you've got things lined up in that area too. But you enjoy this kind of chaos and usually do just fine bringing everything together.

Thursday, November 25 (Moon in Cancer) Happy Thanksgiving! How appropriate that the moon is in Cancer, the sign that traditionally is about family, home, your roots,

parents, and your capacity for nurturing others and yoursel
So enjoy it. You're creating memories today.

Friday, November 26 (Moon in Cancer to Leo 2:0
a.m.)   With the moon entering dramatic Leo today, you'r
in rare form. You and the people with whom you are spendin
the long weekend may get out and about to take in the sight
The one place you probably won't go? The mall to shop. Yo
aren't crazy about the crush of crowds.

Saturday, November 27 (Moon in Leo)   Your though
turn toward relatives or toward your neighborhood and com
munity. If you're working in the arts, then you may be trollin
the Internet for opportunities to strut your stuff. Or you ma
hear about an opportunity through a community paper.

Sunday, November 28 (Moon in Leo to Virgo 5:34 a.m.
Getting ready for your week ahead? Then today is the day t
organize and prioritize. Whether you're tending to family c
professional matters, you bring attention to detail. All planet
are in direct motion now, so take advantage of it.

Monday, November 29 (Moon in Virgo)   As you mov
into the last month of the year, you may want to take stoc
of where you have been this year, what you would like t
achieve in December, and where you would like to go in th
year ahead. It's the first step to coming up with New Year'
resolutions. You know, the resolutions that by March of th
New Year are forgotten?

Tuesday, November 30 (Moon in Virgo to Libra 8:16 a.m.
Mercury enters Capricorn, teaming up with Pluto in you
eighth house. This combination could lead to some strang
experiences today—feelings of déjà vu, synchronicities, an
even psychic experiences. And you're able to take it all in an
somehow use what you gain in a practical way.

Wednesday, December 1 (Moon in Libra)   The moon joins Saturn in your fifth house, firing up the romantic and creative sides of your life once again. You go through these periods where things hum along at a perfect pace, and then suddenly you have a very bad day—or a very good one. Today is the very-good variety. So treat yourself to something you really enjoy doing.

Thursday, December 2 (Moon in Libra to Scorpio 10:44 a.m.) You're digging around through old papers and files, searching for a particular piece of information. There's a strange symbolism to this search that is connected intimately to who you are and what you desire for yourself and your life. You're working up to a new moon and may be very open and willing at this time to stop a bad habit or to try a new exercise or nutritional program. The maintenance of your health is front and center of the day's concerns.

Friday, December 3 (Moon in Scorpio)   Intense emotions and passions swirl around a work issue. If it's a problem with an employee or coworker, the best way to deal with it is avoidance. Wait until after the new moon to solve the problem. Keep your gripes and concerns to yourself for now.

Saturday, December 4 (Moon in Scorpio to Sagittarius 2:00 p.m.)   The moon enters your seventh house of partnerships. A business partnership needs your attention. But you may want to wait until Uranus turns direct tomorrow before you sit down for discussions. Whatever has been delayed or stalled professionally will begin to straighten out once Uranus is functioning as it should be.

Sunday, December 5 (Moon in Sagittarius)   Today's new moon in Sagittarius ushers in new partnership opportunities. Mars forms a wide conjunction to the degree of this moon, suggesting more activity than usual around this time. If you're single and looking, this new moon may bring in a new romantic interest. If you're searching for a business partner, then the person is closer than you think!

Monday, December 6 (Moon in Sagittarius to Capricorn 7:17 p.m.)   Holiday shopping and plans are on your mind. You may decide to shop through the Internet this year, perhaps looking for special gifts for the special people in your life. If you're planning to travel this holiday season, remember that Mercury turns retrograde on December 10 and doesn't turn direct again until December 30. Stay home for Christmas and travel for New Year's? Perhaps that's the best option.

Tuesday, December 7 (Moon in Capricorn)   Mars enters Capricorn and your eighth house, where it will remain through the end of the year. This transit suggests a lot of activity concerning mortgages, insurance, and taxes, but also with the invisible side of life: ghosts, past-life memories. Your career should benefit from this transit too. Others are more willing to help you out.

Wednesday, December 8 (Moon in Capricorn)   Ambition combined with focus can be a powerful motivating force. You bring it all to the table today, and the people to whom you're presenting your ideas or project are duly impressed. You win supporters easily. At the end of the day, you're pleased with all the progress.

Thursday, December 9 (Moon in Capricorn to Aquarius 3:32 a.m.)   Mercury turns retrograde tomorrow. By now you know that means to back up all computer files, finalize travel plans, buy travel tickets, and touch base with clients, employees, and family members. It's beginning to sound like you're going to disappear. But for a Gemini and Mercury retrograde, that's sometimes how it feels!

Friday, December 10 (Moon in Aquarius)   Mercury turns retrograde in Capricorn. Mercury goes to sleep. However, the other planets are all moving in direct motion, giving you the opportunity to make strides in many areas of your life. During this retrograde period, just be sure to communicate clearly to avoid misunderstandings!

Saturday, December 11 (Moon in Aquarius to Pisces 2:41 p.m.)   The moon enters your tenth house, joining Uranus and Jupiter. Expect the unexpected professionally. Even though it's Saturday, surprising news may arrive in your inbox. In some way, this news or the events that occur expand and broaden your horizons and your career opportunities.

Sunday, December 12 (Moon in Pisces)   Using your imagination and intuition, you're on the fast track toward something big today. Just remember that Mercury is retrograde, so don't sign contracts. Explore and brainstorm all you want. Coworkers, peers, bosses—all must be dealt with early in the week. Be prepared.

Monday, December 13 (Moon in Pisces)   Time to touch base with family and friends about the holidays. Who is going where? Are you staying home or traveling? You may get tapped to help organize an office party or some sort of fundraising venture through your office or company.

Tuesday, December 14 (Moon in Pisces to Aries 3:15 a.m.) You're fired up about something today. Perhaps a friend has suggested an idea or a project, and you recognize just how good it is. You're eager to be a part of it. With your ability to communicate and network, you would be an asset to this project.

Wednesday, December 15 (Moon in Aries)   Your social life is booming right now. What with the holidays, the office parties, and the general goodwill that people show each other this time of year, your time is of the essence. Pick and choose carefully, so you don't get overextended.

Thursday, December 16 (Moon in Aries to Taurus 2:49 p.m.) This is the time of month when you may feel like retreating into yourself. But you may not have a chance to do it because you're clearing off your desk, rearranging furniture, and basically getting things prepared for the holidays. Be resolute in whatever you're doing. Complete what you start.

Friday, December 17 (Moon in Taurus)   On December 21, there's a lunar eclipse in your sign. You may be feeling the impact of it already. This eclipse will trigger emotions concerning something in your personal life. So pay attention to what occurs during the next several days. You may recognize patterns in your behavior.

Saturday, December 18 (Moon in Taurus to Gemini 11:38 p.m.)   The moon finally enters your sign. You're in great shape now, in a strong position generally in your life. Even though Mercury is still retrograde, the Gemini moon should help you communicate what you feel with greater clarity.

Sunday, December 19 (Moon in Gemini)   You may be trying to clarify something you feel concerning a relationship. It could be the impact of the lunar eclipse manifesting itself. So gather information, talk to other people, get other opinions. By the end of the day, your feelings will be much clearer.

Monday, December 20 (Moon in Gemini)   News and insights come your way today. It may concern holiday plans. Remember, with Mercury retrograde, plans may change suddenly, or guests could be delayed in arriving. Or you could be delayed if you're the one who is traveling.

Tuesday, December 21 (Moon in Gemini to Cancer 5:22 a.m.)   Today's lunar eclipse in Gemini receives harmonious angles from Saturn and Neptune. Saturn helps to strengthen the structures in your life, and Neptune emphasizes your compassion and idealism. So the inner event that triggers your emotions could be connected to your ideals. An older person may challenge you about your beliefs.

Wednesday, December 22 (Moon in Cancer)   Last-minute shopping? Go for it. But with the moon in the financial sector of your chart, you may be concerned about expenses. Rather than fret about money, pay cash. That way, in the New Year, you won't be among those people freaking out when the credit card bills arrive.

Thursday, December 23 (Moon in Cancer to Leo 8:51 a.m.)
In some way, shape, or form today, you shine, you rock, you're *on*! It could be something as simple and informal as a family gathering or as complex as a theater production. If someone you know is celebrating a birthday today, make the event special.

Friday, December 24 (Moon in Leo) Whether you celebrate Christmas or not, there's a certain feeling in the air, a generosity of spirit. It's evident in your surroundings, perhaps through the gifts that are exchanged, the stories that are told, and the laughter that rings out. There could be a bit of drama played out as well.

Saturday, December 25 (Moon in Leo to Virgo 11:15 a.m.)
Merry Christmas! How appropriate that the moon enters Virgo, your fourth house of the home. So today you stick close to home and family. Even if you're out of town, your thoughts are there, perhaps swimming through the memories of past Christmases. There could be someone in your midst who is overcritical.

Sunday, December 26 (Moon in Virgo) Presents being returned? People say the day after Christmas is like the day after Thanksgiving when it comes to shopping and the malls. You may want to avoid the crunch and go tomorrow. Now is a perfect day to plan for your New Year's celebrations. Don't firm up anything, though, until after Mercury turns direct on December 30. It may be a New Year's on the fly.

Monday, December 27 (Moon in Virgo to Libra 1:39 p.m.)
Today is fun, fun, fun. Do whatever captures your interest and passions. If you're out of town for the holidays, then take in the sights. If you're at home, then get out and do something the entire family will enjoy.

Tuesday, December 28 (Moon in Libra) Balance, teamwork, and cooperation are Libra's hallmarks. Today, all three will come into play with a creative project or a romantic relationship. Or both. If you have children, you may have to be tactful and diplomatic about a particular concern one of your kids has.

Wednesday, December 29 (Moon in Libra to Scorpio 4:50 p.m.)   As the moon enters Scorpio, you can feel the deepening of your emotions, a kind of inner brooding. You may experience jealousy in a relationship with a coworker. Perhaps that person lands a promotion or a raise that you had hoped for. Try not to cling to the injustice of it all.

Thursday, December 30 (Moon in Scorpio)   Mercury turns direct! Usually, the wisdom is that you should wait a day or two until Mercury stabilizes before you move ahead with projects, travel plans, and all the rest of it. But if you're pressed for plans for tomorrow night, by all means move ahead. Sometime before tomorrow night, review your list of New Year's resolutions.

Friday, December 31 (Moon in Scorpio)   There's a certain intensity to the day. Honor it through meditation, a yoga class, something that requires both mind and body. Line up your desires for the New Year. Then step aside so the universe can work its magic.

HAPPY NEW YEAR!

SYDNEY OMARR

Born on August 5, 1926, in Philadelphia, Pennsylvania, Sydney Omarr was the only person ever given full-time duty in the U.S. Army as an astrologer. He is regarded as the most erudite astrologer of our time and the best known, through his syndicated column and his radio and television programs (he was Merv Griffin's "resident astrologer"). Omarr has been called the most "knowledgeable astrologer since Evangeline Adams." His forecasts of Nixon's downfall, the end of World War II in mid-August of 1945, the assassination of John F. Kennedy, Roosevelt's election to a fourth term and his death in office ... these and many others are on the record and quoted enough to be considered "legendary."

ABOUT THE SERIES

This is one of a series of twelve *Sydney Omarr® Day-by-Day Astrological Guides* for the signs of 2010. For questions and comments about the book, go to www.tjmacgregor.com.